M000234668

Jasta Boelcke

Jasta Boelcke

The History of Jasta 2, 1916-18

Norman Franks

GRUB STREET · LONDON

Published by
Grub Street
4 Rainham Close
London
SW11 6SS

Copyright © 2004 Grub Street, London
Text copyright © 2004 Norman Franks

British Library Cataloguing in Publication Data
Franks, Norman L R (Norman Leslie Robert), 1940-
   Jasta Boelcke: the history of Jasta 2, 1916-1918
   1. Germany. Luftstreitkrafte. Jadgstaffel 2
   2. World War, 1914-1918 – Aerial operations, German
   I. Title
   940.4'4943

ISBN 1 904010 76 8

All rights reserved. No part of this publication may be reproduced,
stored in a retrieval system, or transmitted in any form or
by any means, electronic, mechanical, photocopying, recording,
or otherwise without the prior permission of the copyright owner.

Typeset by Pearl Graphics, Hemel Hempstead

Printed and bound in Great Britain by
Biddles Ltd, King's Lynn

Acknowledgements

I would like to thank Greg VanWyngarden, an authority on WW1 German
aircraft and their markings, for his help with information and
photographs, Michael O'Brien Browne for translations of old German
documents, Peter Amodio for supplying some interesting letters, and Mrs
Kaethe Foster for translating them for me. Also to Paul Leaman, Rick
Duiven, and the late historians Neal O'Connor and Ed Ferko.

Contents

Introduction

It is difficult now, some 90 years after the events of the Great War of 1914-18, to imagine a world without warplanes. This was a world where the airmen who were then only starting to take to the air in craft designed merely for flight, not for war, had little concept of how things would develop in a few short years.

By late 1914 and early 1915, armaments had begun to be taken into the air in somewhat frail aircraft to be used to fight other airmen, or to drop explosive devices on targets on the ground, whether they be soldiers, artillery positions, methods of transport, or buildings which might house something of military significance.

In the spring and early summer of 1916 air warfare had developed significantly from August 1914. In just those 20-odd months, aeroplane numbers on both sides had increased, although compared to 1918 they were still relatively small. Airmen had become more adventurous and aggressive, and to a degree, the craft in which they risked their lives had become a little more reliable. Nevertheless, it was still all very new. This was the first air war and each day was, as we say today, part of a learning curve.

When looking back we tend to forget the newness of it all. We now have knowledge of several wars in which aircraft have played a major role; we also have that wonderful thing called hindsight. Therefore it is sometimes difficult to read about the early days in isolation, and not ignore the very real difficulties the early airmen faced. If then one starts talking about the successful fighter pilots and their victory scores, even though in the beginning such things as scores had not yet been contemplated as a yardstick of success, it is easy to forget that they were the pathfinders, the men who found the way, the innovators.

Try, if you will, to read this book as if there was no known futuristic horizon, no knowledge of what went on the next month, let alone the next decade or the next half century. None of us know what tomorrow might bring, and the airmen of WW1 knew just as little, although they could hazard a good guess that tomorrow might mean a grizzly end to their life. It is often said that the airman has a fine, clean death, the combat being compared to a knight of old battling one-against-one. The reality is not like this at all.

The airman, especially one of WW1, had less heroic visions of death, which could encompass his own, his comrade's or his opponent's.

Aeroplanes fell apart, lost wings and shed fabric, all of which meant a horrendous fall to a very solid earth and oblivion. Protection against bullets was minimal. An attacker would fire at the cockpit area knowing how vulnerable the pilot was. So many airmen, hit and wounded – mortally or not – saw death approaching minutes ahead of time, knowing they were powerless to avoid the final impact with the ground. There were no self-sealing petrol tanks. Fire in the air in a contraption made of wood, doped fabric, oil and petrol, fanned by rushing air, quickly consumed man and machine. There was no escape. Men may have cried for their mothers or their God in those last moments, but there were few who survived such infernos. The only – temporary – escape was a leap into space to avoid the burning, and they also knew that was just as fatal.

That these airmen could daily pit their strength of purpose and character against both hostile forces and often equally hostile environments says a great deal about them. Those who survived that conflict came home sadder but wiser men. They had been tested, just as the men who fought in the degradation and filth of the trenches had been too. As all wars are, WW1 was a grim business.

This is the story of one military formation, an air formation, born in that conflict and environment, and led by one whose enemies would not consider to be a beastly Hun if they had had the opportunity of knowing him. Boelcke was a product of his time, and once faced with his chosen destiny did his utmost to do his best for himself, his men and his country. He was far-sighted too, even though his horizons could only be guessed at. Oswald Boelcke accepted his lot, fought to improve it, tried to be humane and forthright, and, in a lesser degree than some chose to be, was successful and modest, yet magnanimous.

Soon after his death his Staffel was by decree referred to by the use of his name rather than its number. Perhaps no finer tribute can be found than this, that from October 1916 onwards, Jasta 2 – the unit he had formed – was known as Jasta Boelcke.

Chapter One

Formation

In the summer of 1916, Hauptmann Oswald Boelcke was already well known among the German Air Service fraternity and a legend in the making. Along with another early successful airman, Max Immelmann, he had received Germany's highest award for bravery, the Ordre Pour le Mérite, on 12 January 1916. Each had managed to bring down eight British and French aeroplanes. In fact both achieved their eighth victories on the 12th, Boelcke a British RE7, Immelmann a British Vickers FB5. At the time, both airmen were comrades in Flieger-abteilung 62 based at Douai.

Although Flieger-abteilung 62 (FA62) was a two-seater Staffel, whose aircraft were used for reconnaissance sorties, the arrival at the front of the nimble single-seater Fokker E-type monoplanes changed things in the air. They were fitted with a single fixed machine gun, set to fire through the arc of the propeller by way of an interrupter gear. Few in numbers, the Fokker Eindeckers (one wing rather than the more usual biplanes) were sent in ones and twos to various two-seater abteilungen so they could be used as escorts and, if free to do so, fly hunting missions to the front-line areas to seek out Allied two-seaters whose crews would be operating against the German army.

Not every pilot was enthused with the idea of flying these early fighters, but those who were certainly had that aggressive and adventurous spirit. They enjoyed the freedom of the hunting sorties where they were masters of their own destiny and could teach themselves the techniques of engaging French and British aeroplanes, and send them scurrying back across the lines, or even, perhaps, knock them from the sky.

Everything happening in the air war was new. In the war so far, a number of aircraft of both sides had been brought down in aerial actions, but in the beginning there was no thought of anyone gaining a reputation by bringing down several opposing aircraft. It was an achievement to secure even one such success. However, with the arrival of the Fokker monoplanes, the fighting pilots had the chance to bring down several.

The fact that Boelcke and Immelmann had accounted for sixteen of the enemy was amazing, and there were a few others like them who had managed to down two or three, mostly flying the Fokkers. These achievements brought fame and glory. Not only publicity but medals and decorations too. The German states and duchies of Prussia, Saxony, Bavaria, Würrtemburg, Anhalt, Baden and Oldenburg, as well as the eight states of Thuringia, all had their own special decorations for bravery and in many ways they each vied for chances of showering their military heroes with physical rewards. That a new breed of national hero – the aviator – was available gave an additional chance to shower such men with medals. And unlike Britain, Germany did not shrink from honouring their heroes publicly. Looking back today, one has the picture of those men depicted in such films as *The Prisoner of Zenda*, with their decorative uniforms, shiny boots, medals and awards dangling from neck and breast, and some with the occasional duelling scar or monocle.

Oswald Boelcke was aged 25, having been born on 19 May 1891 near Halle in Saxony, situated near the River Saale, 20 miles north-west of Leipzig. However, while Oswald was still a youngster the family moved to Dessau, a town in Anhalt, just north of Leipzig, so he was considered a native of that duchy. Oswald was the third child of six, his father was a schoolmaster. In those days it was not unusual for sons to decide on a military career, and parents would support rather than hinder such a desire. Thus in March 1911, still short of his 20th birthday, he entered the Prussian Cadet Corps, and was assigned to Nr.3 Telegrapher's Battalion at Koblenz. During early army manoeuvres he saw for the first time an aeroplane, and not for the first time was a youngster's head turned to the possible adventure of flight.

Desiring to fly he entered aviation in May 1914 and by July was a pilot. When the war began in August of that same year he went to fight and within a very short time was assigned to Flieger-abteilung 13 in France, with his older brother Wilhelm Boelcke flying as his observer. For his good work on reconnaissance missions he received the Iron Cross 2nd Class in October, then the Iron Cross 1st Class in February 1915. Oswald then moved to FA62 which had LVG two-seaters, and in one – numbered 162/15 – with Leutnant Heinz von Wühlisch as his observer, he gained his first official victory on 4 July. This was over a French Morane Parasol, which went down over Valenciennes, near Beauvicourt. The machine came from Escadrille MS15, its crew being Lieutenant Maurice Tétu and observer Lieutenant LeComte Georges de la Rochefoucauld Beauvicourt, both of whom died, the latter falling into the grounds of his own estate.

Once the first Fokker monoplanes arrived, Boelcke and Immelmann volunteered to fly them (Boelcke took one up on 7 July) and it was not long before both men began to achieve success against opposing airmen over the battle front.

One award that was exclusively Boelcke's was the Prussian Life Saving Medal, awarded following the rescue of a 14-year-old French boy who had fallen into the canal that ran in front of FA62's mess building, on 28 August. The local townsfolk actually wanted the German to be given the Legion d'Honneur.

On 22 September, Boelcke, who had by then achieved three victories, was moved to Metz, where he was to join a unit known as Brieftauben-Abteilung-Metz, leaving Immelmann at Douai. Both air fighters received the Knight's Cross with Swords of the Royal House Order of Hohenzollern in November 1915, which would later generally become the prerequisite before an airman could be considered for the Pour le Mérite. As we have read, this came in early 1916.

The odd thing here is that being the highest award Germany could bestow to its military men, whatever else a man receiving this award might achieve, over however long a period, he could expect to receive no better award. Such men could, and did, receive further if lesser awards, but once the attractive gold and blue-enamelled 'Blue Max' dangled from his neck, he had reached his peak as far as rewards went.

Boelcke returned to FA62 in December and from then on he and Immelmann battled for top dog in the scoring race, although Boelcke was again moved south on 21 January 1916, to take command of a fighter detachment at Verdun. Immelmann brought his score to 15 on 16 May 1916 but was killed just over a month later, on the evening of 18 June. Boelcke by this date had 18 victories, and scored one more on 27 June, but then, not wanting to risk further the life of its surviving hero, the German High Command ordered Boelcke away from the front.

He was ordered to undertake an inspection tour of south-eastern areas, notably Vienna, Budapest, Belgrade and finally Turkey. This did not please him at all, having expected a call to come to move back to the British Front where the great Somme Offensive was underway. Rather than just staying on the ground, he decided the inspection tour would at least give him a proper task to perform. On his way he went via Berlin and attended breakfast with the Kaiser. Another award he received at this time was the Knight's Cross 1st Class with Swords of the Ernestine House Order from Saxe-Coburg and Gotha, on 31 July 1916.

By mid-August he was on his way home. He dined with General Erich von Ludendorff and was later presented to Field Marshal Paul von Hindenburg. By 18 August he was again in Berlin with a new posting authority in his pocket. He would soon be back in action in France, and in command of a new unit.

*   *   *

Jasta 2

While Boelcke had been away from the Western Front he had been formulating his ideas about air fighting. Although the overall numbers of Fokker Eindeckers had slightly increased, they had never been numerous to start with. However, in a few units, certainly in FA62, they had had three or four Fokkers which had enabled the pilots flying them to develop some early tactics.

Despite the fact that the numbers made it more practical to fly lone sorties, it had been found that flying in company with at least one other pilot nearby gave some protection from hostile aircraft in that another pair of eyes could search the vast sky to hopefully avoid being attacked by surprise. While the British and French flyers too often flew lone sorties, it was becoming increasingly evident that they also were beginning to operate together for mutual protection against the predatorial Fokkers. So as Boelcke had left France, air fighting in small numbers was already starting to be the norm, although the day of the lone fighter, out looking for trouble, had not totally ended.

There was also the emergence of grouping fighter types together. It seemed more appropriate to have fighting units rather than merely attach a few Fokkers to two-seater abteilungen. Boelcke put his ideas down on paper and, because of his unique position as well as his being in favour with the higher echelons of the Air Service, sent them in for consideration. In essence he was advocating the establishment of a number of small fighting units, each equipped with the latest fighter types. These units would still hunt out the enemy and help escort two-seaters, although he saw the latter as being in the general area in which the two-seaters operated, rather than close escort to individual aircraft or formations. Provided the fighters were able to dominate sections of the sky, the two-seater crews would be able to fulfil their tasks in a hopefully safer environment.

These small groupings had started in early 1916, known as Kampfeinsitzer Kommandos – abbreviated to Keks. Bavarian Inspektor Major Friedrich Stempel, the Stabsoffizier der Flieger (Staff Officer in charge of Aviation) with the German 6th Army, commanded by Prince Rupprecht of Bavaria, had been the first to put the idea forward. Those groups that were formed were generally known, and named, by the bases they occupied, such as Kek Vaux or Kek Bertincourt. Initially they were tasked with Luftwachtdienst – aerial guard duty. Boelcke wanted the single-seaters to be more aggressive, and to hunt out the enemy.

However, what had already become an established tactic was that of fighting almost totally on the German side of the trench lines. Because the Fokker Eindeckers had been few in number, and because in the early days it was desirable not to risk the loss of one on the Allied side, nobody had been allowed across the lines in one. The Fokker's interrupter gear was still something of a secret and more or less remained so until a new delivery pilot lost his way and landed his Fokker intact on the wrong side of the lines, and was captured. Once this defensive stance began where the German fighter pilots waited for the opposition to come to them, offensive actions across the Allied lines became few and far between, except for assaults on observation balloons. Two-seater photo-reconnaissance machines of course continued to cross into Allied airspace, relying mostly on height or cloudy conditions to help them escape interception.

Oswald Boelcke returned to France. In part his ideas for autonomous fighting units had dovetailed with events and the suggestions of other air leaders and there were also new aeroplanes about to come into play. The Fokker monoplanes had run their course. They were never especially good as they were not initially designed for air-fighting, but were unique because of the fitting of a gun and an all-important interrupter gear. The French and British had several improved fighter types arriving at the front too: the DeHavilland 2, the FE8, the Nieuport Scout, and two-seater types such as the Sopwith 1½ Strutter and FE2b.

The new German types, which came under the general heading of Jagdeinsitzers, were all biplanes. These were the Albatros DI, Halberstadt DI and Fokker DII and DIII. By Imperial Decree came the formation of the first Jagdstaffeln in August 1916, seven at first, followed by a further eight in September, and nine more during November. By the end of the year, there were 33 Jastas in being.

Most of the early Jasta units were formed around existing groups of pilots and aircraft, such as the Keks, or training units, or even sections taken from two-seater abteilungen. Jasta 1 was formed at Bertincourt on 22 August and attached to the 1st Army, with personnel from Kek Nord, Army Flugpark 1 and a 1st Army FA Staffel, and was equipped with Fokker DI and DII fighters.

Jasta 2, however, had no parent unit, and no mass transfer of men from existing staffeln, it merely came into being, was assigned to the 1st Army and provided with a leader. This leader was Oswald Boelcke.

Hand-picked Men
It is often said that Boelcke was able to hand-pick his initial pilots and no doubt in part this is true. Presumably he was also able to influence another's choice, but common sense says that some would have just been assigned, and that they and those others he did select from personal knowledge, he quickly welded together.

The official formation date of Jasta 2 is recorded as 10 August, while Boelcke was still in the East. By the time he arrived on the scene at Velu some 17 days later, the decision had already been made to move to Bertincourt, just a short walk up the road, due north – in fact the other end of the flying field. According to his biographer, Professor Johannes Werner, he had received a telegram whilst still in Kovel: 'Return to west front as quickly as possible to organise and lead Jagdstaffel 2 on the Somme front.'

His biographer also confirms that he was able to pick out some suitable pilots for his Staffel, and without question he began at once to do so, but surely he would not have had the time to select every one personally. His brother Wilhelm was at Kovel and he is supposed to have recommended two officers he knew of, one was a young Uhlan by the name of Manfred von Richthofen, and the other was Erwin Böhme, whom Wilhelm had met some years earlier, whilst both were working in

East Africa. At 37, Böhme was no youngster.

According to von Richthofen he had first met Boelcke in October 1915, in the dining-car of a train in France. At the time the latter must have been on his way to Metz. Because his own pilot – von Richthofen was then still only an observer – had recently gone over to flying a Fokker, leaving him temporarily in limbo, he was taking an interest in not only becoming a pilot himself but possibly getting himself a single-seater fighter too. Boelcke was yet to become famous, but having by this date downed three hostile aircraft, he was something of a celebrity and Richthofen, never shy in coming forward, decided to ask the unassuming and almost insignificant-looking Leutnant – except for his penetrating bright steel blue eyes – how it was done. In reply, Boelcke had apparently said: 'Well, it's quite simple. I fly close to my man, aim well and then of course he falls down.' Von Richthofen spent some time in Boelcke's company and within a few days he had started to learn to fly, initially under the tutelage of his pilot, then at flying school.

On becoming a pilot he flew not single-seaters, but bombers on the Eastern Front. Thus in August 1916, whilst stationed at Kovel, he was told the now famous Boelcke was due to visit the airfield to meet with his brother. During the visit Boelcke mentioned that he was about to command a new unit in France and was looking for men to fly with him. Richthofen was not unhappy with his lot, so said nothing, but on the morning Boelcke was to leave, the great hero knocked on Richthofen's door, and asked him if he would like to join him in France. He obviously said yes, for within a couple of days von Richthofen was on a train to the west.

Erwin Böhme had been flying on the Russian Front for some time too, and on 16 August 1916 he wrote to his fiancée:

> Today there's some big news that I must report to you immediately. The famous Boelcke is here for two days on his journey back from the Balkans in order to visit his brother. He spoke very interestingly of his impressions and experiences in Turkey, and then, what interested me even more, that he was now putting together on the Somme a single-seater fighter squadron. He would be selecting from all of the air service what appeared to him to be the best qualified people. That evening I fell asleep with the thought – too bad you're such an old boy and not fifteen years younger! Such flying in the latest single-seater; that would be your downfall.
>
> So, imagine my surprise in the morning when Boelcke suddenly walked up beside me and simply asked, "Do you want to go with me to the Somme?" In my entire life, I have not voiced a happier "yes".
>
> Besides myself, Boelcke also selected here a young

Leutnant out of the lancers, Richthofen, a splendid person
who has already proved at Verdun and also here to be a brave
and steady pilot.

Although it is recorded that Böhme and Richthofen went with Boelcke
from Kovel there appears to have been three others as well. As Dr.-Ing.
Niedermeyer records in one of his several splendid articles over the
years in *Over The Front*[1], Böhme later recorded in a letter that:
'...besides von Richthofen and me he took three others...'
Unfortunately he does not name the three but it can be deduced that they
were probably Leutnants Hans Imelmann, Christian von Scheele and
Herwarth Philipps. The 21-year-old Philipps was the son of a doctor who
had been the medic with Wilhelm Boelcke and Böhme in East Africa. If
true that these additional three were returned to France, it was some
while before they joined Jasta 2, so we can perhaps assume they had first
to gain some experience on single-seaters. Von Scheele had already been
decorated for bravery, having received the Mecklenburg-Schwerin
Military Merit Cross 2nd Class in September 1914. However, his name
does not feature in Jasta 2 until January 1917.

On the Somme
By the time almost everyone had been selected or assigned, and
assembled at Velu, it was late August. The Somme battles had raged
continuously for the last two months and were not going well. The
German defenders had inflicted horrendous casualties on the Allied
attacks since the first day, but on the whole the familiar stalemate was
starting to show.

Boelcke arrived to find nothing except that his 'paper' unit was at the
airfield used as the Velu aircraft park. There were four permanent hangars
that had previously been used by Flieger-abteilung 32, and a few ground
mechanics that had been assigned to him. The date was 27 August and he
was starting from scratch. With him were just two other officers,
Leutnants Hans-Joachim von Arnim and Wolfgang Günther, and 64
NCOs and other ranks. Von Arnim was a former hussar from Pensiz
Gotlitz (Saxon Hussar Regiment Nr.19), aged 22, who was a pilot with
FA(A)207. The three officers were billeted in Bertincourt itself while the
men slept in huts. There were no aeroplanes.

Jasta 1's CO, Hauptmann Martin Zander, at the main Bertincourt
airfield, helped by giving Boelcke a few more mechanics and Leutnant
Otto Walter Höhne, on the 29th. Höhne had some experience, having
been with Kek Nord but when this had become Jasta 1, he stayed just six
days before being sent up the road to Velu. He was 21-years-old. Others
arriving in August were Leutnant Ernst Diener, from Kamfgeschwader
Nr.6, aged 20, and Leutnant Winand Grafe, also from Kek Nord/Jasta 1,
aged 22, who had achieved two possible victories.

[1] *Over the Front* is the quarterly journal produced by the League of WW1 Aviation
Historians.

The new unit suffered its first loss on the 28th, although in actual fact the pilot concerned was not flying with the Jasta. Von Arnim, while assigned to Jasta 2, had decided to continue flying with his two-seater outfit until such time as Jasta 2 at least got some aeroplanes. Thus on this day he was piloting one of two Roland CIIs south-east of Bapaume.

They were unlucky enough to be spotted by a pilot often termed as 'the British Boelcke' – Albert Ball – seated in a 60 Squadron Nieuport Scout. Ball was the master of stalking opponents, always trying to close in without being seen, generally underneath his target, so as to be able to pull down his top wing Lewis gun and fire upwards into an unsuspecting enemy. Ball's combat report records:

> Nieuport Scout A201. 9.15 to 9.45 am. OP Bapaume – Cambrai roads.
> Two Rolands seen SE of Bapaume. Nieuport chased and got underneath nearest machine, which had a three-ply fuselage. Nieuport fired one drum at about 20 yards, turned to change drums and fired half a drum, after which the Roland dived and landed in corner of cornfield. Machine did not fire when diving, although Nieuport followed it down to 3,000 feet. The second machine ran, and fired off back mountings.

In fact it was the observer, Leutnant Böhne, who landed the machine after a struggle to fly the Roland down and straighten it out from its downwards plunge. It was to have been von Arnim's last sortie before moving over to Jasta 2's billet in Bertincourt.

Pilots at the end of August 1916:	Name	Victories
	Hauptmann Oswald Boelcke	19
	Leutnant Wolfgang Günther	–
	Leutnant Otto Walter Höhne	–
	Leutnant Ernst Diener	–
	Leutnant Winand Grafe	2 (?)

September 1916

Two more pilots arrived on the 1st, von Richthofen and two NCO pilots, Feldwebel Leopold Rudolf Reimann and Offizierstellvertreter Max Müller. To confuse matters, there is another Reimann noted as joining on this first day of September, Leutnant Hans Reimann, aged 22, from Minden, previously with Kasta (Kampfstaffel) 8 of KG2. Leopold Reimann had been with FA32, recently moved from Bertincourt.

Many Jasta 2 pilots were destined to become well-known fighter aces, none more so than Max Müller, a Bavarian from Rottenburg. However, he was older than most of the youngsters around him – 29. He had joined the army before the war and had been a motor driver, a job where he could use his knowledge of mechanics. In 1913 he had even had the job of chauffeur to the Bavarian War Minister. The story goes that Müller had become entranced with flying, and every time he ran to open the car door for the minister, he requested a transfer to aviation. He obviously succeeded, or the minister got fed up with him, for by December 1913 he was learning to fly at the school at Schleissheim, where he gained his 'ticket' on 4 April the following year.

When war started he flew with FA1b (the 'b' denoting a Bavarian unit) but within days he crashed on take-off following engine failure, and broke both legs. Recovering, he returned to his unit and by 1916 had flown 160 front-line missions, receiving both classes of the Iron Cross and the Bavarian Military Merit Cross 3rd Class with Crown and Swords. Following a particularly hazardous photographic sortie on 13 December 1915 he had been awarded the Bavarian Bravery Medal in Silver. Moving to fighters he joined Kek B (Bertincourt), which was the attachment to FA32, and then moved to Jasta 2.

NCO Reimann was from Oberhohnsdorf, near Zwicken, and was therefore a Saxon. He had won the Iron Cross 1st and 2nd Class with Pioneer Battalion Nr.12, but was wounded in the spring of 1915. However, his bravery gained him the Silver St Henry Medal in June. He then went into aviation and flew Fokkers with Kek B too. He survived a crash on 30 June and had now come to Boelcke's new Staffel.

Next to arrive were Böhme, and Oberleutnant Günther Viehweger, on the 8th. Viehweger, as his rank suggests, was a long-serving officer and he had previously flown with KG2. Böhme, of course, was the father-figure and had seen much of life thus far. An engineer from Holzminden on the Weser, he had worked in both Germany and Switzerland before going out to East Africa. Returning as the war started, he had served in a Jäger Regiment prior to requesting pilot training. At 35 he was retained as an instructor for a year but finally snapped himself clear and reported to Kagohl 2 on the Eastern Front, which was commanded by Boelcke's brother Wilhelm, whom he knew. No doubt one reason why Oswald had been happy to take brother Wilhelm's advice about Böhme was that he had shown a particularly aggressive streak and had claimed three enemy aircraft shot down, although only one had been officially confirmed. Again, no doubt due to his age and experience, he and Boelcke became good friends.

Something else happened on 1 September; the first aircraft arrived. Reimann flew across an Albatros DI from Jasta 1 and two Fokker biplanes were ferried in from the aircraft park – one being taken over by Boelcke himself (a DIII, serial number 352/16). This aircraft would later be exhibited in the Berlin Zeughaus armoury museum, but would be lost in the bombing of World War Two. Boelcke wasted no time in testing his new fighter, and in the most spectacular way, by downing his 20th opponent on the 2nd. Officially his Jasta was not yet operational, but that did not stop Boelcke from taking a trip to the front, air test or not. He wrote to his family on the 4th:

You will be astonished to read of my 'twentieth', because you will have imagined me still organising my Staffel but not yet flying.

A few days ago Fokker sent two machines for me, and I made my first flight in one of them the day before yesterday. There was a fair amount of enemy aerial activity at the front. These fellows have grown very impudent. One of them tried to have a go at me when I was flying peacefully behind our lines, but I refused to let myself be drawn – he was flying much higher than I. Somewhat later in the day I saw shell-bursts west of Bapaume. There I found a BE, followed by three Vickers single-seaters, i.e. an artillery plane with its escort. I went for the BE, but the other three interrupted me in the middle of my work, and so I beat a hasty retreat. One of those fellows thought he could catch me and gave chase. When I had lured him somewhat away from the others, I gave battle and soon got to grips with him. I did not let him go again; he did not get another shot at me.

When he went down his machine was wobbling badly, but that, as he told me afterwards, was not his fault, because I had shot his elevating gear to pieces. The machine landed north-east of Thièpval; it was burning as the pilot jumped out and beat his arms and legs about because he [his flying coat] was on fire too. I then flew home and took off again with fresh supplies of ammunition because other Englishmen had appeared, but I did not score any further successes.

The machine, a DH2 of 32 Squadron, was piloted by Captain R E Wilson. Wilson, upon his return from Germany at the end of the war, noted:

Engaged enemy aircraft whilst protecting photographic machine. Drove enemy machines away several times. Gun jammed and was then attacked by this hostile machine. Endeavoured to regain lines but controls were shot away, engine hit, crashed out of control and machine fired. Crashed on fire.

Boelcke wrote:

Yesterday I fetched the Englishman I had forced to land – a certain Captain Wilson – from the prisoners' clearing depot, took him to coffee in the mess and showed him our aerodrome, whereby I had a very interesting conversation with him.

Captain Robert E Wilson was with 32 Squadron RFC, flying a DH2 'pusher' scout – the engine is at the rear, pushing the machine through the air. He and the others were escorting a 4 Squadron BE2c, the crew seeing Wilson land safely and appear to set his machine on fire. Boelcke's reference to an artillery machine meant that he thought it was a two-seater that would direct artillery fire onto a German target, whereas Wilson says it was a photo-machine – one using a camera to take pictures of the ground positions. Wilson was later to record:

It is some consolation to me that I was brought down by Captain Boelcke, the greatest German airman, and that my life was preserved in a fashion that is almost miraculous.

I fly a fast Vickers Fighter[2]. When out on reconnaissance work I saw a German scout intending to polish off one of our slow old BEs and came just in time to rescue it. After I loosened off a couple of shots at the German, he went into a turn and flew home. I was fool enough to chase him and failed to spot that he only wanted to lure me further in to his territory. When I followed him about 15 miles behind the German lines, he turned round and attacked me by climbing above me at a fabulous speed; he was flying a machine I had never seen before, and I had no idea of its speed or climbing capacity. I hardly let off a couple of shots before my gun jammed, so that I could not fire a single round more.

Under these circumstances I did the only thing left to me and fled to get out of the way of a better machine and a superior pilot. I tried to shake him off by all sorts of tricks, but he followed all my movements magnificently and sat on my neck [tail] the whole time. He shot away all my controls, with the exception of two that were jammed, shot holes in my machine, shot the throttle away when I had my hand on it; then he put some holes in my tank and a couple in my coat so it was soaked in petrol. Naturally I lost all control over my machine, which whizzed down in a nosedive – a most uncomfortable sensation! I sat there, pretty dizzy and waiting for the crash when I would hit the ground below, but when at about fifty feet up I made a desperate tug at the stick and somehow obtained enough control at the last moment to dodge the crash and bring off some sort of a landing, which however, set the machine and my coat on fire. I managed to jump out and pull my coat off without getting burnt.

---

[2] This is an odd term for Wilson to use for his aircraft. At various times the Germans tended to give certain types a sort of group name. In this early period, a type that was met fairly often was the Vickers FB5 'pusher' – later known as the Gunbus. Thus most pusher-types became known as Vickers, be they DH2s, FE8s, or FE2s. The term 'sitting on my neck' is also a German term, British pilots usually saying 'sitting on my tail'.

The German came down quite low and flew away as soon
as he made sure I was settled. Next day Boelcke invited me
to his aerodrome and entertained me in his mess. We were
also photographed together. I got a very fine impression of
him both as a pilot and a man, and this fight will remain the
greatest memory of my life, even though it turned out badly
for me.

During the period 8 to 15 September, Boelcke showed that he was back
into his stride by downing six further opponents, an FE2b on the 8th,
another DH2 on the 9th, and doubles on 14 and 15 September. Boelcke's
second claim of the 14th was a DH2 from 24 Squadron. Its pilot, Second
Lieutenant John V Bowring, was brought down and taken prisoner. He
recorded upon his release from Germany in 1918:

> Whilst on Offensive Patrol near Bapaume machine hit
> several places by enemy aircraft. Previous to this I had been
> slightly wounded in the foot; attacked EA but engine failed
> and [was] forced to land. Surrounded at once, could not burn
> machine.

The victory on the 8th was over a machine from 22 Squadron which went
down in flames north of Le Sars. The next day was a DH2 of 24
Squadron, again falling on fire, near Bapaume. The other three were
Sopwith two-seaters of 70 Squadron.

The crew of the 'Strutter' on the 14th was on a recce mission to Douai-
Le Quesnoy-Marcoing-Bapaume. It was seen to be attacked by a German
fighter, went into a nosedive and collapsed in the air south of Bapaume.
This victory can be seen through the report of another 70 Squadron pilot,
Captain W J C K Cochrane Patrick, a future ace. Some squadrons used to
write their reports in the third person, no doubt due to the fact that the
Recording Officer would do the writing after jotting down notes from
the pilots concerned:

> While returning from reconnaissance over Bapaume, Capt.
> Patrick's and 2/Lt E W Burke's machine was about 1,000
> feet above 2/Lt S H Gale/Sapper J M Strathy. Six hostile
> machines were seen to come up at the same height as 2/Lt
> Gale. Capt. Patrick turned and dived on a hostile machine.
> After a running fight with three machines, Capt. Patrick saw
> 2/Lt Gale's machine go down in a spinning nosedive. The
> next he saw of it one of the planes had come off.
>
> 2/Lt Burke was hit and killed, and Capt. Patrick headed
> for the lines going down to 6,000 feet. Four HA followed
> him a short way over the lines and then turned back.

One of the two Sopwiths he shot down on the 15th was piloted by Captain G L Cruickshank DSO MC, an experienced flight commander and air fighter. Guy Cruickshank came from Eastbourne, Sussex, was aged 26 and had been flying since 1913. He and his observer, Lieutenant R A Preston, were killed. A report made out by another pilot, Second Lieutenant N Kemsley, shows that he was lucky to survive Boelcke's attentions:

> Whilst on patrol two HA dived on my machine, one coming on the tail, the second coming alongside. My observer, 2/Lt C J Beatty, fired ¾ [of a] drum at the second machine when his gun jammed. He changed drums and got off a full drum at the second machine. I then discovered that my petrol tank had been hit twice, so I broke off the fight and made for the lines, where I landed at Barleux. My observer had been hit through the head and was alive on landing, but died later in hospital.

Alan Bott MC was the author of the book *An Airman's Outings*, written under the penname of 'Contact'. This followed the story of 70 Squadron in 1916, Bott being the observer to A W 'Bunny' Vaucour. In his book he recalls Guy Cruickshank:

> C. [Cruickshank] we learned was down at last after seventeen months of flying on active service, with only one break for any appreciable time. He destroyed one more enemy before the Boches got him. In the dive he got right ahead of the two machines that followed him. As these hurried to his assistance, they saw an enemy plane turn over, show a white, gleaming belly, and drop in zigzags. C's bus was then seen to heel over into a vertical dive and to plunge down, spinning rhythmically on its axis. Probably he was shot dead and fell on to the joystick, which put the machine into its last dive. The petrol tank of the second machine to arrive among the Huns was plugged by a bullet, and the pilot was forced to land. Weeks later, his observer [actually the pilot – 2/Lt F H Bowyer] wrote to us a letter from a prison camp in Hannover. The third bus, perforated by scores of bullet-holes, got back to tell the tale.
>
> C. was one of the greatest pilots produced by the war. He was utterly fearless, and had more time over the German lines to his credit than any one else in the Flying Corps. It was part of his fatalistic creed that Archie [AA fire] should never be dodged, and he would go calmly ahead when the AA guns were at their best. Somehow the bursts never found him. He had won both the DSO and MC for deeds in the air.

Only the evening before, when asked lightly if he was out for a VC, he said he would rather get Boelcke than the VC; and in the end Boelcke probably got him, for he fell over the famous German pilot's aerodrome, and that day the German wireless announced that Boelcke had shot down two more machines. Peace to the ashes of a fine pilot and a very brave man!

Perhaps of interest, the RFC order (dated the 14th) that had sent them out read:

Operation Order No.488
by
Major-General H M Trenchard CB DSO ADC
Commanding Royal Flying Corps,
In the Field

Tuesday,
September 14th, 1916.

1. The 4th and Reserve Armies are taking the offensive at zero [hour] pm the 15th instant with a view of gaining in the first instance, the line Morval–Les Boeufs–Guedecourt–Flers, and thence south of Martinpuich to our present front-line R.54.b.

   The French are attacking on the right of the 4th Army. When the infantry are established on the above line, the cavalry corps will push through to the high ground between Rocquigny and Bapaume.

2. The C-in-C considers that the situation is so favourable as to justify and demand very bold and vigorous action on the part of all arms, including the RFC.

3. The 9th Wing will co-operate as shown in table 'A' attached.

   Pilots will fly low should weather or other reasons render it necessary to do so. In the event of any sign of disorganisation or retreat on the part of the enemy, every endeavour must be made to harass his troops and transport with machine-gun fire and bombs, with a view of turning his retreat into a rout.

4. If the weather is bad, the bomb raids (1) and (2) on table 'A' will not start, but all machines detailed for them will be held in readiness to go out in pairs and act as in paragraph 3 above, east of the line Mory–Frémicourt–Barastre exclusive.

   The Sopwith patrol (3) will be carried out whether (1)

or (2) start or not.

5. The Officer Commanding, 2nd Wing, will, in addition, detail three BE12s for contact patrol work. The first will leave the ground in time to be over the 4th Army trenches at zero hour which will be notified to OC 9th Wing.

One of these machines will constantly patrol in rear of our attacking troops, and will watch for flares lit or signals sent by them. The pilot will report in person to Adv. HQRFC immediately on landing, giving the positions reached by our own troops as far as he has been able to ascertain them.

The cavalry are using green flares and the infantry red flares.

6. Acknowledge.

Item 3 on the attached table 'A' read:

3. Eight Sopwiths. Escort to (1) and (2). As soon after BE12s as possible.

Remain out – three hours. During bombing will patrol E. of Bourlon and Havrincourt and will subsequently patrol in the area Havrincourt-Epehy-Roisel-Bapaume.

Reading this order today it gives the feeling that this assault was little more than a 'walk in the park' and that there would probably be little difficulty in reaching the objectives. If nothing else it probably instilled some sort of confidence from the top.

*   *   *

Boelcke's pilots were eager to emulate their leader but without sufficient aircraft to mount patrols there was nothing else to do but to make the odd practice flight while their Staffelführer took the opportunity to ease his Fokker biplane towards the front when in the air. Their time would soon come.

Jasta 2 now had an adjutant – an Offizier zur besonderen Verwendung (OzbV) – by the name of Leutnant Hellmuth von Zastrow. Zastrow was a Berliner, aged 25, and had also served in Prussian Infantry Regiment Nr.129. Boelcke had met him earlier at the Fokker unit at Jametz, which was also shared by von Zastrow's unit, FA(A)203 – an artillery spotting flieger-abteilung, denoted by the (A). Since their meeting he had been badly wounded and was now unfit to fly. He had arrived on the 10th, the same day another pilot arrived, Leutnant Herwarth Philipps, posted in from Kek Vaux. He came from Kiel. It is assumed that he had initially gone to Vaux whilst awaiting a posting to Jasta 2.

Böhme had arrived on the 8th, disappointed to find that apart from

Boelcke's personal machine, none of the promised new aircraft were available. These 'new' machines were the Albatros DIs. In all the Jasta had five aircraft, the Albatros that Reimann had come with, a Fokker DI, a 'refurbished' Halberstadt, a Fokker DII and at least one Fokker DIII.

Straining at the Leash

There can be little doubt that Boelcke's young pilots were eager to emulate him, eager to get into the air in the new fighter planes, and eager to clash with the British airmen along their section of the front. Suddenly the aircraft were ready for collection from the aircraft park at Cambrai. On Saturday 16 September the pilots drove there, collected six machines and flew them back to Bertincourt. That same evening, Otto Höhne secured the Jasta's first victory by someone other than their leader. By this date Boelcke had increased his own score to 26 and at around 6 pm, Höhne downed a British FE2b of 11 Squadron RFC.

The Jasta encountered the FEs, which were out on a reconnaissance mission west of Marcoing and Höhne's fire crippled one pusher, forcing its pilot, Second Lieutenant A L Pinkerton, to make a hasty landing – trailing smoke – which put him and his observer, Lieutenant J W Sanders, into a prisoner of war camp. When both men were released from captivity at the end of 1918 they recorded the action which seems to give more credit to anti-aircraft fire than to a fighter:

> Alfred L Pinkerton: While on reconnaissance patrol near Cambrai heavy AA fire was directed on us, propeller being very badly damaged, engine hit. Three enemy aircraft also attacked, riddling the machine and forcing us down to the ground.

> James Wm Sanders: Flying in formation when propeller was hit by EAA [enemy anti-aircraft] – forced to land unwounded. Shot-up by enemy aircraft after being hit by AA. Machine wrecked.

Whatever the real facts of the action, there was jubilation at Velu. It had worked. Someone had brought down one of the enemy. If anything it made the rest of the pilots even more keen to start combat actions. If Höhne could do it, so could the others. Boelcke wrote home on the 17th:

> The Staffel is not quite up to strength yet, as I am still without about half of our machines. But yesterday at least six arrived, so that I shall be able to take off with my Staffel for the first time today. Hitherto I have generally flown Fokker biplanes, but today I shall take up one of the new Albatroses. My pilots are all passionately keen and very competent, but I must first train them to steady teamwork – they are at

present rather like young puppies in their zeal to achieve something.

No one was more eager or zealous than Manfred von Richthofen. He had been brought up a hunter and saw this new way of waging war very much like being pitted against a stag or a wild boar. What had once been man against animal, was now man against man – the supreme hunt. In his book *The Red Air Fighter*, von Richthofen recorded:

> We were at the butts trying our machine guns. On the previous day we had received our new aeroplanes, and the next morning Boelcke was to fly with us. We were all beginners. None of us had had a success so far. Consequently everything that Boelcke told us was to us gospel truth. During the last few days he had, as he said, shot for breakfast every day one or two Englishmen.
>
> The next morning, the 17th of September, was a gloriously fine day. It was therefore only to be expected that the English would be very active. Before we started Boelcke repeated to us his instructions, and for the first time we flew as a squadron commanded by the great man whom we followed blindly.

Heading for the front on the morning of the 17th, Erwin Böhme achieved his first victory by downing a Sopwith $1^1/_2$ Strutter of 70 Squadron at 07.45 near Cambrai. His attack sent the two-seater down to crash north-west of Hervilly, its pilot dead, the observer badly injured and taken prisoner. Again jubilation back at the airfield. Re-armed and refuelled, the Albatros fighters took off again late morning; a British squadron had been reported crossing the lines.

FE2b machines of 11 Squadron ran into the grinder. Boelcke and his eager fledglings fell on the big pusher two-seaters west of Marcoing. 3 Brigade RFC had ordered a bomb raid upon Marcoing railway station, and four BE2d aircraft from 12 Squadron had been bombed up and flown out without observers in order to maximise the weight of their bomb loads. Instead of observers, the aircraft would be protected by the FEs. And protect them they did. None of the BEs were lost but the FEs suffered. Boelcke, Hans Reimann and von Richthofen each despatched one, while Leutnant Wilhelm Frankl of Jasta 4 accounted for another.

The battle had drifted some way south of the target area. Boelcke's victim – which he noted carried streamers, denoting a leader or deputy leader – force-landed near Equancourt where the crew set fire to their machine before being captured. It was flown by Captain D B Gray, a flight commander. Reimann's FE came down near Trescault, its crew dead or dying. Von Richthofen shot his victims down at Villers Plouich, its observer dead, the pilot dying later:

Apparently he was no beginner, for he knew exactly that his last hour had arrived at the moment I got at the back of him. I was curious to see whether he would fall.

My Englishman twisted and turned, flying in zigzags. I did not think for a moment that the hostile squadron contained other Englishmen who conceivably might come to the aid of their comrades. I was animated by a single thought: "The man in front of me must come down, whatever happens." At last a favourable moment arrived. My opponent had apparently lost sight of me. Instead of twisting and turning he flew straight along [ahead]. In a fraction of a second I was at his back with my excellent machine. I gave a short burst of shots with my machine gun. I had flown so close that I was afraid I might crash into the Englishman. Suddenly I nearly yelled with joy, for the propeller of the enemy machine had stopped turning.

The historian H A Jones recorded in his work *The War in the Air*:

At the same time as the German fighters were getting into the air, eight BEs of 12 Squadron, carrying eight 112lb, and 32 x 20lb bombs, escorted by six FEs of No.11 Squadron, were leaving for a visit to Marcoing station.

Boelcke saw them soon after they had crossed the lines and followed to cut them off. But the British pilots reached Marcoing and, taking deliberate aim, dropped their 40 bombs about the station, which was set on fire. Just outside the station an explosion which followed the burst of a bomb sent clouds of smoke high in the air. Almost as they released their bombs the aeroplanes were mixed up in a fierce fight. In addition to Boelcke's five, some seven other German fighters appear to have joined in. The FEs did all they could to protect the bombing aeroplanes and in doing so four of them were shot down. In spite of the self-sacrifice of the escorts two of the bombers also fell victim to their more speedy opponents.

The problem with FE2 machines, along with other pusher types, was that while the big engine behind the gondola which housed the crew helped protect them from bullets fired from a stern attack, the engine itself was also extremely vulnerable to this fire. At the same time, the observer in the front section of the gondola found it difficult to defend against a hostile machine behind them. He had a splendid field of fire of 180 degrees in the front, but his only recourse against a rear attack was to man a backwards-firing Lewis gun on a pole, stand himself up precariously on his seat or even the edge of the cockpit, and hammer a burst in the general direction of the enemy behind. It was more in hope than in judgement, little more than a scatter-gun effect which may or may not score a hit or put off an attacker. An experienced attacker would merely lose a little bit of height and continue to fire slightly upwards into his target. Engine and fuel tank then took the full force of his fire.

Von Richthofen's victim came down near the airfield at Flesquières, so there was a convenient place for him to land and inspect his first kill. Men from that airfield were already running towards the downed machine and von Richthofen soon joined them. Soldiers had arrived too and when von Richthofen inspected the two-seater it confirmed his view that he had smashed the engine, but his fire had also mortally wounded both airmen. One had already died – the observer – the other, pilot Lionel Morris, dying shortly afterwards. Fate decreed another disaster on the family of the dead observer, Tom Rees, for on the very same day – incongruously – his brother John was killed. He was struck by lightning!

The crew of Boelcke's FE, Captain D B Gray and Lieutenant L B Helder, said they had force-landed at Nurlie. Leonard Helder had this to record after his return home in 1918:

> Engine hit by machine-gun fire from enemy aircraft [Boelcke]. Formation became broken up on account of one machine dropping behind, and others turning to support [it]. Whilst continuing with the other machine, attacked in rear and underneath. Engine hit and forced to land on return journey. Escorting bombers.

Captain David Gray was flying a brand new FE, one delivered only the previous day. So new he had not even recorded its serial number. As yet the mechanics had not really had much time to give it the once over and Gray must have been only too aware of the newness of the machine as he had flown out. 'Munshi' Gray was sent to Osnabruck, then Crefeld, ending up at Holzminden prison camp. With others he began a tunnel from the camp and in July 1918, he and two companions escaped and got back to England, for which Gray was awarded the MC.

On the 18th Boelcke wrote to his father:

> Dear Father,
> I forgot to answer your questions.
> (1) My colleagues are very efficient and ambitious. Day before yesterday, a number of aircraft arrived. Yesterday, they had already brought down 4 Englishmen.
> (2) None of the well-known names are with me.
> (3) The squadron is not complete yet, half of the aircraft are still missing.
> (4) Quarters fine. Good bed, nice room.

> (5) I have now flown Fokker Biplane. In yesterday's battle
>   an Albatros.
>
> Max is between Tahure and Argonne. I don't know exact
> location either.
>
> > Best regards – Oswald.

Max was one of his brothers.

   Boelcke shot down a Morane on the 19th which broke up in the air as
it fell in flames into a wood near Grévillers. This action too appears in H
A Jones' work:

> An attempted reconnaissance by FEs of No.11 Squadron
> escorted by fighters of No.60 Squadron, was attacked by
> Boelcke's formation near Quéant. A Morane flown by Capt.
> H C Tower was shot to pieces in the air by Boelcke, the pilot
> of one of the FEs was wounded and another FE with a
> damaged engine and wounded observer had to be landed in
> Delville Wood where it was destroyed by shell fire.

*   *   *

Erwin Böhme wrote to his fiancée on the 21st:

> Today, before anything else, I can report to you that our new
> fighter squadron is now properly organised. Our planes
> finally arrived; first, to be sure, only six. On Saturday, we
> collected them from Cambrai. On Sunday morning, we
> tried them for the first time. We happened across an English
> squadron at the same time, eight large biplanes together,
> and immediately shot down six (*sic*). Only one or two
> escaped.
>   Meanwhile, Boelcke had another, his 28th. The
> composure and guts with which he flies and fights are simply
> marvellous. Our new aircraft border likewise on marvellous.
> Compared to the single-seater which we flew before Verdun,
> they are improved. Their rate of climb and turning radius are
> amazing. It is as if they are living, feeling creatures that
> understand what the pilot wishes. With them one may risk
> everything and succeed.

Boelcke had scored number 28 on the 19th, a Morane Scout of 60
Squadron, but then on the 22nd Leutnant Grafe did not survive an
encounter with a BE12 of 19 Squadron soon after 8 am. He was shot
down by Second Lieutenant V R Stewart, and seen to fall and burst into
flames near Bapaume. Jasta 2 had suffered its first real loss and no doubt

this gave the fledglings pause for thought. The Jasta got its revenge later that morning, four pilots meeting 19 Squadron again. Höhne and both Reimanns each downed a BE12. Stewart's combat report read:

> 22 September 1916. 8 am, OP 11,000 ft. Between Bapaume and Cambrai. Rotary engined biplane.
> I was on OP under Lt [G B A] Baker, 1st Leader, and Lieut. [T] Davidson, 2nd Leader.
>   East of Bapaume a rotary engined biplane attacked me on the right. I fired my Vickers gun first and then about 8 rounds with my Lewis gun. He disappeared, diving, and about a minute later burst into flames, and dived to earth, evidently having been hit by some other machine's fire. I engaged two more machines and fired two or three rounds from the Vickers gun at each and they both dived. I lost the patrol for a few minutes and attached myself to an FE8 patrol.

It is interesting that Stewart was so self-effacing that he assumed someone else must have caused the enemy machine to catch fire, but nobody else had shot at it so he was given the victory. Nor does he mention that he was still carrying his bombs during the action! From his combat report we can assume that Grafe was flying a Fokker DIII – this type having a rotary engine. 19 Squadron Record Book:

> 07.01 – 09.01 am. Attacked by biplane and replied and HA dived. Was seen in flames a few minutes later. BE12 6588. Failed to drop bombs owing to hostile aircraft.

Vernon Radcliffe Stewart, aged 23, was killed in a flying accident while with 28 Training Squadron in England on 5 December 1917.
    The BE12 was a fighter version of the BE2, with the observer's front cockpit covered over and a Lewis gun fixed to the top wing, and/or a Vickers gun fixed to the port side of the pilot's cockpit. Despite downing Grafe, it was not a fighter, merely a BE2 being used as a fighter. It did not last long as a combat machine. On this same day, Boelcke wrote home:

> I have not yet been able to put up sheds for our machines, which must be accommodated in tents at present, as we haven't the men to do the work. My first aim is to get huts built for my officers so they can be housed on the aerodrome instead of living in the village, and be always ready for take-off. What a lot of work it means!
>   Besides that I have to give my pilots some training. This isn't easy because they are all inspired with such fiery zeal that it is difficult to put the brakes on them. They have certainly all learnt that the main thing is to get the enemy in

your power and beat him down at once instead of arguing
with him. But until I get it into their heads that everything
depends on sticking together through thick and thin when the
Staffel goes into battle and that it doesn't matter who
actually scores the victory as long as the Staffel wins it –
well, I can talk myself silly and sometimes I really have to
get tough with them. I always give them some instruction
before we take off, and deal out severe criticism after every
flight and especially after every fight. But they take it all
very well.

Boelcke may have tried to insist it didn't matter who shot the enemy
down so long as he fell, but the nature of these new fighter pilots was to
register their own kills for the glory of themselves rather than for the
Staffel.

The reason Boelcke remarks about accommodating men in tents and
wanting huts for his officers was that the officers had been moved out of
their living quarters in the village of Bertincourt due to it being shelled a
number of times by British artillery.

The next day, the 23rd, von Richthofen and Hans Reimann were each
credited with a Martinsyde G100 (27 Squadron), while Erwin Böhme
claimed another but did not have it confirmed. However, 27 Squadron did
lose three aircraft. Von Richthofen shot down Sergeant H Bellamy, who
was killed, while Reimann collided with Lieutenant L F Forbes and fell
to his death. In fact, Forbes deliberately rammed the Albatros and
managed to get his damaged machine back across the lines. He tried to
reach the airfield at Bertangles, north of Amiens, but hit a tree, injuring
himself and smashing his G100. Forbes, who received the Military Cross,
later became an air marshal.

It is unclear what happened to the other Martinsyde. As mentioned,
three were lost but only two credited. It is assumed that the Germans must
have concluded that Reimann's collision had accounted for one of the
wrecks on their side of the lines and Richthofen's was the other, so why
did the third loss not go to Böhme? Possibly Reimann had accounted for
one before the collision, and the third one, the one attacked by Böhme,
was the one seen going down smoking across the trenches to come down
near Le Transloy, on the British side. If so, this was the one flown by
Second Lieutenant E J Roberts, who was killed. It was sometimes
difficult to gain confirmation of a victory in cases where aircraft fell on
the Allied side of the lines, although never impossible.

While it was gratifying to have achieved further combat successes, it
had cost the Jasta the life of Hans Reimann, who had just achieved his
fourth victory moments before Leslie Forbes rammed him.

A Move to Lagnicourt

The next day, the 24th, Jasta 2 completed a change of base. From Velu/Bertincourt it went to Lagnicourt, about eight kilometres due north of Bertincourt. British artillery fire was again the culprit, their guns starting to lob shells near to the airfield itself making it an unsafe place from which to operate. In the nearby village, near to the church, the officers occupied a small château. The church steeple was a good landmark being right next to the landing ground.

Boelcke was not well. He was suffering from the damp autumn weather which was aggravating an asthmatic condition, but he refused to leave his command and go into hospital for some treatment. He was back on the flying roster by the 27th.

That same day he downed a Martinsyde for his 29th victory and the Jasta scored another that was not credited to any individual. RFC Operation Order No.500 had requested six Martinsydes and six Sopwiths to leave the ground at 9 am or as soon after the weather permitted, for three hours, and patrol the area Bapaume-Fins-Lagnicourt. Boelcke was on patrol with four of his men in the Bapaume area and spotted a squadron of British machines to the south-east. They were higher than the Albatri so Boelcke turned to the north and began to climb. Getting into a position from which to attack, Boelcke led his men into a dive and shot down one of the Martinsydes almost immediately.

He curved in behind another and opened fire, whereupon the British pilot went into a series of steep turns. Boelcke could not match the turns and then came to the conclusion the pilot was dead, or at least unconscious at the controls, which were now locked in position. Closing in to one side of the circling machine, Boelcke could see the man was indeed slumped in his cockpit. Noting the serial number on the tail – 7495 – Boelcke left it to its fate. He then fired at another Martinsyde, seeing his bullets slash into the fuselage, but the pilot got his machine back across the lines.

Back at base Leopold Reimann claimed to have fired into a Martinsyde with the tail number 7495, so, in order to do nobody an injustice, the victory was merely added to the Jasta's total and not credited to any individual.

27 Squadron had certainly been through the mill. One machine had been lost, its pilot killed. Two others had been shot-up and one of the pilots returned wounded, while another was missing. One pilot had claimed to have sent one of the attackers down in a vertical nosedive, but Jasta 2 had no losses.

The missing pilot in 7495 was Second Lieutenant S Dendrino. Stephen Dendrino came from Essex and was 27. His machine eventually ran out of petrol and came down. Wounded and unconscious, he was made a captive but later died, being buried at Neuville-Vitasse by the Germans.

On the last day of the month, Manfred von Richthofen brought down an FE2b near Frémicourt for his third victory, shortly before noon. It was a machine from 11 Squadron, whose crew were killed.

However, Jasta 2 lost Leutnant Ernst Diener on this day, shot down by a French Nieuport Scout near Bapaume mid-morning. It is probable that he was the victim of René Dorme of Escadrille N.3. Dorme, who at age 26 was known as 'Père' by his comrades, had been in the army pre-war and rejoined in August 1914. He moved to aviation in April 1915 to become a reconnaissance pilot. Almost as soon as he became a fighter pilot, he was wounded, but after recovery he began a rise to fame as an air fighter. France had strict rules on victory confirmations and as Dorme often flew out on lone patrols, many of his claims were not made official. So too was his claim for Ernst Diener whose aircraft fell, as Dorme saw it, near Bertincourt, but without anyone else seeing it go down, he could only request a 'probable'. As he had twelve official victories already and at least three other probables, it has to be fairly certain that he was the cause of Diener's fall.

September ended with the Jasta having achieved 21 victories for the loss of three pilots, four if one counts von Arnim. The fledglings were riding high having tasted victory while at the same time realising only too well that fate always flew with them.

Chapter Two

Autumn 1916

Pilots at the start of October 1916:	Name	Victories
	Hptm Oswald Boelcke	29
	Ltn Manfred von Richthofen	3
	Ltn Erwin Böhme	2
	Ltn Otto Höhne	2
	Ltn Wolfgang Günther	–
	Offz Max Müller	–
	Offz Leopold Reimann	2
	Oblt Günther Viehweger	1
	Ltn Herwarth Philipps	–
OzbV	Ltn Hellmuth von Zastrow	–

Base: Lagnicourt   Front: 1st Army

On 1 October 1916 the Battle of the Ancre Heights began, and would rumble on until 11 November, to be followed two days later by the Battle of the Ancre (a river which runs through the town of Albert north-east of Amiens) which lasted till 18 November.

Boelcke brought his score to a round 30 on the first day of October, bringing down a British aeroplane north-west of Flers. Jasta records note this as a BE2c, but in his Field Book, Boelcke himself says he surprised a scout, or häschen (rabbit) as the Germans called them, which went down and disappeared. The Jasta also noted it came down by the lines. Captain H W G Jones MC of 32 Squadron, flying a DH2, was shot down by a German fighter, falling into a shell hole during a line patrol between Pozières and Courcelette, which all fits with the claim. Jones abandoned the DeHavilland and scrambled into the British front-line trenches without serious injury.

There appears to have been quite a scrap, 32 Squadron also forcing a German fighter out of the fight in a steep dive, leaving a smoke trail. Hubert Jones, from Llandudno, Wales, had won his MC with the Welsh Regiment before transferring to the RFC. With 32 Squadron he had already claimed a couple of victories and later this same day would be flying again and gain his third. By early 1917 he would have achieved seven victories before being wounded in March.

The day was marred by the loss of another Staffel pilot, this time Leutnant Herwarth Philipps who was brought down, it is noted, by anti-aircraft fire near Bapaume. The time of his loss is unclear and one has to wonder if in fact this was the machine forced down by 32 Squadron's Captains G N Martin and H W von Poellnitz, flying DH2s. Their Squadron's Combat Record Book notes the patrol time as 10.10 am, north of Bapaume, and records:

> Pilots attacked firing 3 drums. Before Captain von Poellnitz fired his second drum, both pilots saw smoke coming from the enemy machine's fuselage. After Captain von Poellnitz fired his second drum, the hostile machine was diving very steeply, completely enveloped in a cloud of smoke, and was seen still diving like this at about 1,500 feet.

Perhaps it was seen falling below cloud and then being fired at by AA gunners who also made a claim for it. One imagines that Hermann Walter von Poellnitz had to suffer much ragging by his RFC pals because of his German name, although he came from Sidcup in Kent and had previously served with the 2nd Lincolnshire Regiment. He later commanded 72 Squadron in Iraq but was killed in an accident in May 1918. He is buried in Baghdad.

Boelcke and von Richthofen scored the next victories but had to wait until the 7th to achieve them. Bad weather till the 6th curtailed flying on both sides. Von Richthofen claimed a BE12 over Equancourt on the German side, while the Staffelführer bagged a Nieuport two-seater east of Morval which came down on the Allied side. It was always difficult to get confirmations on the occasions aircraft went down in Allied lines unless they were seen to be on fire, to smash to pieces on hitting the ground, or the aircraft, once down, was still in view and could be blasted to matchwood by artillery fire. Even this was sometimes not good enough to get confirmation. On some occasions, confirmations were made on less positive results, where records show that aircraft and crew remained virtually unharmed. Sometimes it depended on who was doing the claiming!

With most of the falling aircraft ending up inside German lines due to the very nature of their defensive fighter war, the wreckage could often be located. So too the dead, injured or captive airmen. Things were far less clear cut if aircraft went down on the 'wrong' side. Von Richthofen's victim was a pilot of 21 Squadron, who fell and died near Ytres (not to be confused with the more famous Ypres) – his fourth victory. There were no Nieuports of any description lost by the RFC, so Boelcke's victim had to be French. The British and French sectors joined not far from Jasta 2's area of operations, and the French did lose a Nieuport XI Ibis on the 7th, and a crew, from Escadrille F.24, which, as the 'F' denotes, normally flew

Farman machines. Commandant Maurice Challe and his observer Sous-lieutenant Henri Mewius were the luckless airmen. Boelcke recorded:

> Suddenly far below me, I saw one fellow circling about, and I went after him. At close range I fired at him, aiming steadily. He made things easy for me, flying a straight course. I stayed 20 or 30 metres behind him and pounded him till he exploded with a great yellow flare. We cannot call this a fight because I surprised my opponent.

There was more of a fight on the 10th, a day which saw Jasta 2 gain four kills. The first two were claimed as FE2b pushers downed by Böhme and Müller, although only the latter's fell inside German lines. In point of fact Müller's victim was a DH2 of 24 Squadron whose pilot, Second Lieutenant Norman Middlebrook, was taken prisoner. Böhme's victory was over an FE though, an 18 Squadron machine that came down east of Longueval, in British lines, its crew unhurt and able to fight another day.

There was often confusion between DH2s and FE2s. The DeHavilland was a much smaller single-seater as opposed to the big two-seater FE, but as both were pusher types, the nature of their design meant both had no fuselage in the conventional sense. In order to have the whirling propeller behind the cockpit and engine gondola, the tail assembly was fixed to two large frameworks connecting wings to tail. The Germans called all pusher types gitterumpfs – lattice-tails (or hulls). As this was a general term, German records often show the type rather than the name, confused even further by, as stated earlier, also calling all such types as Vickers. Therefore historians cannot take such recorded types for granted without studying the RFC losses. Nevertheless, the two Boelcke fledglings had scored their third and first victories respectively.

Next came the first victory of a new pilot, Leutnant Hans Imelmann (not to be confused with Max Immelmann). Imelmann came from Hannover and was 19. He had served with Kek Metz flying Fokker monoplanes and while he had no successes, his experience showed when he downed a Sopwith two-seater of 70 Squadron near Bapaume in the late afternoon of the 10th so soon after joining the Jasta.

Boelcke brought down the fourth of the day, and his own 32nd victory, in the shape of another DH2 of 32 Squadron, flown by Second Lieutenant M J J G Mare-Montembault. Hit by Boelcke's gunfire, 'Monty' crash-landed with his controls shot away, at Mouquet Farm, near Pozières. He scrambled to the safety of the British trenches as German gunfire began destroying his aircraft. Having survived this encounter, Mare-Montembault went on to survive being shot down by Adolf von Tutschek in March 1917.

New Pilots

Apart from Hans Imelmann, amongst other new arrivals in October were Vizefeldwebel Paul Bona and Leutnant Bodo Fr von Lyncker. Bona was 21 and from Berlin, and he arrived sometime early in October but did not last long. On 13 October he was sent off to Army Flug-park Nr.1, so one must assume his flying was not up to Oswald Boelcke's required standard. However, Bona went to Jasta 1 in December and scored six victories – in spite of a wound in December – but was killed on 6 June 1917. Chasing an Allied aircraft the wings of his fighter tore off and he plummeted to his death.

Freiherr von Lyncker was another Berliner, 22-years-old on 22 October. He lasted a month more than Bona, being injured in a crash on 13 November. He later served with Jasta 25 in Macedonia, but was killed in a collision with an Allied Nieuport on 18 February 1917.

Leutnant Karl Heinrich Otto Büttner was another October arrival and so was Oberleutnant Stefan Kirmaier, who came on the 9th. Kirmaier, from Lachen, was 27 and had previously been in the infantry prior to transferring to aviation. He was already a well-decorated soldier with Infantry Regiment Nr.8, where he collected the Bavarian Military Merit Order 4th Class with Swords in October 1914, the Iron Cross 2nd Class, the Knight's Cross with Swords of the Order of the Zähringen Lion, and then the Iron Cross 1st Class. After serving with KG6, he went to an artillery spotting abteilung where he had also flown Fokkers, the formation becoming Kek Jametz. With them he claimed three victories in July 1916. His first move following the formation of the Jagdstaffeln was to Jasta 6, but he was soon on the move to Jasta 2. It is possible that he was being groomed to take over from Boelcke in the near future, Boelcke perhaps being earmarked for higher command.

Leutnant Erich König arrived in October also. From Oberhausen, in the Ruhr, this Westphalian would become a minor ace with Jasta 2 over the next few months. He had trained alongside Kirmaier at Schleisshiem in 1915, known as the home of the Bavarian Air Service. Another to arrive was Leutnant Jürgen Sandel, posted in from FA39.

October continued with another batch of four victories on the 16th. Shortly after 2 pm Boelcke and Reimann both sent BE2c machines down into the British lines, but as only one loss occurred, a BE of 15 Squadron whose crew both died, this might be a case of over-claiming, unless another BE made it down without becoming a total loss. The BE that came down fell in the front-line trenches and was shelled to total destruction. Boelcke said his came down at Hébuterne, which is where the 15 Squadron machine in fact crashed. Reimann reported his down south-west of Thiepval about a quarter of an hour prior to Boelcke's claim. These two spots are some way apart. The 15 Squadron machine had flown out at 12.15 pm and was seen to be brought down in combat with five hostile aircraft and fall in wire entanglements in front of the trenches where it was shelled by German artillery.

A 34 Squadron BE was shot-up near Warlencourt, which is a little to the east between the two locations, and the time of the combat, if correct, is a little different. Times are often difficult to reconcile due to the differences between Allied and German times, which at this point in the year had the Germans one hour ahead of the Allies. Over the years times have been noted, adjusted to adhere to the proper times, then readjusted in error to try and match something up. A minefield really!

In the late afternoon von Richthofen shot down yet another poor BE12 from 19 Squadron, over Ytres at 4 pm – 5pm German time. Another BE12 was also lost, but the only claim was made by Leutnant Sandel, which was not confirmed, so obviously he did not get the required number of witnesses. 19 Squadron had mounted a bomb raid on Hermies railway station, eight aircraft in all, although one dropped out soon after take-off with engine trouble.

Just why Sandel failed to get his kill confirmed is unclear. Von Richthofen later had the serial number of his victim nailed to the wall of his room, so we know which one he downed. The pilot from the other 19 Squadron loss was buried just south of where Richthofen's man fell, still inside German lines. Did AA gunners also put in a claim?

Three quarters of an hour later Boelcke shot down number 34, a DH2 from 24 Squadron, coming down near Beaulencourt. The British pilot was Lieutenant P A Langan-Byrne DSO, the commander of C Flight. The RFC Squadron was on a 4th Army Front OP, four aircraft taking off at 15.15. Front-line observers saw them attacked by 12 enemy machines north of Transloy and one DH go down out of control. As Tyrell Hawker wrote in his book about his brother Lanoe Hawker VC, who commanded this British squadron:

> Langan-Byrne led his patrol with his usual hair-raising élan straight into the middle of the twelve machines of Jagdstaffel 2, and Boelcke, in his vastly superior Albatros Scout, shot him down after a short dogfight in which the DH2s were hopelessly outclassed.

Oddly enough, Boelcke noted in his Field Book:

> The day was a good one for my command. Leutnant R [Richthofen] brought down his fifth, and Leutnant S [Sandel] got one, so that in all we got five that day.

This certainly seems to indicate that at one stage even Boelcke believed Sandel had achieved his first kill, but things turned out rather differently.

In the same Field Book, Boelcke recorded that his 35th victory fell on the 16th, although it actually was the 17th.

> After some fruitless flying I saw six Vickers over our lines.

These I followed, with Leutnant B [Böhme]. From command there were also three machines present. Leutnant Leffers attacked one and forced him to earth (his eighth). The others were all grouped together in a bunch. I picked out the lowest and forced him to earth. The Englishmen did not try to help him, but let me have him, unmolested. After the second volley he caught fire and fell.

Gustav Leffers was another old hand, a former Fokker Eindecker pilot with Kek Bertincourt, later AKN (Abwehr Kommando Nord), which later still became Jasta 1. He and Boelcke must have attacked the same FE2b as there is only one loss, a machine from 11 Squadron. Boelcke noted 'his' FE down west of Bullecourt, Leffers says his went down south-west of Bapaume – both inside German lines. To confuse matters still further, Kirmaier claimed an FE too, his going down north-east of Bapaume, while Leutnant Renatus Theiller of Jasta 5 also put in a claim for an FE in the same area.

Leffers was to gain one more victory before falling in combat on 27 December 1916 and Theiller survived till 24 March 1917, after achieving 12 victories, the one above being his third.

Of the four men from 11 Squadron who were shot down in this fight, only one survived as a prisoner, Second Lieutenant Cecil Leon Roberts, from Liverpool, one of the two pilots. He was lucky to have survived and unlucky to be captured. When he came home from captivity he said he had come down close to Le Sars, and recorded:

Attacked by seven EA whilst flying outside right of formation. Observer killed, self wounded and engine hit. Attempted to regain lines, landed in no-man's-land. Obtained shelter until midnight. Walked into German lines by mistake owing to thick fog.

* * *

On the 18th, Erwin Böhme wrote to his fiancée about Boelcke:

You admire our Boelcke. Who wouldn't do that? But all of you admire only the war hero – you cannot know about his rare personality. This personality can only be known by the few who have the luck to live together with him. This simple young man is far from being emancipated by glory, and possesses an unparalleled maturity and tolerant nature.

This unpretentious young man, far from allowing fame to turn his head, exhibits a maturity and detached presence that is straightaway incredible if one considers that in his short life before the war he experienced nothing unusual. I assure you, I admire Boelcke not only as my commander, however strange that may seem since I am 37 and he is 25 years old, but I also look up to him as a man. I am proud of the fact that between us a friendship has grown. It is probable that he sees in me an aged, experienced man and is happy that, in spite of my age, a youthful enthusiasm burns in me for the same cause for which his heart glows.

It is somewhat unique how Boelcke conveys his spirit to each and every one of his students, how he carries all of them away. They follow him wherever he leads. Not one would leave him in the lurch. He is a born leader! No wonder that his Staffel blossoms! We presently have received as reinforcements a number of excellent young men. The victories of our Staffel are piling up. At the same time, and in spite of many battles and many a bold venture, we have not suffered a single loss in the last two weeks.

Every victory which I achieve is counted not only for me, but also for my Staffel, and in its service we strive to achieve successes. It is called esprit de corps. That prevails the more so in the Boelcke Staffel and our outstanding young men are totally committed to it. It may indeed seem strange that I, an old character, have been so set on fire – but it is a holy flame.

Manfred von Richthofen was equally enthused over the achievements and his hunting spirit enjoyed every moment of it. He wrote later:

During my whole life I have not found a happier hunting ground than in the course of the Somme Battle. In the morning, as soon as I get up, the first Englishmen arrive, and the last disappear only long after sunset [as darkness fell]. Boelcke once said that this was the El Dorado of the flying men.

There was a time when Boelcke's bag of machines increased within two months from 20 to 40. We beginners had, at that time, not yet the experience of our master, and we were quite satisfied when we did not get a hiding. It was a beautiful time. Every time we went up we had a fight. Frequently we fought really big battles in the air... but unfortunately the Germans were often in the minority. With [us] quality was more important than quantity.

Two more FE2s went down to Jasta 2 on the 20th, one for Boelcke, another to Böhme. No problems this time, both 11 Squadron aircraft were indeed lost, even though Boelcke's victim went down inside British lines. The pilot survived the crash although he was wounded, but the unfortunate observer had fallen out during the plunge earthwards. Both aircraft were on a photographic mission that morning. The observer was Second Lieutenant G K Welsford who had earlier been a despatch rider with the Royal Engineers, before transferring to the RFC in June 1916. He had been educated at Harrow where he had been the champion lightweight boxer and a school swimmer. H A Jones recorded:

> The 3rd Army reconnaissance sent out by No.11 Squadron had completed its photography at Douai and was moving off to the south when Boelcke's Jagdstaffel attacked. The German leader severely wounded the pilot of one of the FEs and shot many of his controls away. As the aeroplane went down the observer was thrown out and fell behind the German lines. The FE crashed in the British lines south of Arras, and was completely wrecked. Another of the FEs was shot down, but was seen to land under control west of Douai, whilst a third, with its petrol tank smashed by bullets, got back to its aerodrome.

Müller got his second kill that evening, another BE12 'fighter' from 21 Squadron, whose Canadian pilot was killed.

Next day two more, achieved by Kirmaier and Reimann, then five on the 22nd; Boelcke two, Böhme, Reimann and Imelmann one each. Boelcke's first was a Strutter of 45 Squadron. He and Böhme attacked the British machines from 45 Squadron which were seen coming from the east, south of Bapaume. In company with four other Staffel pilots, they cut off two of the Sopwiths, Boelcke's being seen to fall in flames and disintegrate. This victory, Boelcke's second, had been a BE12 from 21 Squadron. Coming in for a crash-landing, the pilot, Second Lieutenant W T Willcox smashed into a shell hole and was hurled out in a high curve. He was captured but not seriously hurt. Within a short time his wrecked BE was blasted by British gunfire. Walter Willcox's post-war report stated:

> Offensive Patrol. Flight intended to be in formation of five machines. Formation was not maintained owing to irregular speed of machine of Flight Commander. Having become detached I observed two LVG machines and attacked the nearest. While attention on attacking said machine I was attacked by a German scout machine, which, with another one had come up unobserved from the right. [My] gun on BE12 [was] on the left of machine. My engine was shot and I was forced to land. This happened over Bapaume. I tried to make the line but failed to do so and landed in shell hole 100 yards behind German lines. Machine crashed. Myself unwounded.

Reimann was wounded in the right knee during a later action that day and his growing skill was lost to the Jasta. Recovering from his wound he was married on New Year's Eve and then posted to the Jastaschule at Valenciennes as an instructor. On 24 January 1917, his aircraft suddenly, and for no apparent reason, dived into the ground from 2,500 feet and he died instantly.

Von Richthofen got his sixth on the 25th, while Leutnant Höhne got his third, and Boelcke his 39th – a BE2c crew ranging for the 165th Siege Battery – over Miraumont. On the 26th he made it an incredible 40, while Imelmann got his third, and Kirmaier bagged two, which brought the Jasta total to 50. Boelcke wrote:

> October 25, 1916. This morning, near M [Miraumont] I brought down an English BE biplane.
> October 26, 1916. About 4.45 seven of our machines of which I had charge attacked some English biplanes west of P [Puisieux]. I attacked one and wounded the observer, so he was unable to fire at me. At the second attack the machine started to smoke. Both pilot and observer seemed dead. It fell into the second line English trenches and burned up.

Boelcke did not see it actually crash, but a later report noted the fall and so he had made it to 40 victories. It had been a machine from 5 Squadron which came down in the front-lines south-west of Serre, its pilot wounded and observer dead.

One of Kirmaier's victims was Lieutenant W Bertram Clark of 29 Squadron in a DH2, who came down near Valenciennes. Upon his return after the war he made no mention of the air action, only recording:

> Offensive Patrol. Engine cut out, probably petrol trouble, but had only two minutes to set machine on fire so could not ascertain.

From this we must assume that his engine and petrol trouble originated from fire from Kirmaier's machine, and that after landing he was not certain if he had managed to properly set light to his pusher before being hustled away by German soldiers.

Hans Imelmann had been in action with 60 Squadron, as H A Jones recorded:

> Captain E L Foot of No.60 Squadron was returning alone in his Nieuport from chasing a German formation when he saw, from a distance, the attack on the artillery aeroplanes. He dived straight down towards a single-seater which was on the tail of one of the BEs; he was too late to save the BE, but he got a burst of fire into the enemy aeroplane from close

range. The German turned head-on to the Nieuport, got slightly above it and, with his first few rounds, put the Nieuport's gun out of action; he then got on to the tail of the Nieuport and easily held it in the quick manoeuvring which followed. Foot dived steeply but could not shake off his enemy, who followed him down and set fire to his petrol tank when he was no more than a few feet from the ground. The Nieuport crashed at once and burnt itself out but the pilot escaped without injury.

Captain Ernest Leslie Foot – known as 'Feet' – had scored five victories up to this time and was about to receive the MC. He had earlier flown with 11 Squadron alongside Albert Ball. Soon after his encounter with Imelmann he was sent back to England for a rest.

The Master Falls
Nothing of interest occurred on the 27th. On the afternoon of Saturday 28th the Jasta pilots engaged a patrol of DH2s of 24 Squadron between Pozières and Bapaume. It seems that some Allied pilots were still not totally aware of the new Albatros scouts that the Jastas were starting to use, for 24 Squadron described the German formation as a mixed bunch (they said 12) of Halberstadt and Aviatik Scouts. Jasta 2 was mostly flying the Albatros DIIs now, and Boelcke was in D386/16.

In the fight that developed, Boelcke went to engage the DH2s flown by Lieutenants A G Knight and A E McKay. Erwin Böhme went for them too but failed to see Boelcke's machine just below him and to the right. His right undercarriage wheel appeared only to brush Boelcke's upper left wing but caused damage to both wing and aileron. Boelcke endeavoured to glide away to the east but shortly afterwards his top wing broke away and the Albatros fell to the ground. 24 Squadron's combat report, which was signed by the CO, Major Lanoe G Hawker VC DSO, read:

> It was after about five minutes strenuous fighting that two HAs collided. One dived at Lieut. Knight, who turned left-handed. The HA zoomed right-handed, and its left wing collided with the right wing of another HA which had started to dive on Lieut. Knight.
> Bits were seen to fall off; only one HA was seen to go down and it glided away east, but was very shortly lost to sight, as the DHs were too heavily engaged to watch it.

Everyone in Jasta 2 was devastated, especially Böhme. Not only had Boelcke been his commanding officer but in the short time they had been together they had developed quite a friendship. To fall in combat was one thing, but to die as a result of a fateful collision was another. Nobody could believe that Boelcke had gone. Three days later Böhme wrote to his fiancée:

> On Saturday afternoon we were sitting around our small airfield quarters on combat alert. I had just begun a game of chess with Boelcke. We were then called shortly before 4 o'clock during an infantry attack on the front. Boelcke himself led us, as usual. We came into contact over Flers very quickly with a number of English aircraft, fast single-seaters, that skilfully defended themselves.
>
> In the ensuing wildly gyrating mêlée in which we could always only get into range for brief moments, we attempted to force our opponents downward by alternately blocking their path, as we had previously done so often with success. Boelcke and I had the same Englishman between us, as another opponent being chased by our friend Richthofen cut in front of us. In our abrupt mutual efforts to dodge, with Boelcke and my views obscured by our wings, we did not see each other for a moment. Here is where it happened.
>
> How can I describe my feelings from that moment on, when Boelcke suddenly appeared just a few metres to my right, how he dived, how I jerked upward, and how we nevertheless grazed each other, and both plummeted downward! It was only a light touch, but at such breakneck speeds that also meant a strong impact. Fate is usually so horribly irrational in its choice. Only a portion of my undercarriage was torn away. He lost the outermost portion of his left wing.
>
> After falling a couple of hundred metres I regained control of my aircraft and could follow Boelcke's. I saw his aircraft in a gradual glide, left wing drooping a bit, drifting towards our lines. First, in a layer of cloud in lower regions, where his aircraft was buffeted by strong winds. Then he went into an ever steepening glide and I saw before the landing how he could no longer keep the machine facing straight forward, and how he struck the ground near a gun battery.

Unable to land nearby because of the shell-torn terrain, Böhme returned to Lagnicourt where, due to his damaged wheel, he turned over on landing. Several pilots were quickly driving a car to the spot where Boelcke fell, but upon their arrival, soldiers from the battery could only present them with the body of their late leader. He had apparently died immediately on impact. Böhme's letter continued:

Now everything is so empty for us. Only gradually are we beginning to realise what a void Boelcke leaves behind, that without him the soul of the whole Staffel is lacking. In every relation he was our unparalleled leader and master. He had a compelling influence upon everyone who had anything to do with him, even his superiors, simply through his personality, the simplicity of his character. We never had the feeling that something could go awry if he was there amongst us, and almost everything that we tried succeeded.

This afternoon he was conveyed to Cambrai, from whence his parents and brother will accompany him to his burial in the war memorial cemetery in Dessau. His parents are wonderful people – valiantly bearing all the pain of that which is irrevocable. That gives me a bit of consolation. However, nothing can take away the sadness over the loss of this extraordinary man.

Manfred von Richthofen had been in the action over Flers, and wrote in his book:

Suddenly I noticed an unnatural movement of the two German flying machines. Immediately I thought of a collision. I had not yet seen a collision in the air. I had imagined that it would look quite different. In reality, what happened was not a collision. The two machines merely touched one another. However, if two machines go at the tremendous pace of flying machines, the slightest contact has the effect of a violent concussion.

Boelcke drew away... and descended in large curves. I had not the feeling he was falling, but when I saw him descending below me I noticed that part of his planes had broken off. I could not see what was happening afterwards, but in the clouds he lost an entire wing. Now his machine was no longer controllable. It fell accompanied all the time by his faithful friend [Böhme].

When we reached home we found already the report: "Boelcke is dead!" We could scarcely believe it.

Oberleutnant Stefan Kirmaier was given command of Jasta 2 on the 30th. If he was indeed being groomed to take over from Boelcke at some stage, he would not have wanted it in this way. However, Boelcke had gone. The Fatherland was certainly no stranger to tragedy and death, but the loss of Boelcke was a massive blow, not only to his pilots but to the German Air Service as a whole.

He had received virtually every medal and decoration that could be bestowed upon him: the Pour le Mérite; the Knight's Cross of the Royal

Hohenzollern House Order with Swords; Iron Cross 1st and 2nd Class; Military Merit Order, Knight's Cross – from Würrtemburg; the Knight's Cross, 1st Class with Swords of the Ernestine House Order, from Saxe-Coburg and Gotha; House Order of Albert the Bear – Knight's Cross 1st and 2nd Class with Swords, and the Friedrich Cross 2nd Class, all from Anhalt; the Mecklenburg-Strelitz Cross for Distinction in War, 2nd Class; the Austrian Order of the Iron Crown 3rd Class with War Decoration; from Bulgaria the Bravery Award 4th Class, 2nd Degree, and the Ottoman (Turkish) Empire gave him the Imtiaz Medal in Silver, and of course there was his Pilot's Badge.

There was also another bravery award, but not for fighting in the air. This was the Prussian Life Saving Medal, given in recognition of Boelcke saving the life of that 14-year-old French boy who had fallen into a canal. That was back in Boelcke's Fokker Eindecker days.

The great hero's funeral took place at the cathedral in Cambrai, following which his body was taken back to Germany to be buried in Dessau. Von Richthofen was Jasta 2's official representative and carried the Ordenskissen (a cushion upon which was placed the dead hero's medals and awards – 15 in all). In a letter to his mother, Manfred von Richthofen wrote:

Jagdstaffel Boelcke, 3 November 1916.

Dear Mama!
Unfortunately, I missed the train after Boelcke's funeral, where I was ordered as a representative of the squadron. Now I can't come to you until the middle of the month. Boelcke's death came as follows: Boelcke, a few other gentlemen of the squadron, and I were entangled in an air battle with Englishmen. Suddenly I see how Boelcke, attacking an Englishman, is rammed in the air by one of our men. Nothing else happens to the other poor man. Boelcke went down quite normally at first. I followed him immediately. Later a wing broke off, and he plunged into the ground. His skull was fractured in the impact, so he was dead at once. At the ceremony, I carried the pillow with his medals. The funeral was like that of a reigning prince. In six weeks we have six dead and one wounded; two have lost their nerve.
I shot down my seventh yesterday, after I had just previously despatched the sixth. Up to now my nerves have not yet suffered all the bad luck of the others.

Under the New Commander
Oberleutnant Kirmaier officially took command of Jasta 2 on 30 October. Two days later, on the first day of November, he shot down a BE2e over Le Sars for his eighth victory – a machine from 9 Squadron RFC seen to

go down near Rocquigny, which is just to the east of Le Sars. The crew were on a photo op and both died. It was the Jasta's 52nd victory.

Pilots at the start of November 1916:	**Name**	**Victories**
	Oblt Stefan Kirmaier	7
	Ltn Manfred von Richthofen	6
	Ltn Erwin Böhme	5
	Ltn Otto Höhne	3
	Ltn Hans Imelmann	3
	OffStv Max Müller	2
	Oblt Günther Viehweger	–
	Ltn Karl H O Büttner	–
	Ltn Wolfgang Günther	–
	Ltn Erich König	–
	Ltn Bodo Fr. von Lyncker	–
	Vfw Paul Ostrop	–
	Ltn Jürgen Sandel	–
OzbV	Ltn Hellmuth von Zastrow	–

Base: Lagnicourt   Front: 1st Army

As related earlier, the newcomers were Leutnants Karl Heinrich Otto Büttner and Bodo Freiherr von Lyncker. Büttner had arrived sometime during October, around the time von Lyncker, a Berliner, who had celebrated his 22nd birthday on the 22nd turned up. Vizefeldwebel Paul Ostrop was another new arrival, with Jürgen Sandel arriving from a two-seater unit, FA39. Hans Wortmann arrived in early November.

The day that von Richthofen had written to his mother, the 3rd, saw Jasta 2 back in the scoring with no fewer than five victories. Von Richthofen shot down an FE2b inside German lines at 14.10; the crew of the 18 Squadron FE were both killed. Twenty-five minutes later Höhne had despatched a BE2c into the British lines, although the only casualty appears to have been a 16 Squadron machine shot-up (but not shot down), south of Lens in action with two LVG two-seaters. It seems therefore that Höhne's victim probably escaped serious damage.

Nearly an hour later Jasta 2 engaged a formation of FEs of 22 Squadron, Müller claiming one south-east of Bapaume, while König shot down another near Barastre. In all, 22 Squadron lost three FEs, (although also claiming was a Jasta 5 pilot – west of Le Mesnil) and a two-seater crew near Mory. All are in the general area of Bapaume, but one of the claims was duplicated.

As far as can be ascertained, Müller downed the FE piloted by Captain A T Lord Lucas, who was killed, with his observer Lieutenant A Anderson surviving as a prisoner. Again H A Jones makes mention of this combat in his *War in the Air*:

Five of our aeroplanes were shot down in the German lines during the day, three of them from a photographic reconnaissance formation of No.22 Squadron led by Capt. A T Lord Lucas who, it was afterwards known, had been attacked by three enemy pilots and shot in the head and leg. His aeroplane was landed by the wounded observer, Lt A Anderson. Lord Lucas never regained consciousness after he was hit, and died the same day.

The fifth victory was by Hans Imelmann who shot down a Nieuport Scout of 60 Squadron over Adinfer Wood/Douchy at 16.45, its pilot dying of his injuries.

It took six more days before Jasta 2 were again successful – mainly due to very bad weather – yet this time they claimed six British machines. Von Richthofen, Kirmaier and Imelmann each scored around 10.30 am, Höhne twenty minutes later, while Wortmann achieved his first success just before the hour, a Nieuport sent down into the Allied lines south-west of Le Transloy. This may well have been Captain J D Latta MC of 60 Squadron who nevertheless got back home although he further damaged his fighter in landing.

That same afternoon Erwin Böhme claimed an FE8 pusher, one of two machines lost from 40 Squadron – their first losses – the other being brought down by AA fire. These claims brought Kirmaier's score to nine, von Richthofen's to eight and Böhme's to six. Much of these morning actions had centred around a large raid by RFC aircraft against an ammunition dump at Vraucourt, engaged by Jasta 1 as well as Kirmaier's gentlemen.

Von Richthofen's victim was the pilot of a 12 Squadron BE, who was flying without an observer in lieu of a larger bomb load. The pilot died. Kirmaier got a second BE from the same unit, whose pilot was taken prisoner, while Imelmann recorded the downing of a DH2 inside German lines which was probably one of the four aircraft 29 Squadron lost, although there are other claimants for all of them. H A Jones noted the day's action as follows:

A raid on the ammunition dump at Vraucourt north-east of Bapaume, made by twelve bombers with fourteen escorting machines, was attacked by thirty or more aeroplanes, and led to the biggest air fight which the war had yet seen. Some of the enemy pilots attacked soon after the lines were crossed, but most of the eighty 20lb bombs carried by the aeroplanes of Nos. 12 and 13 Squadrons were dropped on their objective. As Vraucourt was neared the German attacks were intensified, some fighters getting inside our formation, and over the village itself the fighting became general. The escorting aeroplanes were supplied by Nos. 11, 60 and 29 Squadrons.

The first casualty was suffered by No.60 Squadron soon after the trenches were crossed. Lieutenant A D Bell-Irving, in the last of three flights, was wounded in the leg, and had his Very lights set on fire and his engine and petrol tank hit, but he was able to land near the trenches, where his aeroplane was wrecked. Meanwhile, the remainder of the escorting machines were fighting hard to protect the bombers, but two of these, both from No.12 Squadron, were shot down, and the pilot of another was wounded but got home. Two of the escorts, both DH2s of No.29 Squadron, were fought down by several enemy fighters, and were last seen still keeping up the fight close to the ground. Lastly, one of the FEs of No.11 Squadron, with a dead observer and a wounded pilot, crashed into no-man's-land whence the pilot escaped into the front-line trenches.

A New Offizier zur besonderen Verwendung

Leutnant Hellmuth von Zastrow had left the Jasta on 4 November and after being promoted to Oberleutnant, moved to Berlin in the new year, serving in the office of the Inspector General for Air. His replacement was Oberleutnant Karl Bodenschatz.

Born in December 1890, his birth place is given as Rehau/Ober Franken, Germany. Entering military service in 1910 with the 8th Bavarian Infantry Regiment, he was commissioned in 1912, which was backdated to 1910, and made Oberleutnant in March 1916. He saw action at Verdun and following no less than four combat wounds, moved to aviation. For a month, between October and November 1916, he was with Flieger-abteilung 3b before being given something of a prize job with Jasta 2. He actually reported for duty on the day Boelcke – an old classmate of his – was killed and it was he who accompanied his body back to Dessau. He arrived back on 4 November to take up his new position.

The Battle of the Ancre began on 13 November, which was to be the last significant fighting of the Somme battle, which had dragged on since July. Poor weather and fog kept both side's airmen mostly on the ground and there were no real air actions for the next three days.

Kirmaier and Müller scored kills on the 16th and Höhne brought his score to six the next day. The Staffelführer's claim was over a 70 Squadron Sopwith 1½ Strutter, Müller's was a BE of 9 Squadron, while Höhne scored a DH2 from their old antagonists, 24 Squadron. Kirmaier made it 11 for himself on the 20th around 09.00 hours, von Richthofen claiming one too for his ninth. However, only one BE was lost in this action – from 15 Squadron – so somehow in the mêlée close to the front-lines, confirmation was given for two BEs downed. Richthofen got an

FE2b during the afternoon, bringing his score to ten.

The 16th also saw the next loss by the Jasta – Leutnant Karl Büttner being brought down during an engagement with a BE2c of 8 Squadron RFC. He came down near Pommies, close to Arras in Albatros DII 391/16, his captured machine becoming one of the most photographed of the period, with its 'Bü' motif on the fuselage sides. The crew that got him were Captain G A Parker and his observer Lieutenant H E Hervey, and it was the first Albatros DII captured intact following a sustained air fight above the lines. More in the German tradition than the British, Parker landed close to the downed fighter to secure the pilot's capture. George Parker and Hamilton Hervey both received the Military Cross for their efforts. Büttner ended up in a prison camp in Manchester (prisoner no.5579), England. 8 Squadron's Record Book records:

> BE2d 5735. 10.10-11.15 am. Engaged with hostile machine which was eventually forced down on our side of the line near Pommies. Our machine followed the Hun right down and landed alongside. German machine had a bullet through radiator but otherwise undamaged. Machine was an Albatros Scout. German pilot, who was unhurt, was taken prisoner.

Von Richthofen gained his ninth victory on the morning of 20 November, a BE2c machine of 15 Squadron, both crew members being taken prisoner. The pilot, Lieutenant Thomas H Clarke, put in this report upon his return from captivity in late 1918:

> Artillery Observation Patrol from Lealvillers. We were sent up at dawn in a very strong west wind which rendered escape when attacked impossible. Whilst over enemy territory we were attacked by five enemy single-seaters, believed to be Albatros [Scouts]. After engaging them for some time our engine was hit and observer wounded in [the] leg. We received no protection from our own scouts. One enemy machine fired into at low altitude fell apparently out of control.
>
> Machine landed outskirts of Miraumont (Somme). Could not burn machine as Lt. [J C] Lees had to be slowly extricated from it owing to his wound, and by this time German soldiers captured us. I am informed by officers of my Squadron met since my return to England that the machine was seen later on lying on its back and as the shellfire was intense at the time of landing in this area, have no doubt it was turned over by a burst. Machine was badly crashed on landing. Germans exhibited surprise that 'so old fashioned a machine' was still in use by the British.

James C Lees later reported:

> On artillery shoot attacked by five Huns, wounded in right
> leg. Lost height and engine went dud at about 800 feet and
> could not reach lines. Machine crashed on landing and
> shortly afterwards machine destroyed by one of our own
> shells.

Von Richthofen made it 10 that afternoon with an 18 Squadron FE2b
down at Grandcourt at 16.15, ending the lives of two young airmen, one
from Derbyshire, the other from Edinburgh. The pilot, Gilbert Hall, had
only joined his squadron less than two weeks earlier and his observer,
George Doughty, had lasted less than a month. Von Richthofen's report
(he was flying Albatros DII 491/16) stated:

> Together with four planes, I attacked a Vickers two-seater
> type above the clouds at 2,500 metres altitude. After 300
> shots adversary broke through the clouds, pursued by me.
> Near Grandcourt I shot him down.

Kirmaier Falls

The Staffel gained its 70th victory on 22 November, but lost its leader.
Thick mist over the front precluded much flying until the afternoon.
Böhme scored the 70th by shooting down a Morane Parasol at 14.10 in
the afternoon over Longueval, a 3 Squadron machine flown by Second
Lieutenant E P Roberts and his observer Captain G L Watson, who were
both killed. At 16.50 König got his second by downing a 'Vickers' near
Hébuterne – an FE2b of 11 Squadron. However, Kirmaier fell to the guns
of a DH2 pilot near Flers at 14.00 hours. Again it was the Staffel's
antagonists, 24 Squadron, that hurt them. Their combat was timed at
13.10 (German time being one hour ahead of Allied during this period),
the successful pilots being Captain J O Andrews MC and Second
Lieutenant K Crawford. They recorded the Albatros DI going down over
Les Boeufs, in Allied territory. It was John Andrews' seventh victory, and
Kelvin Crawford's second. Examination of Kirmaier's body showed one
bullet to the back of the head. 24 Squadron also shot down a Jasta 12 pilot
this date, between Gueudecourt and Ligny-Thilloy, again in British lines.
It was unusual to bring down German aircraft inside Allied lines, so two
in one day was exceptional.

Tyrell Hawker mentions this combat in his book *Hawker VC*:

> Captain J O Andrews MC, on his way back from a fight in
> which his engine had been damaged, was dived on by a flight
> of HA Scouts which, however, did not fire at him.
> Dexterously he turned on the tail of the lowest machine and
> emptied a drum into it at short range. It was Kirmaier's

Albatros, and it crashed heavily just behind our front-line trenches near Flers.

This same date came the announcement to Kirmaier of the award of the Knight's Cross of the Royal Hohenzollern House Order with Swords. With 11 victories, at a time when the award of the Pour le Mérite required 16 victories, the Hohenzollern was, as mentioned earlier, the necessary prerequisite to the final prestigious award of the Blue Max.

*   *   *

There can be little doubt that Boelcke's protégés – von Richthofen, Böhme, Reimann, Müller, et al, were all very conscious of the prestige, fame and awards that came with success in air fighting. They had been close to it with Boelcke, had seen for themselves the medals showered upon him, and knew of similar decorations heaped on such men as Max Immelmann, Max Ritter von Mulzer, Otto Parschau, Kurt Wintgens and others. They were household names in Germany, the pop-stars or sports heroes of their age. For those with the necessary skills and with the will to kill it would not be too difficult to emulate such men and walk among them.

Karl Bodenschatz, as senior ranked officer, took temporary command of Jasta 2 following Kirmaier's failure to return. One of his first duties was to ensure a new arrival had settled in. The previous day Leutnant Werner Voss had become the latest addition to Jasta 2's roster of pilots.

Voss was all but unknown at this stage. Born in the town of Krefeld in April 1897, this 19-year-old had been in the army since the start of the war, assigned initially to the 11th Westphalian Hussar Regiment, with which he served on the Eastern Front. He was promoted to the rank of an NCO and won the Iron Cross 2nd Class prior to requesting a move to aviation, starting his flight training in August 1915 in Cologne and then Krefeld. He was found to be a good pilot, and as such was retained as an instructor for a few weeks before finally being posted to Kampfgeschwader Nr.4 – Kasta (Kampfstaffel) 20 – on 10 March 1916. At first he flew as an observer, but upon receipt of his Pilot's Badge on 28 May began to fly as a pilot.

Promoted to Leutnant on 9 September his obvious skill marked him for better things and so in November he was sent to Jasta 2. It did not take him long to make his mark.

Meantime, a new commander for the Jasta had to be found. It was still a time for rank and position rather than experience 'in the job', so it was no real surprise that a senior airman was given the position a week after Kirmaier's death, on the 29th. Not that the new man was totally devoid of operational experience, far from it. He had already achieved six victories with Kampfstaffel 2, before the advent of the Jastas.

Hauptmann Franz Josef Walz was nearing his 31st birthday and came from Speyer, a town south of Mannheim. He had been in the army since 1905, with a Bavarian Infantry Regiment, and was commissioned in 1908. He had learnt to fly pre-war and on the outbreak of hostilities was given command of Feldflieger-abteilung Nr.3, becoming an Oberleutnant in November 1914. Just over a year later he took command of Kagohl 1's Kampfstaffel 2. Kagohl was the abbreviation for Kampfgeschwader der Obersten Herresleitung – Fighting Unit of the Army High Command – formed with several fighting staffeln. Most of his six victories were in company with his observer, Oberleutnant Martin Gerlich, later to become the adjutant of Kagohl 3. (Later still he served with Bombengeschwader 5, Bombenstaffel 6, before becoming a prisoner of war on 30 June 1918.)

Just prior to coming to Jasta 2, Walz had been given command of Jasta 19 on 3 November, shortly after its formation. Prior to that he had been with FEA 1 – Flieger Ersatz Abteilung – an aviation replacement unit. He may have acquired rank and air fighting experience but his time in command of Jasta 2 would not prove a happy one.

Another newcomer to the Jasta was Leutnant Dieter Collin, coming in from Jasta 22. Collin was 23 and from Luben. He had hardly settled with Jasta 22 before he was transferred to Jasta 2. He would score two victories with them before he returned to his former unit, and prior to his death in 1918, would achieve 13 victories in air combat.

Collin did not waste his time, claiming his first victory on 23 November and the second one on 26 December. On the 23rd he downed a DH2 in the late morning, with another falling to von Richthofen during the afternoon. Both were from 24 Squadron. Collin's went down over the lines, its pilot killed. In the afternoon, Jasta 2 fell on three DH2 fighters and following a well-documented air battle, von Richthofen finally downed the machine flown by 24's CO, the famous Major Lanoe George Hawker VC DSO.

The air fight was evenly matched, both were experienced air fighters and they circled and battled it out for some time until Hawker had to make a decision, knowing that with his fuel beginning to run low he would soon have to get back across the lines or risk a landing and almost certain captivity. Finally he had to make a dash for it, but a long burst from a chasing von Richthofen sent a bullet into the head of Hawker and he fell dead at Luisenhof Farm, just south of Bapaume.

Another of the DH2s, flown by Captain Andrews who had killed Kirmaier the previous day, was badly shot-up and with his engine stopped and leaking petrol, he was chased back over the lines by another Albatros Scout. Only the timely intervention of the third DH pilot, Lieutenant Robert Saundby, saved him, and denied a third 24 Squadron loss this day.

It did no harm to von Richthofen's rising star that he had shot down Hawker, known apparently as 'the British Immelmann'. He had no way of knowing during the combat who was in the British machine and it took a day or so to get news of who the pilot was. With a Victoria Cross and the Distinguished Service Order, his name was well-known among both

British and German airman.

On the 27th Werner Voss opened his scoring with two victories, a Nieuport Scout at 09.40, Max Müller shooting down another, and then Voss shot down a DH2 at 14.15 in the afternoon. However, only one Nieuport appears to have been lost by their opponents of 60 Squadron, Captain G A Parker DSO MC falling dead, and the 'DH2' (Vickers?) was in reality the larger 'gitterumpf' – an FE2b from 18 Squadron. Müller reported 'his' Nieuport going down inside Allied lines, but the pilot obviously got away with it as there is no obvious casualty. George Parker, it was recalled, shot down Büttner on 16 November while with 8 Squadron. Jasta 2 had now got its revenge.

Chapter Three
Jasta Boelcke

December 1916
Pilots at the start of December:

	Name	Victories
	Oblt Franz Walz	6
	Ltn Manfred von Richthofen	11
	Ltn Erwin Böhme	7
	Ltn Otto Höhne	6
	Ltn Hans Imelmann	5
	Ltn Erich König	2
	Ltn Hans Wortmann	1
	Ltn Dieter Collin	1
	Ltn Wolfgang Günther	–
	Ltn Jürgen Sandel	–
	Oblt Günther Viehweger	–
	Ltn Werner Voss	2
	OffStv Max Müller	5
	Vfw Paul Ostrop	–
	Ltn Amann ?	–
OzbV	Oblt Karl Bodenschatz	–

Base: Lagnicourt   Front: 1st Army

There is a record that a Leutnant Amann, in an Albatros DI of Jasta 2, was brought down and taken prisoner on the first day of December, but no details of who he was, when he joined or how he was lost are known. The weather from late November to early December was poor, with a good deal of fog, which made flying almost non-existent. One wonders if he actually lost his way and landed on the wrong side of the lines. With no RFC comment or reference on this machine, and no one of this name as a prisoner, perhaps he came down and was captured by the French.

Pronville

Other than some action on 4 December, there was little real air activity on the British front early in the month, and in any event, the Jasta was busy moving its base. On the 5th it went to Pronville, situated just a couple of kilometres to the north-east of Lagnicourt, and just to the south-east of

54

Quéant. With this and the weather, it was not until the 11th that Jasta 2 was back in the scoring game. That day Manfred von Richthofen bagged a DH2 of 32 Squadron, but then it was not until the 20th that combat was resumed.

By this time Jasta 2 had become, by Royal Decree (on the 17th), Jasta Boelcke, and although officially it was still Jasta 2, it was from this time forward more commonly referred to as Jasta Boelcke, or simply Jasta B.

The 20th saw four victories – two by von Richthofen, one by Imelmann and the fourth by Wortmann. Von Richthofen's first was another DH2, this time a machine from 29 Squadron, but flown by an experienced air-fighter, Captain A G Knight DSO MC, from Canada, although he had been born in England. Jerry Knight had earlier been with 24 Squadron, gaining six victories during the summer of 1916. Promoted to captain he became a flight commander with 29 Squadron in November scoring victory number seven before falling to von Richthofen.

The other three victories were all FE2b pushers from 18 Squadron on a fighting patrol. Von Richthofen despatched one machine while his comrades sent down two more. Richthofen had now achieved 14 victories and as the apparent target for the Blue Max was 16, he was eager to make that total before the goal posts were moved again.

Voss made his third claim on the 21st, a BE2d of 7 Squadron, which was the only Allied aircraft shot down that day. Then the day after Christmas – the 26th – Jasta 2 scored three, one each by Böhme, König and Collin. The latter two were DH2s in another fight with 24 Squadron, although only one was lost, and indeed, Collin reported his going down over British lines. König's was also claimed by a two-seater crew of FA6b, whose pilot was Oberleutnant Adolf von Tutschek. Von Tutschek and his observer, Leutnant Fr. von Stein, lost the argument and the victory was given to Jasta 2. Von Tutschek later became a successful fighter pilot and his first single-seater unit was to be Jasta 2.

Böhme's claim was against a BE from 5 Squadron, although this too went down inside British lines near Courcelette. The crew survived although the pilot, Canadian Lieutenant W H Hubbard, was wounded. William Hubbard was later a Camel pilot with 73 Squadron, winning the DFC and Bar in 1918 as a flight commander.

Jasta B gained its last victory of 1916 on 27 December. Due to a variety of reasons, the victory appeared to be something of a mystery, von Richthofen being credited with an FE2b for his 15th victory. However, it fell inside Allied lines so there was no convenient wreck to inspect, but front-line observers confirmed they had seen a gitterumpf going down in a spin from height and so it was confirmed as having crashed.

In the event it did not crash, nor had it even been hit by von Richthofen's fire. We know that because the British pilot was Sergeant J T B McCudden, later to become a highly successful and highly decorated fighter pilot himself. McCudden had been part of a three-man patrol that had engaged Jasta 2's aircraft, but after a bit of a tussle McCudden's gun had jammed and with no future in scrapping with von Richthofen's Albatros, he had kicked his DH2 into a spinning nose-dive and headed earthwards. He kept the spin going from around 10,000 feet to about 800 feet, knowing he was inside his own lines. Obviously Richthofen did not go down after the DH2 simply because he too was over Allied lines and would have come under ground fire. Anyway, as far as he could judge, the DH2 was only seconds away from smashing into the ground. Another of the DH2 patrol, having landed before McCudden returned, had already reported seeing the NCO pilot spinning down near the ground and said he appeared to be lost.

Von Richthofen, keen to get to the magic 16 victories before someone decided a score of 16 was now becoming too easy, requested confirmation of his 15th kill and got it. He would have to wait over a week before number 16 came. As it happens, von Richthofen's victory this day was the last for the year of 1916, and his next would be the Jasta's first for 1917. It brought the Staffel's total claims since its formation to 86 for the loss of nine pilots.

December also saw two pilots posted out, both virtual founder members: Oberleutnant Günther Viehweger, and Leutnant Wolfgang Günther. The latter was sent to an artillery two-seater flieger-abteilung, FA(A)205. Günther Viehweger was posted to Army Flug Park Nr.7, probably to instruct. In April 1917 he moved to Jasta 17 and the following month took command of Jasta 31, which he led till September. He then went to the Inspectorate of Military Aviation (Idflieg) where he appears to have remained until the war ended. He had not achieved any victories, but obviously he had learnt the art of command during his time with Jasta Boelcke.

January 1917

Pilots at the start of January:	Name	Victories
	Hptm Franz Walz	6
	Ltn Manfred von Richthofen	15
	Ltn Erwin Böhme	8
	Ltn Otto Höhne	6
	Ltn Hans Imelmann	6
	Ltn Erich König	3
	Ltn Hans Wortmann	2
	Ltn Werner Voss	3
	Ltn Dieter Collin	2
	Ltn Jürgen Sandel	–
	Vfw Max Müller	5
	Vfw Ostrop	–
	Ltn Albert Dossenbach	9
	Flgm Gustav Kinkel	–
OzbV	Oblt Karl Bodenschatz	–

Base: Pronville   Front: 1st Army

The new names on this month's list were Gustav Kinkel, who, as his rank of Flugmaat (Aviation Petty Officer) indicates, was a Naval aviator, and Albert Dossenbach. Most Naval airmen were either operating with the German Navy or the Marines, over the North Sea or along the Belgian coast. Several Naval pilots crop up from time to time in German (Army) staffeln, probably gaining experience of operations with the army air service. He arrived in late December.

Dossenbach arrived on New Year's Eve. This 25-year-old from the Black Forest region was a former medical student and the initial war months saw him in the army where his bravery brought him the Iron Cross 2nd Class for carrying his wounded CO from the battle area, followed by the Mecklenburg-Schwerin Military Merit Cross 1st Class (1914), and Iron Cross 1st Class. He moved up through the ranks until he was commissioned in January 1915, but then moved to aviation. Once a pilot he flew two-seaters with FA22, then Schutzstaffel 9, claiming, in company with his observer, nine victories by 3 November 1916. Dossenbach received the Knight's Cross 2nd Class with Swords to the Order of the Zäringen Lion, the 2nd Class of the Mecklenburg-Schwerin Military Merit Cross (September 1916), the Knight's Cross of the Hohenzollern House Order (October 1916), and finally the coveted Pour le Mérite, on 11 November. Thus he arrived with the Blue Max dangling at his throat, which probably had von Richthofen's eyes riveted to the blue and gold painted enamel cross, with himself having the award of this decoration so tantalisingly close. Dossenbach had front-line combat experience but needed to gain knowledge of single-seater action prior to taking command of one of the several new Jastas being formed at this time.

A new pilot who would arrive on the 27th was Leutnant Franz Christian August von Scheele. From Schwerin, he came four days after his 21st birthday and had moved to aviation from the Lieb-Granadier Regiment Nr.8 – König Friedrich Wilhelm III (1st Brandenburg).

Von Richthofen's Last Victory with Jasta B

Four days into the new year, Manfred von Richthofen finally downed his 16th victory and eight days later he was awarded the Blue Max. The goal posts had not been moved, but they soon would be. He had received the requisite Knight's Cross with Swords of the Royal Hohenzollern House Order on 11 November, coincidentally the same date Dossenbach had received his Pour le Mérite. So now Jasta Boelcke had two of its men wearing the famed medal.

Victory number 16 had been a Sopwith Pup of 8 Squadron, Royal Naval Air Service, which went down near Metz-en-Coûture where its pilot died. Richthofen noted in his combat report that it was the first time he had seen this type of aeroplane and decided it was a superior machine to his own. Only because there were three Albatros Scouts to one Pup did they manage to overcome it, the Sopwith breaking up as it fell earthwards. Pups were indeed fairly new, having only started equipping fighter squadrons in October 1916. Naval 8 had received theirs at that time too, having been flying Nieuports previously.

Three days later, on the 15th, von Richthofen received orders to leave Jasta Boelcke and take command of Jasta 11 at Brayelles airfield near Douai. Jasta 11 had been in existence since October 1916 but had only achieved one confirmed victory. Its CO was posted away to another Jasta and von Richthofen became its new Staffelführer. Jasta 11, under his command, became one of the most successful fighter units of the German Air Service, and later part of the first Jagdesgeschwader – JGI – commanded also by von Richthofen.

Another away posting was for Max Müller on the 19th, who was sent to Jasta 28w (a Würrtemberg unit) upon its formation. He would spend the spring and summer with it but would return to Jasta Boelcke in the late autumn. Leutnant Jürgen Sandel had already left ten days earlier, returning to a two-seater unit, FA(A)259. It has to be assumed that he had not proved good fighter pilot material.

Changing Fortunes

January 1917 proved a sparse month as regards victories. On the 7th Böhme scored his ninth by downing a DH2 west of Beugny. On the 23rd, Jasta Boelcke suffered a double blow, losing Hans Imelmann and Paul Ostrop. Imelmann was attacking a BE two-seater, crewed by Captain J C McMillan and Lieutenant J R Hopkins of 4 Squadron. The time was 14.05. Hopkins' fire hit Imelmann's fuel tank and he went down in flames. He fell near Miraumont, where the Albatros was seen burning on the ground.

Ostrop was flying an Albatros DII and again it was the Jasta's 'thorn' – 24 Squadron – that was in the action. Lieutenant E C Pashley killed him at 14.40 hours not far from the same Miraumont area; it was Eric Pashley's sixth victory. Strangely enough Ostrop was trying to shoot down the same Captain McMillan of 4 Squadron who had been the pilot of the BE engaged by Imelmann shortly beforehand. According to Pashley the German pilot fell from his Albatros over Grandcourt following the loss of a wing, his body and the wreckage falling in British lines. John McMillan, aged 24, from Essex, did not survive long after his fight with Imelmann and Ostrop, dying on 6 February of wounds that he had received in combat three days earlier.

Pashley's combat report:

> 23 January 1917. 1.30 pm. DH2 9730. Escort to BE2s. Grandcourt. Halberstadt Scout.
> At 1.30 pm Lieutenant Pashley was flying over Grandcourt at a height of 12,000 feet when he saw a BE2e at about 4,000 feet directly below him with a HA on its tail. He dived with engine full on to within about 25 yards of tail of HA and

fired a burst of 15 to 20 rounds. The HA nose-dived vertically and the pilot was seen to fall out of his machine.

Lieutenant Pashley, owing to pressure failure, was unable to see the machine hit the ground. Captain Long saw Lieutenant Pashley engage this machine closely. Owing to a double feed he did not see the actual combat but immediately afterwards saw Lieutenant Pashley flying alone. Lieutenant Cockerell also observed the HA to nosedive vertically.

This was the third blow to Jasta Boelcke in January, for earlier, on the 10th, Otto Höhne had been wounded in the chest and arm during a fight with a Sopwith 1¹/₂ Strutter at 10.30. He did not fly again for some time, but as we shall read, he did serve with the Jasta again. So, following a period of exceptional success, January had seen the loss of three pilots for just three victories. Had Jasta Boelcke's fortunes begun to fade? The unit's fourth loss was to follow.

Gustav Kinkel claimed (or to be accurate it was claimed for him) his first victory on the 25th, an FE2b north-east of Moislains, although in doing so, he was himself shot down by a DH2. However, it is far from clear who or what he shot down, for no FE2s were lost in the area on this day (one was shot down by Jasta 18 and flak near Menin – too far north to be in Jasta 2's territory). Even if the usual gitterumpf confusion is in issue, no DH2s were lost either.

Kinkel fell to the guns of Lieutenant A E McKay of 24 Squadron, in his Albatros DIII 1982/16, which came down in British lines – a sector held by Australians – and Kinkel was taken prisoner. He ended up in a prison camp in Southampton, England. This was Alfred McKay's fourth victory, and last with 24 Squadron. The Canadian received the MC and became a flight commander with 23 Squadron, flying Spads. Before the year was out he had increased his score to ten but was then killed in action on 28 December, the day after his 25th birthday. McKay's combat report records:

> 25 January 1917. 10.35 am. DH2 7884. Offensive Patrol. Single-seat Albatros with Nieuport struts and planes. Large K on side of fuselage.
> About 10.35 am Lieutenant McKay saw one HA coming from the East just south of Bapaume, at same height – 6,500 feet. Lieutenant McKay attacked HA at 30 yards range. HA dived so as to swing on to the tail of another DeHav which was flying below. Lieutenant McKay followed him down, driving him off DeHav's tail. He continued to follow HA down to within 500 feet of the ground, when HA crashed at T.26.a. [west of Combles]. Captain Wood, Lt Sedgwick and Lt Woollett followed HA down at rear of Lieutenant McKay.

For aircraft that came down on the British side of the lines, the RFC gave most of them a G-prefixed serial number, even if it was little more than a wreck. Kinkel's machine, which, as McKay spotted, was decorated with a large letter 'K' on the fuselage, became G5, just as Büttner's had become G1.

The Jastas had only just started to receive the mark DIII Albatros, and this one was one of the first to fall inside Allied lines. It copied the Nieuport Scout's sesquiplane wing layout, in that the lower wing was of a much narrower cord than the upper wing. Like the Nieuport, this necessitated the use of a 'V-Strut' between the two wings, and it was not long before RFC pilots were calling the new Albatros the 'Vee-strutter'.

February 1917

Pilots at the start of February:	Name	Victories
	Hptm Franz Walz	6
	Ltn Erwin Böhme	9
	Ltn Dieter Collin	2
	Ltn Albert Dossenbach	9
	Ltn Erich König	3
	Ltn Franz von Scheele	–
	Ltn Werner Voss	3
	Ltn Hans Wortmann	2
	Oblt Adolf Ritter von Tutschek	–
OzbV	Oblt Karl Bodenschatz	–

Base: Pronville   Front: 1st Army

Following the postings and losses of the previous month, only two new pilots had arrived. Leutnant Franz Christian von Scheele from Schwerin, aged just 22 (born 23 January 1895), previously a Grenadier, then an observer with FA32 in 1915, then finally a pilot with Kasta 11 of KG2, and Leutnant Adolf von Tutschek. Both arrived in late January.

Von Tutschek was a Bavarian, from Ingolstadt, born 16 May 1891, and had been in the army since 1910, starting as a cadet. Commissioned in 1912, he was wounded in the infantry soon after the war commenced and in 1915 was serving on the Eastern Front. Wounded again, he had nevertheless received a number of decorations: the Iron Cross 1st Class, the Bavarian Military Merit Order 4th Class with Swords, and the Military Max-Josef Order, which gave him the title of Ritter (Knight) and a promotion to Oberleutnant. He then fought at Verdun on the Western Front but was badly gassed, having to spend a long period in hospital.

Obviously having had enough of trench warfare, he transferred to aviation and becoming a pilot flew with FA6b in October 1916. On 17 January he was decorated again, this time with the Bavarian Military Merit Order 4th Class with Crown and Swords. About a week later he arrived at Pronville to start a successful career as a fighter pilot. Another pilot to boost the Jasta's ranks during February was Vizefeldwebel Thiel, posted in from Kasta 15 of KG3. Johannes Wintrath arrived on the 20th.

Von Tutscheck's letters home have survived and were translated into English by the late Kelly Wills Jr some years ago. They help give an insight into his days with Jasta Boelcke:

> 26 January 1917. Pronville. Yesterday I made my first four test flights since joining Jasta Boelcke, in Albatros DI 1708/16. After lunch I made an overland flight to Le Cateau and returned the next morning. The leader of the Boelcke Staffel is Hauptmann Walz.

> 27 January 1917. First patrol with Jasta Boelcke flying from Pronville.

> 29 January 1917. Yesterday only a short trial flight in Albatros DI 438/16. This morning and this afternoon one patrol each.

February began more promisingly with Werner Voss scoring his fourth victory on the 1st, a DH2 of 29 Squadron at 17.30 in the afternoon. Von Tutschek wrote:

> 3 February 1917. Yesterday and today we shot down three. Among them was an English captain who had lunch with us today before moving off to a PoW camp. Ltn Voss had shot his motor up. Otherwise there isn't much news. The weather seems to be getting worse.

Despite being dated the 3rd, it seems clear this was in fact written on the 4th as there were no claims on the 3rd. Voss's guest would appear to be Captain A P V Daly, who was not only brought down but also wounded in the shoulder, a fact von Tutschek does not mention. It is also recorded that Voss visited Daly in hospital a few days later, with a gift of some cigars.

On the 4th the Jasta saw a return to its autumn heydays with four kills, although all four went down on the Allied side. All occurred shortly after 3 pm, Böhme shooting down a DH2 and a BE2, Erich König another BE, and Voss a third. Apart from a victory by Jasta 1, these four were the only claims this date. Von Tutschek recalled his part in these combats:

> I was terribly angered. I sat on the tail of a BE from 3,000 metres down to 1,800 and powdered him from close range. Just when he began to trundle downwards, Ltn König came and gave him his final dosage.

There were no shared claims between German fighter pilots, so either the Jasta sorted out who got the credit amongst themselves, or it went to arbitration on the evidence before a final confirmation was given. No doubt in this case König got the victory without too much squabbling.

However, Jasta B did not get off scot-free. In the air battle, von Scheele was shot down west of Le Mesnil and he fell to his death. Eric Pashley of 24 Squadron, who had downed Ostrop ten days earlier was again the culprit. Pashley wrote in his combat report:

> 4 February 1917. DH2 7930. Albert. 2 pm. Offensive Patrol. About 2 pm Lt Pashley observed six or eight HA dive upon five FEs flying between Fricourt and Maricourt. Lt Pashley approached the HA and chose to attack one which was upon the tail of an FE crossing the lines at [map ref] U.1. He got onto the tail of the HA, which then left the FE and turned East, closely followed by Lt Pashley. For more than half a minute Lt Pashley followed the HA firing continuously at a range of about 20 yards. The HA finally turned over and fell at about U.3. Lt Saundby who was nearby fired a few shots into the HA at about 70 yards range. He stopped firing owing to Lt Pashley being so near to the HA and observed the latter to side-slip and eventually turn over and crash.

Von Scheele had lasted just nine days. The next day Vizefeldwebel Thiel was wounded in combat, but was able to remain on duty.

Eric Pashley, who came from Yarmouth but had lived in Croydon pre-war, was 24 and this was his seventh victory. He would gain one more in March but was killed in a flying accident on 17 March. His older brother Herbert, serving in a Balloon Company, had been killed in an accident on 26 December 1916. Eric Pashley had just been recommended for the Military Cross, but with his death it could not be proceeded with, so he ended up with just a mention in despatches for his eight victories.

On the 10th Böhme and Voss scored again with an FE and a DH2 respectively, although again both went down inside British lines. As far as can be seen, only one DH2 of 32 Squadron was lost. The RFC patrol had spotted Jasta Boelcke's machines above them at around 11.15 British time but being unable to climb to their height immediately, they traversed their Lewis guns upwards and began to fire. The German pilots, not unnaturally, took umbrage and immediately fell on the four DH2s. A fight developed. Captain L P Aizlewood's machine was badly shot about, and he was also wounded in the right shoulder.

Lieutenant A V H Gompertz in another DH2 was also shot-up badly and there is no doubt that the German pilots saw both DH2s heading down and 'apparently' out, low over the British lines. In the event both pilots survived and so did their aircraft, although badly damaged. Aizlewood reported his fire hitting one of the German aircraft which had streamers at its wing struts and a BE2 pilot later confirmed seeing it going down vertically 1,000 feet from the ground. Jasta Boelcke recorded no losses.

On the 11th the Jasta did suffer a loss, with Böhme being wounded in the left arm, the third Jasta pilot to be wounded by a Sopwith 1½ Strutter. He ended up in Cambrai hospital. He wrote:

> ... and I am in hospital, because the day before yesterday such a malevolent Englishman, who was defeated theoretically, shot me maliciously in the left arm. It was a Sopwith two-seater, which I had already fought down so far that he intended to land, and, as a fair hunter, I protected him in a kind of magnanimity – that is the result of my politeness.

Another of Boelcke's originals had departed. König, however, evened the score with a victory over a BE2c of 13 Squadron, shot down above the trenches at 15.30 German time, not far from Arras.

*   *   *

It was two weeks before the next claim, and again it was König who scored, a DH2 of 29 Squadron for his sixth victory. The 25th also saw Voss claim two others inside British lines in the same action, but apart from the one 29 Squadron loss, that was it. All three had been seen to fall towards the ground over the lines.

The six-man DH2 patrol's first intimation of danger was when Lieutenant J H R Sutherland, in the highest machine, was attacked from behind. Turning to face the danger his gun jammed and he was forced to dive away, all the while being chased and attacked. Sutherland had his rudder post smashed so headed down and only at the last moment did he straighten out and head for base. Was this König, who being senior to Voss might have had the first chance of attack? Lieutenant R J S Lund was also engaged by what he later described as 'a cleverly flown Albatros'. He was wounded and crashed into the British lines near Arras.

Meantime, Captain H J Payn was struggling with another Albatros. A DH2 pilot came to his aid and managed to 'persuade' the German pilot to break off his attack. Payn's machine was badly hit and the engine was spluttering as he edged over the trenches, his predicament no doubt observed by German soldiers and reported upon. He put down safely near Duisans.

In terms of attack timing, König reported his attack as being at 14.45, while Voss recorded his attacks as being 14.55 and 15.00 so if Sutherland was indeed the first to be engaged, then it looks like König shot him up and Voss splattered the other two – Lund and Payn. As a matter of interest, it had been Payn who reported McCudden as being shot down on 27 December, the day von Richthofen claimed his pusher as his 15th victory. These victories brought Jasta Boelcke's total claims to over 100. Voss may have been the man to actually get the 100th, although König may have sneaked in and got it as he may have brought down his DH2 before Voss got his two.

Werner Voss completed the month's scoring by downing three BE two-seaters, one on the 26th and a brace on the 27th. Again all three were noted as falling inside British lines, but all three were indeed RFC casualties. An 18 Squadron FE was brought down in combat near St Catherine, Arras, falling near Guillemont, its pilot dead, the observer mortally injured. This claim does not appear in the German communiqués (the Nachrichtenblat) and no other claims are made for it, so all that can be said is that the Jasta's score had reached over 100 during February 1917.

Albert Dossenbach left the unit on 19 February, going to Jasta 36, to command this newly formed unit. He gained five victories with it before being wounded during a bomb raid on his airfield. Recovering, he was given command of Jasta 10 with JGI, scored one more victory but was killed in action on 3 July 1917. Another pilot was posted out during the month, Dieter Collin being sent to Jasta 22 on the 21st.

March 1917

Pilots at the start of March:

	Name	Victories
	Hptm Franz Walz	6
	Ltn Erich König	6
	Vfw Thiel	–
	Oblt Adolf Ritter von Tutschek	–
	Ltn Werner Voss	11
	Ltn Johannes Wintrath	–
	Ltn Hans Wortmann	2
	Ltn Fritz Otto Bernert	7
OzbV	Oblt Karl Bodenschatz	–

Base: Pronville   Front: 1st Army

Leutnant Fritz Otto Bernert had arrived on 1 March. From Upper Silesia he was just five days from his 24th birthday and had been wounded four times with the infantry, the last – a bayonet wound – had severed the main nerve in his left arm leaving it virtually useless, but it had not stopped him transferring to the air service, firstly as an observer, then making the transition to pilot. When he arrived at Jasta Boelcke he had scored seven victories with Kek Vaux and then Jasta 4, and had already received the Iron Cross 1st and 2nd Class, the Saxon Albert Order, Knight 2nd Class with Swords, then on 25 January 1917, the Knight's Cross with Swords of the Hohenzollern House Order.

Werner Voss opened the March account with another BE2 shot down on the 4th. Two days later von Tutschek started his scoring run with a DH2 of 32 Squadron. The British pilot was a minor ace, Lieutenant M J J G Mare-Montembault, whose MC was about to be announced. He had claimed his sixth victory this same day. Mare-Montembault, it will be recalled, had been shot down before, on 10 October 1916, by none other than Oswald Boelcke – the German's 34th victory. This time however, he had come down on the wrong side of the lines and was captured. Von Tutschek wrote:

> On patrol from 16.01 to 17.12 hours and scored my first air victory in Albatros DI 1994/16 over a Vickers single-seater. Witness reports: "Today, at 16.30 hours 6 March 1917 was an air battle between a German and an English pilot over the Hindenburg positions north of Beugnâtre in which the Englishman was forced to land. The occupant of the aircraft was taken prisoner and was not wounded. According to his statement he received a shot in the fuel tank forcing him to land. Before anyone could reach him he succeeded in firing his machine. Motor No.30059. Signed Aszmuth, Adjutant to Fusilier-Regiment Nr. 3/90."
>
> "K-Flak Batterie 21 reports the shooting down of a Vickers near Beugnâtre at 16.40 hours on 6 March 1917. The enemy pilot was forced down by an Albatros D aircraft in the direction of Beugnâtre. Flak-Gruppe II and signed A.B. Offizier, Leutnant Mais."
>
> At 16.30 the Boelcke Staffel attacked a Vickers squadron which was flying eastwards over the front at 2,800 metres altitude. I took on an English one-seater over Beugnâtre and forced him away from his squadron in a northerly direction. After about 100 rounds the enemy craft went down in a dive but caught himself when 600 metres from the ground, whereupon I immediately attacked him again and forced him down in a dog-fight north of Beugnâtre. The occupant was captured by Fusilier-Regiment No.90. No other German machine engaged in the combat. The occupant was Lt M J Mare-Montembault, who was taken prisoner unwounded.

Voss had bagged another DH2 in the same fight, Captain H G Southon who was also taken prisoner. It was Voss's 13th victory. The Jasta Boelcke War Diary records:

> 6 March 1917.
> Weather: morning hazy, afternoon cloudy, clearing later.
> Ready to take off: 11 machines. 15 combat flights were carried out.

Take-off on command of the Staffelführer. Five aerial battles occurred, of which two were successful.

Oberleutnant Ritter von Tutschek forced, at 4.30 in the afternoon, a Vickers single-seater No.7882, to land north of Beugnâtre. Rotary engine no. 30059, occupant Lieutenant M J Mare-Montembault unwounded and captured. Aircraft was burned on landing and was salvaged by A.Fl.P.I. [Army Flug Park 1]. A built-in machine gun was located in the machine.

Leutnant Voss forced to land a Vickers single-seater No. A.M.G. 7941 Havilland type north-west of Bapaume, near Favreuil. Occupant Captain J C Southon, C.F.E, wounded, shot in the foot, captured. Aircraft salvaged by A.Fl.P.I.

Enemy aerial activities very lively. Opponents appeared in strikingly strong flights.

Airfield established at Eswars.

His Majesty the Kaiser and the King was pleased to bestow Leutnant der Reserve Böhme the Knight's Cross of the Royal House Order of Hohenzollern with Swords.

With this victory came the start of a run of ten victories for Voss during March. Two victories on the 11th, two on the 17th and two more on the 18th firmly established Voss as the leading ace of the Jasta. During the late morning of the 11th he downed an FE2b into the British lines, and in the afternoon shot down a Nieuport Scout of 60 Squadron, flown by Lieutenant A D Whitehead. Whitehead's companion was Second Lieutenant F Bower, who reported:

I was escorting BEs with Lt. Whitehead, when I saw him dive onto a HA. I saw another close by to him, dived on it and fired a burst but he dived away. I turned to see what had become of Lt. Whitehead and saw him attacked by four other Scouts. He was almost immediately brought down in flames.

Arthur Whitehead survived the attentions of Voss to become a prisoner. After the war he recalled his last flight yet did not mention anything about being set on fire. He was hit in the left knee, the bullet then going into his right leg, and he lost control of the Nieuport. Falling in a spinning nose-dive he managed to regain control, but Voss was on him again and a stream of bullets smashed into his machine, hit his engine and cut his elevator controls. Due to shock and loss of blood Whitehead fainted when at about 3-4,000 feet and did not regain consciousness until a week later. He woke up in Douai hospital having added a fractured skull to his injuries. Perhaps some flames had appeared from the damaged engine after he had passed out? That would explain why he did not mention a fire.

His injuries ensured an early repatriation from Germany which occurred in January 1918. He wanted to remain in the service but he was

finally released on medical grounds in late 1919. He was never to regain
his full strength and fitness and died an early death in 1933.

Then came the announcement of the award of the Knight's Cross with
Swords of the Hohenzollern House Order to Voss. Amongst his kills had
been two BEs, two FEs, a Nieuport and a DH2, and on the 19th he and
Bernert both scored over RE8 Corps machines.

The RE8 was a fairly new RFC aircraft to the front, and these were the
first Jasta Boelcke had encountered successfully. So new to them in fact,
that both German pilots had claimed a 'Sopwith', perhaps confusing them
with Strutters, although they must have looked more like BE2s in the air.
They were reconnaissance and artillery observation machines and while
a little better than the BE2s were still vulnerable to German fighter attack.

Both machines came from 59 Squadron and both fell within a short
time of each other. The crew of Voss's RE8 were Captain E W Bowyer-
Bower and Second Lieutenant E Elgey. Eldred Bowyer-Bower's father
was also a captain, in France with the Royal Engineers, and was of course
devastated to hear of his son's loss. When it became apparent his boy had
fallen to his death behind the German lines, he was determined to search
for his grave when this became possible. In due time the front-line moved
sufficiently for him to find and locate the crash-site. He found the remains
of the RE8 with numerous bullet holes through it and nearby the graves
of the two men beneath a cross made from pieces of the aircraft.

To be certain he had to excavate the graves, identify the remains of his
son and bring them, together with his observer's, to a better resting place.
One can only imagine the experience of the father in these severely tragic
circumstances, but he must have been very proud to have given his son a
decent burial before the area of his fall was forever obliterated by the
turmoil of war. Both his son and Eric Elgey lie in Mory Abbey Military
Cemetery.

The second of Voss's two RE8 victories on 18 March provided him
with the chance of securing a trophy from the wreck, to aid the
confirmation process. Voss wrote the following report:

> While I was continuously spiralling upwards over Neuville
> together with Leutnant Wortmann, who was always behind
> me, a BE two-seater came towards us somewhat to the north
> and much higher than we, and then continued in a southerly
> direction. As I later determined, he was engaged in artillery
> spotting.
>
> I had soon reached the height of the BE and approached
> closer to him from behind. 150-200 metres behind me was
> Leutnant Wortmann, and quite farther away the remaining
> machines were also following.
>
> The opponent shot at me from about 200 metres' distance
> and dived steeply back to his front. Because of my continual
> fire, which I began at about 100 metres' distance, and which

I held until I was right behind him, the BE went into banks and spirals. I stayed behind him almost continuously and could get off good bursts at the closest distance.

After I had followed him down with many bankings, suddenly a second Albatros from my Staffel dived in between us from the left, and a crash almost happened. This Albatros turned upwards once more while I followed the opponent all the way down till right over the ground and shot at him. During an emergency landing the BE (No.5770) got quite smashed up.

I recognised the cavalrymen running about by their steel helmets and field caps to be Germans and so I decided to land on a grassy area nearby. Here I discovered this cavalry patrol were the last Germans before the advancing enemy whose patrol was staying close by. I took out the two Lewis machine guns from the aircraft and had them brought back to the First Company of Infantry Regiment Nr.107, to be stored there. I then shot one of the gas tanks of the BE, set it on fire and took off again.

He does not mention that both RFC airmen had survived and been taken prisoner – Captain G S Thorne and Second Lieutenant F E H Van Baerle of 13 Squadron, but they had been. Unfortunately, Guy Thorne had suffered a severe wound in the back from which he died later that evening. He was 35-years-old and had spent some years working in China. He had been married for less than four months. Upon his return from captivity, Van Baerle had recorded that while the two men were sat defenceless on the ground after crash-landing, the German fighter had shot them up. He was in praise of his pilot who managed to get them down despite his terrible wound.

During this period, the Jasta had moved its base from Pronville to Eswars on the 14th, which was just north of Cambrai. It moved again on the 23rd, this time to Proville, on the western outskirts of Cambrai. (This should not be confused with the airfield at Pronville, spelt with an 'n'.)

The Prince
Prince Friedrich Karl of Prussia was one of two aviator sons of Louise Sophie, third daughter of Friedrich, Duke of Schleswig-Holstein-Sonderberg-Augustenburg, of the house of Oldenburg, a second cousin to Kaiser Wilhelm. The younger of the two, Friedrich Karl, had earlier been with the Lieb-Husaren-Regiment Nr.1, whose insignia was that of a 'Death's Head' skull and crossbones. Becoming a pilot he was, by 1917, deputy leader of Artillery Flieger-abteilung 258. However, he took every opportunity to fly single-seaters, having an Albatros DI machine with the adjacent Jasta Boelcke.

On 21 March he went out looking for trouble with others of Jasta B and they found it in the shape of a patrol of DH2s from 32 Squadron. In the fight that ensued the Prince's machine was hit in the engine during an attack by Lieutenant C E M Pickthorn. Being over the lines with a crippled machine he had to quickly find a place to put down, and during a further attack he was wounded in the right foot. Landing close to the trenches, he decided to make a run for it but was fired upon by Australian troops and badly wounded. He was taken prisoner, and his aircraft towed away intact. Much was made of the victory once the wounded captive's identity became known.

He wrote a note after his capture, confirming his name and what had happened to him. Taken to a hospital in Albert (Baracen Lazarette), he was able to write a letter to his father on 30 March:

Now something about my air fight. You know I started with Walz's Staffel. We cruised along the front a long time without seeing anything. We went as far north as Arras and south in the direction of Bapaume and Péronne flying very low. On our return to the lines we all of a sudden discovered some 900 or 1,000 metres below six or eight Vickers single-seaters. Our leader immediately went for them and I followed, not willing to leave him alone, the enemy numbering so many more machines. That our other fliers did not follow can only be explained by assuming that they did not see the enemy in the dark clouds.

How we went for them! I sometimes lost sight of the leading German machine, but always managed to find it again. Suddenly one enemy flier came my way and I attacked him. He fled, I after him. Thus I lost my only comrade.

The enemy fliers around me increased still more in numbers. They must have noticed the dangerous condition of the man I was chasing. Meanwhile, I had succeeded in manoeuvring my opponent pretty close to earth, when all of a sudden I heard the tack-tack-tacking, with the result that soon I was wounded in the right foot. Thank heaven my controls remained intact.

Gliding over badly battered villages and trenches, I succeeded in landing, as the Australians who captured me said afterwards, not far from the German lines. I should have liked to destroy my machine, but the enemy gunfire prevented it. My second thought was to reach our lines, but the enemy at once directed his fire at me. Still I seemed to have luck until finally a bullet pierced my spine and came out at the right of my stomach. I went down like a log.

When finally the Australians found me, they treated me

very tenderly. I had lost so much blood and was freezing
cold. Two soldiers kindly offered their greatcoats and
covered me with them. They carried me an endless
stretch until we found a doctor, but they were very careful
with me.

Friedrich Karl did not survive. He succumbed to his wound on 6 April.
His elder brother, Friedrich Sigismund served on the Eastern Front with
FA46, and later with FA 22, between 1915-18. Friedrich Karl's Albatros
– serial 410/16 – was well photographed after its capture, with its skull
and crossbones insignia on the rear fuselage, and became G17 on the list
of captured German aeroplanes. Von Tutschek wrote a letter about the
episode:

21 March 1917. Eswars. Today at 16.30 hours I took off with
a flight [Kette] from Jasta Boelcke in weather where one
could fish in the dullness. The clouds were hanging at 500 to
600 metres when Voss, Wortmann and I, in succession, found
a hole in the clouds over Cambrai and climbed through the
mountainous mists. We found beneath us a sea of clouds
once we were through, while above was the most beautiful of
blue skies. Ltn Voss was up ahead with the leader, and we
followed closely behind. As I glanced backward I suddenly
spied a strange Albatros to the left, coming towards us. I
quickly recognised it as the green Albatros DI of Prince
Friedrich Karl of Prussia as he joined us, happily waving his
hand. The Prince commanded a [nearby] Flieger-abteilung
but was to join our Staffel in the near future. In the meantime
he was practicing on an Albatros from our Staffel. He had
painted a large skull on both sides of the fuselage and the
same on the propeller boss. The Prince was a frequent visitor
and we all liked him a lot. He was a true sportsman, which
was revealed in his flying. Shortly before this flight he had
an experience, the word of which went through the
Jagdstaffeln like wildfire.

[I remember that on this day] Prince Karl was sitting in
his heavy 220-hp Albatros with the motor running at top
speed in order to check the tachometer. To ensure that the
aircraft didn't plunge forward on its nose, two people were
at the back of the machine holding down the tail at the
elevators. On the call, "Free!" the chocks in front of the
wheels were jerked aside and one of the mechanics at the
rear jumped away. The Albatros, which the Prince was flying
for the first time, rolled forward and lifted off after an
unusually long run and became airborne. Immediately, the
Prince found it odd that the craft was so tail heavy and it

displayed an uncommon tendency to climb, in addition to a poor response from the steering while in a turn. He was at about 200 metres altitude when he noticed the people on the ground kept firing flares. He didn't understand the meaning of the flares but since the obstinate Albatros acted strange, he decided to go down and make a landing. The wheels touched the ground and the Albatros came to a stop with hardly a "run out". The Prince glanced around and saw a pale, whitened from fright mechanic clinging to the elevator. The poor fellow had hesitated at the word, "Free!", and so made the flight as a most unwilling passenger on the tail. For his nearly being frightened to death (in a steep climb or dive he would most certainly have slid off) he was handsomely rewarded [perhaps with a stiff drink!]. But back to our flight.

Over Arras we went down in steep spirals hoping to head off an artillery spotter, but there were none. So back we flew just under the clouds over the newly captured Siegfried Line positions towards the south. Coming towards us were the red rumps of the Richthofen Staffel who were returning from an equally unsuccessful hunt. With short greetings we passed each other.

Five of us were in the flight, Voss, Prince Karl, Walz, Wintrath and I. It was clear that we shouldn't become involved in a dogfight as the prevailing strong east wind [it was usually blowing from the west] would surely push us eastward. Despite that, our leader and Voss turned towards a few Vickers lattice-tailed single-seaters that were also flying just under the clouds at our altitude over Lagnicourt. Ltn Wintrath and I followed and the dance began. I went after an Englishman who instantly headed for the clouds just as additional aircraft were coming out of them. The same thing happened to Voss. When I looked back, I noticed the green Albatros of the Prince nearing the ground and spiralling, closely followed by two other enemy aircraft who were protecting him. While Prince Friedrich Karl was in the process of finishing off an Englishman, he was attacked by a second one who shot-up his motor so that his only recourse was an immediate landing.

He climbed out, and while running towards our lines, collapsed. The shots from an Englishman, as we found out later, had ended his life-or-death run as he was struck in the lower torso.

Charles Pickthorn, who brought down the Prince, was to end the war as a major in command of 84 Squadron. He won the Military Cross, and for some years the propeller from the Prince's Albatros hung in his house, the skull and crossbones motif clearly visible. Pickthorn died at a young age in 1938, and the trophy has, unfortunately, been long lost.

*   *   *

Voss and Bernert were to share the laurels over the next few days, with von Tutschek being the only other claimant with a Nieuport Scout for his second victory on 31 March. By the end of the month, Voss had increased his personal score to 22, and Bernert to nine. Voss had received the Hohenzollern House Order on the 26th. By this time von Tutschek had received official credit for his 6 March victory. He wrote of this and of his next victory on the 31st.

> 26 March 1917. Today the following message was received: "Oberleutnant Ritter von Tutschek of Jasta Boelcke is credited with his first victorious air victory, a Vickers single-seater on 6 March 1917. I therefore bestow on Oblt von Tutschek the 'Ehrenbecher' [Honour Goblet] for the 'Vickers in Aerial Combat'. The title of possession is to be taken and handed to the honouree and the receipt is to be signed. There will be further instructions about the transfer of the 'Ehrenbecher'. Hoeppner. Kofl 1."[1]
>
> 31 March 1917. Today at 09.00 hours in Albatros DIII 2004/16, an air combat with success in the vicinity of Loos, north-west of Lens, against a Nieuport single-seater. The shot down aircraft lies behind the enemy lines on the western edge of Loos. The aircraft was silver-grey with pennants on the wings and the occupant was killed.
>
> The Staffel, with Ltn König leading, flew to Lens, since there wasn't any enemy air activity south of Arras. West of Lens at 3,500 metres altitude, I attacked a Nieuport which was close behind an Albatros two-seater. Immediately the Nieuport let up in his pursuit of the Albatros two-seater, which was going down in a steep glide, and attempted to outclimb Ltn König and I, but I managed to get behind him. After 150 shots, the machine suddenly stood on its nose, tumbled over, and went to the ground almost vertically. I observed the impact near the north-west of Loos and saw the debris of the totally wrecked machine laying about as I flew over at 400 metres altitude.

---

[1] The 'Ehrenbecher' was given to an airman, pilot or observer upon achieving his first air

combat victory, but only the first.

April 1917

Pilots at the start of April:

	Name	Victories
	Hptm Franz Walz	6
	Ltn Werner Voss	22
	Ltn Fritz Bernert	9
	Ltn Erich König	6
	Oblt Adolf von Tutschek	2
	Ltn Johannes Wintrath	–
	Ltn Hans Wortmann	2
	Ltn Hermann Frommherz	–
	Ltn Georg Noth	–
	Vfw Thiel	–
OzbV	Ltn Bieler	–

Base: Proville   Front: 1st Army

New pilots arriving during March had been Hermann Frommherz, on the 19th, and Georg Hermann Paul Noth. Frommherz came from Waldshut, Baden, close to the Swiss border, and had been born in August 1891, so was 25. An engineering student at a technical college in Stuttgart, and an army reservist from 1911, he was mobilised just before war began and served in France and then on the Russian Front with an infantry regiment. As an NCO he received the Iron Cross 2nd Class in February 1915. Transferring to aviation in June 1915 he was an NCO two-seater pilot with Kampstaffel 20 of Kagohl 4 prior to becoming a fighter pilot. Before this, however, he saw action at Verdun, the Somme and then, having been commissioned in September 1916, Romania, Macedonia and Salonika.

For his service with Kasta 20, Frommherz received the Iron Cross 2nd Class, and the Knight's Cross 2nd Class, with Swords, of the Zähringen Lion Order, in January 1917.

Georg Noth had also been through the usual route of being in a two-seater unit, flying with Flieger-abteilung 38 before moving to Jasta Boelcke. Also, Leutnant Bieler had arrived to take over the adjutant's duties from 1 April, Bodenschatz having two weeks leave from 1 to 15 April.

In April came Friedrich (Fritz) Paul Kempf, who arrived on the 4th. This 22-year-old (he was a month short of his 23rd birthday) came from Freiburg, in the Black Forest, Baden, and had been a pre-war infantryman, army service interrupting his engineering studies. Wounded in September 1914, upon recovery he joined the Air Service in May 1915 and early in 1916 was flying with Kasta 20 of Kagohl 4, seeing action on the Somme, at Verdun and then in Romania and Macedonia, operating with Gotha G.II twin-engined bombers. His infantry service brought him the Iron Cross 2nd Class and the Silver Merit Medal. With Kasta 20 he won the Iron Cross 1st Class. In Jasta B he found fellow pilot Hermann Frommherz who had been in Kasta 20 with him.

Leutnant Hans Eggers arrived during the month and remained until the start of October, but he doesn't seem to have made much of an impression, and certainly made no claims that were upheld. However, the fact that he stayed alive during his six months with the Staffel says something.

Another Blue Max

Both Voss and Bernert continued their scoring theme into April. Voss gained victories 23 and 24 on the 1st and 6th of April, Bernert scoring his 10th to 19th by 11 April. Voss had now passed the magic figure of 20 victories so nobody was surprised when the announcement came that with effect from 8 April he had been awarded the Pour le Mérite. This, as was usual, brought him an extended leave to Germany. For one thing he had earned a break, and the German publicity machine needed him to parade around as the latest war hero. As he left the front, the next great land battle was about to begin – the Battle of Amiens.

These victories were not achieved without loss, for on 2 April two pilots had died. In mid-morning the Jasta had attacked a formation of FE2d pushers of 57 Squadron on a line patrol between Lens-Arras-Bapaume. Their initial attackers had been Jasta 11, and as the British group broke up and scattered, Jasta 2 came on the scene. The FE2 gunners put up a spirited defensive fire and had the good fortune to score hits on both the Albatros Scouts of Erich König and Hans Wortmann. The former went down in flames over Wancourt, the latter crashing near Vitry-en-Artois. Jasta 11 did however down two of the British machines. Sadly, König fell on his 27th birthday.

57 Squadron crews did not claim any victories – that is, the surviving crews who returned did not claim. One crew saw two go down, one in flames, but it was crews who were themselves shot down that got them. As the one crew that put in a report noted the two falling German fighters, we know they fell in this action, but that is all. The FE crew were Second Lieutenant E E Pope and Lieutenant A W Naismith in aircraft A1959. Their combat report states:

> 2 April 1917. 09.45 hours. Line Patrol SE of Arras. 9,000 feet.
> While on Line Patrol from Le Bassée to Bapaume, three FE2ds were attacked from above by six Hostile Aircraft at 9.45 am about 10 miles SE of Arras. One FE2d dived at by one HA pursued it and it was seen to descend in a vertical nosedive, and then burst into flames. FE2d A/1959 dived at this HA also, and fired one round, then turned and got under the tail of another HA which was circling round above the FE2ds. Both Lewis Guns on FE2d A/1959 jammed and machine had to withdraw from combat and circle round while observer tried to remedy jams.
> Another HA was seen to leave the formation and dive

away apparently out of control, and was not seen to rejoin the combat.

The two remaining FE2ds continued the combat which was progressing in a north-easterly direction owing to the strong wind.

The observer being unable to remedy jams, FE2d A/1959 re-crossed the lines at Arras passing a formation of Nieuports proceeding south-east and immediately afterwards passed the remaining three of the formation of six FE2ds.

In the past this crew have on occasion been credited with these two Albatros Scouts but as we have read, they did not shoot anything down, only reporting seeing two go down during the fight.

Böhme had been forced to go to Düsseldorf in mid-March for orthopaedic treatment on his left arm, which was giving him trouble. He returned to the hospital in Cambrai on 5 April to learn of the deaths of König and Wortmann. Böhme and von Richthofen were now the only two survivors of the original Boelcke Staffel.

Chapter Four

The Battle of Amiens

Bloody April Begins

Werner Voss did not return to Jasta Boelcke until the beginning of May 1917 and one has to wonder what sort of victory score he may have achieved if he had remained. As history now shows, April 1917 and the Battle of Amiens was to give the German fighter pilots a plethora of Allied aircraft to shoot down, and if Manfred von Richthofen and his Jasta 11 is anything to go by, victories there were aplenty. Of course, one could argue that had Voss stayed he might have been killed before he attained another kill, but the odds are that he would have given von Richthofen a far closer contest in the scoring game had he remained and survived. Von Richthofen, at the start of the Amiens Battle, had 39 victories, only 15 more than Voss.

What made April 1917 and the Amiens battle so costly for the Allied airmen was that the German Jasta pilots were just about ready for a major confrontation. They had perfected their tactics since the start of the Jasta era the previous autumn, and had now almost totally equipped with the latest Albatros biplane fighters, each carrying two machine guns firing through the propeller. As the winter weather was starting to ease away, the Jasta pilots along the British front were faced with an offensive and above it, masses of aircraft. It was like a fisherman finding a stretch of river teaming with fish and having his new rod and reel ready.

By April the Jasta had virtually standardised with Albatros DIII Scouts as had most other Jagdstaffeln. The updated versions, the DV and then the DVa would not start to arrive before May. Jasta B also took delivery of a Siemens-Schuckert DI (3754/16) on 12 April (actually the SSW DI – Siemens-Schuckert Werke) for operational testing. Most German aircraft designers had been given captured examples of the French Nieuport Scout to help them with their ideas for new fighters, and Siemens certainly copied it well. It looked exactly like the French machine but it did not live up to the French one in action and only a handful saw active service on the Western Front.

Before the ground battle started, Jasta B added a few more scalps to its tally. Bernert shot down two observation balloons on the 3rd, and on the 6th von Tutschek shot down an FE2, while Voss and Bernert claimed a BE and an RE8 respectively. Bernert followed this with a kill on the 7th, a Nieuport XXIII, then two kills on the 8th, a BF2b and another RE8. Von Tutschek wrote of his victory in a letter dated the 6th, but opened it with an account of an action that took place on 2 April:

>...I took off by myself while the others were peacefully sleeping. The Front was quickly reached, and I climbed to 4,500 metres and waited for something to show up. There was serenity and peace everywhere. Below me the newly constructed Siegfried position with its wire obstacles appeared as a dark veil against the white snow, while 500 metres above me was a layer of cloud.
>
> I searched and searched for an English machine beneath me, and I became so occupied with my searching that it was only after a sudden rattle above me that I looked up and saw five Nieuports diving down on me.
>
> "Too many of them," I thought, so I stood my crate on its nose and tore out. The Nieuports were close behind me but I was faster and I had a head start. I was several kilometres behind our lines and observed with satisfaction how four of my pursuers veered off while the fifth bravely followed.
>
> I throttled my motor and let the enemy catch up. Now I had him close enough and I turned and headed towards him at top speed. Tommy accepted the challenge and we roared around each other. Neither of us was able to get the other in his sights – not even for a second – but I was constantly above him and we were gradually losing altitude. My partner gave up and flew homeward, that is, he banked, looped, and slid as he tumbled westward.
>
> In the meantime another German single-seater arrived and was idly watching our contest but I was unable to recognise him. My competitor was already behind the fellow and after a few shots the Englishman tilted forward with flames shooting from his machine. The wings broke away and the fuselage hit the ground near Quéant. Furiously I stared at the victor. It was Bernert again, and he had the nerve to wink at me cheerfully.[1]
>
> Thinking thoughts of revenge, I [later, on the 6th] lay in the sun while my bird was being readied with petrol, oil and water. Suddenly loud cries were heard from everyone. All eyes and binoculars were directed rearward in the direction of Cambrai where a lone English FE lattice-tail was flying towards the front at 1,600 to 1,800 metres altitude.

---

[1] Bernert's victim was Second Lieutenant V F Williams of 60 Squadron, who was killed.

We knew we would have a little head start if we got up
immediately. I jumped into my craft and without buckling
my belt or testing the motor I raced off. Next to me in the
same second was Ltn Voss. We caught up with the enemy
craft over Bourlon Wood and fired at him simultaneously. I
let go 60 rounds whereupon the propeller of the FE stopped
and the craft made a left bank, gliding in the direction of
Anneux. The proficient "Franz" [German nickname for
observer] hid himself behind the motor and gas tank and
instead of shooting, did nothing. After the FE, with its
immobile propeller, reached the altitude of 100 metres, I let
up and circled over him. Suddenly two strange Albatros
DIIIs from another Staffel joined us, and the one nearest the
ground shot at the landing FE and then landed beside him.
The FE bore the number A652 and was later salvaged by
Jagdstaffel 12.

Despite another Jasta almost horning-in on Jasta B's kill, Voss and von
Tutschek were noted as the victors, and as there were no shared kills, the
two men tossed a coin and von Tutschek won. It was a machine from 57
Squadron, a unit that lost five machines on this date, although there was
no aircraft numbered A652 among them, which in any event was a
Sopwith Pup serial! It was probably A22, whose crew were captured near
Anneux the same day.

The Battle Commences
The Battle of Amiens opened on Easter Monday, 9 April. High ground in
northern France is at a premium, and command of the high ground is
always necessary in war. He who holds the high ground commands the
battle. The high ground at this stage was Vimy Ridge, situated due north
of Arras. Whoever occupied it could see much of the surrounding
countryside. To the east lay Méricourt, Fresnoy and Oppy Wood. To the
north, Givenchy. South-east, was Bailleul-sir-Berthoult.
    The main thrust towards Vimy was in the hands of the Canadian
Corps, part of General Henry Horne's First Army. Just as the opening
salvoes were fired the weather turned bad hindering the attack at first
light – 05.30 hours. Slowed down by cold wind and snow showers the
troops advanced, hoping that the pre-dawn artillery fire had both
pulverised the enemy's trenches and cut the barbed wire sufficiently for
it not to be a problem. In the event, the leading assault troops did get
through, the British barrage lifting and moving foward as they
progressed. Only the smoke from exploding shells gave any cover to the
German survivors who now began to emerge from their underground
bunkers to man their machine guns. Further south, General Edmund
Allenby's Third Army attacked from positions just east of Arras, either
side of the River Scarpe.

Jasta Boelcke remained south of the main battle front, well south of the Scarpe. It flew patrols but it was not to be until the third day – the 11th – that success came against the British in the air. At 09.00 Frommherz shot down a Spad of 23 Squadron, which he claimed as a 'Sopwith'. Three and a half hours later Bernert knocked down a Morane from 3 Squadron, and another Spad. There is no obvious Spad loss, but a 23 Squadron machine that had flown out late morning had its flying wires shot away, and was damaged enough to have its pilot force-land near Ecoust St Mien. Bernert noted his victim as going down into British lines north-west of Lagnicourt, exactly where Ecoust lay. These became his 18th and 19th kills.

Twenty kills was still the approximate yardstick for the Blue Max but somehow Bernert beat the system by being awarded this prestigious decoration on the 23rd. Perhaps it was because his score was all the more creditable because of his useless left arm? He also wore spectacles! This was not a rare event in WW1 but a factor nevertheless.

Frommherz scored the next victory on the 14th, a BE2f of 10 Squadron, without an observer, on a bombing sortie. Again there came a lull in the Jasta's fortunes, for while other units were scoring heavily, Jasta B always seemed on the edge of things. On the southern French front, General Robert Nivelles finally launched his delayed supportive offensive on the 16th as the British assault came to an end. Vimy Ridge had been captured, and so too had 4,000 German soldiers and 54 guns. However, it was another ten days before the next victories were achieved by Jasta B – five in number – and all down to Otto Bernert!

Not only did Bernert score an incredible five victories on the 24th, but they were all shot down within a space of twenty minutes, between 08.30 and 08.50 hours, and all but the last one came down inside German territory. If he was making a point about his recent Pour le Mérite, he made it well.

After a brief lull, the British had reopened the Amiens Battle on the 23rd which put numerous RFC aircraft back in the sky. First down, on the 24th, was a Sopwith two-seater of 70 Squadron at 07.30 British time, falling in flames over Cambrai. The next three were BE2e machines from 9 Squadron, all flying without observers in lieu of extra bomb weight. Two of the pilots were killed and one captured. All fell around Catelet between 07.40 and 07.45 British time. Number five came at 07.50, a DH4 bomber from 55 Squadron. The wounded pilot got his machine down inside British lines near Doullens, his observer having been killed. 70 Squadron reported on their loss thus:

> Whilst the formation was flying south-east of Cambrai, a formation of six Albatros Scouts attacked from the direction of the sun. Lieut. Hulse and 2/AM. Bond were apparently hit early in the engagement, and whilst gliding down under the formation they were attacked and shot down by two HA.

9 Squadron reported:

> 9 Squadron bombed Bohain station from an average height
> of 1,900 feet and some of the bombs were observed to fall on
> the station and in the town.
>   The day proved disastrous – three out of five aircraft
> which set out failed to return. Lts. F A Matthews and C L
> Graves were killed and Lt. G E Hicks was taken prisoner.

This brought Bernert's score to 24[2], and this was to be his last while with
Jasta B. At the end of the month he was promoted to lead Jasta 6. He went
on to score a further three victories with his new command.

    The last victory of the month came on the 30th, and it was the first
victory of a new pilot who had arrived on the 4th, Leutnant Friedrich Paul
Kempf. He came from Freiburg, Baden, and was born in May 1894. He
had enlisted into the infantry in 1913 and moved to aviation in 1915. His
first (flying) war posting was to Kampfgeschwader Nr.4, Kasta 20, in
January 1916. During his time there he received the Iron Cross 2nd Class
and the Baden Silberne Militär-Verdeinstmedaille. His first victory was
over a BE2e from 9 Squadron which he shot down near Le Pavé at 07.45
hours.

                              *   *   *

Adolf von Tutschek received a telephone call on 28 April informing him
he had been named as leader of Jasta 12, due to his rank more than his
combat score. This was despite him refusing the same offer three days
earlier as he was after a new unit where he could hand-pick his pilots, and
take Oberleutnant Bodenschatz with him, having been together at training
school. He was also in danger of losing his May leave. However, he
accepted the inevitable and left on the 30th. In all he had made 140 sorties
with Jasta B, and had had five successful combats with three
confirmations. He filled the vacancy in Jasta 12 left by the loss of
Hauptmann Paul von Osterroht on the 23rd, who had been one of
Manfred von Richthofen's pilots in BAO.

---

[2] Within these pages pilot's scores are noted in chronological order. However, with the
German system of confirmation, victories in numerical sequence show a slightly different
picture. If confirmation of a victory was a long time coming, the number of that victory was
given according to the confirmation date, not the date of the victory. Therefore, as in
Bernert's case here, these five victories were recorded as his 20th, 21st, 22nd, 27th, and
23rd, due to the fourth one taking longer to be confirmed and credited. Bernert's official
24th, 25th and 26th victories were all credited to him in May with Jasta 6, before
confirmation of his 27th came through, scored on 24 April.

May 1917
Pilots at the start of May:

Name	Victories
Hptm Franz Walz	6
Ltn Werner Voss	24
Ltn Hermann Frommherz	2
Ltn Johannes Wintrath	–
Ltn Friedrich Kempf	1
Ltn Georg Noth	–
Vfw Thiel	–
Ltn Hans Eggers	–
Ltn Kurt Francke	–
Oblt Georg Zeumer	4
OzbV Oblt Karl Bodenschatz	–

Base: Proville   Front: 1st Army

Adolf von Tutschek left Jasta Boelcke on 30 April without adding to his score during the month. He was to do great things with Jasta 12 before being wounded on 11 August 1917, and received the Pour le Mérite. Returning to the front in the New Year, he commanded JGII and brought his score to 27 before being killed on 15 March 1918. He was hit by a glancing blow to the head in a combat with SE5s and although he landed safely, collapsed soon afterwards and was found dead next to his Triplane. The SE5s were from 24 Squadron!

Another pilot of note who came and went during April was Vizefeldwebel Josef Mai, previously with KG5. He moved on to Jasta 5 on the 17th and never looked back. He too won the Blue Max and achieved 30 victories by the war's end.

Two other newcomers were Leutnant Kurt Francke and Oberleutnant Georg Zeumer. Kurt Francke came from Lissa, and was born in December 1891. Little is known of his previous history. Georg Zeumer, however, is better known. Born in Nikolei in March 1890, this 27-year-old had been flying two-seaters since the start of the war and had already been awarded the Iron Cross, and the Knight's Cross of the Military St Henry Order, as early as November 1914. With FA69 on the Eastern Front he had been Manfred von Richthofen's pilot, while the latter was an observer. He had later flown with BAO, then with KG2, during which he had achieved four victories, the first being a French Nieuport Scout over Douaumont on 11 April 1916. He had also given von Richthofen flying lessons when the future 'Red Baron' decided it would be better to fight his war in the front, rather than the rear cockpit.[3]

---

[3] Von Richthofen became well known as the Red Baron due to his constant use of red to colour his aeroplanes. Initially, however, he was known to Allied soldiers and airman as the Red Devil. Other German fighters also had a red colour scheme, so it follows that any red machine was believed to be that flown by Richthofen.

Zeumer had had a rough time of it. In June 1916 he had been shot down near Fort Vaux. Injured, he was being taken by car to a field aid station when it was involved in an accident in which Zeumer broke a thigh bone. It did not heal properly and in consequence he was left with one leg nine centimetres shorter than the other, so had to use a stick. By the time he joined Jasta B Zeumer knew his days were numbered. He suffered from diabetes and tuberculosis, and was known amongst his comrades as 'the lunger'! It gave him the motivation to fly and fight harder, not caring if his recklessness ended everything for him. While sympathetic to his plight and his mind set, von Richthofen did not want this kind of pilot in his command, so he had arranged for him to go to Jasta B.

A third arrival in May was Leutnant Rolf Freiherer von Lersner, a former member of the Prussian Hussar Regiment Nr.8. He came from Deutz where he was born in December 1893.

Voss Returns

Werner Voss returned to the Jasta after his Blue Max leave on 5 May. Bloody April was over and although he missed it, Jasta B had only achieved 21 victories during it. Compared to Jasta 11's 89 kills and Jasta 5's 32, they were third on the list. In total the RFC had lost 245 aircraft in war operations and over 300 airmen, of which 211 were killed. There were also over 100 aviators wounded. The French had lost over 50 aeroplanes and more than 70 men.

Bernert had been the star during April, and Voss would be the May star, although scoring during this month was sparse overall. Voss got back into his stride on the 7th by shooting down one of the new SE5 fighters of 56 Squadron. The SE5 was one of the breed of British fighters arriving in France, along with the Bristol F2b two-seater, and later the Sopwith Camel.

The senior flight commander with 56 Squadron was the famed Captain Albert Ball DSO & Bar, MC, victor in over 40 combats. He was due to return to England soon and on this evening he led a patrol into a hostile and very cloudy sky. He was destined not to return from this flight. Jasta 11 were in the fight and Manfred von Richthofen's brother Lothar was incorrectly credited with killing Ball. Actually, Ball became disorientated in cloud and crashed. In the opening rounds of some very confused air fighting, Voss picked off the SE5 flown by 19-year-old Second Lieutenant R M Chaworth-Musters. His remains were never found and his only epitaph is his name carved on the Arras Airforce Memorial to the missing.

Two days later Voss scored three kills. The first was a BE2e from 52 Squadron that went down in pieces near Havrincourt, in the British lines, at 14.00 hours German time. It had been in the air since midday doing artillery observation work and was just about finished. Neither of the crew survived. Almost three hours later Voss was back over the front, this time shooting down a Pup of 54 Squadron, which he forced down intact at Lesdain where its pilot was captured.

This was followed five minutes later, at 16.50, by an FE2b of 22 Squadron, near Le Bosquet. The two-man crew recorded a fight against seven Albatros Scouts, but Voss got the credit and both men joined the earlier Pup pilot into a prison camp. These victories brought his score to 27. The RFC War Diary noted:

> A photographic reconnaissance of No.22 Squadron, with an escort of No.54 Squadron had a big fight with seven German machines. Capt. C M Clement and Lieut. M K Parlee, 22 Squadron, drove down one of the hostile machines out of control and then dived at three others that were following one of our Sopwith Scouts down. They were unable to get there in time, however, and the Sopwith Scout was forced to land in a field, but they eventually succeeded in engaging one of the German machines which crashed quite near the Sopwith.

There is no obvious German casualty recorded. The only suggestion is Hans Klein of Jasta 4 who was wounded this date, location not known. Jasta 4 were operating a little further north, around Douai, but he could have drifted south. Otherwise the German who crashed survived without injury, but not from Jasta B as far as is known.

Voss is Transferred
There was some discontent among the pilots of Jasta Boelcke at this time. The early glory days had passed and they were going through a period best described as lacklustre. Few victories had been scored in recent weeks and most of those by just two pilots, Bernert, who had now left, and Werner Voss. There was a strong feeling this was due to the Staffelführer, Franz Walz, who did not appear to have the same aggressive nature of Boelcke or Kirmaier. However, it has to be said that the pattern of most Jastas was that it was the star performers who led and who scored, supported by the rest of the Staffel. No doubt due to his position as leading ace, Voss led the opposition against Walz, and actually lobbied for his removal. Perhaps encouraged by his position, status and being a Pour le Mérite winner, he went against protocol and used poor judgement, along with another pilot, von Lersner, in going over his CO's head and reporting the perceived problem to 'higher authority'. The result was that he was removed from Jasta B and sent to command Jasta 5. Whether he had hoped to be given command of Jasta Boelcke is uncertain, but obviously his punishment was not as severe as it might have been, given the circumstances.

Amongst the papers of the late Ed Ferko, now housed in the University of Dallas, was found a translation of a document from Kogenluft 2, detailing how Voss and von Lersner got into serious trouble for trying to oust Walz as CO of Jasta B. Voss was in real hot water over this and only his combat record and his youth saved him from more severe punishment.

> **Personal Matter.**
> Subject: Request for a court of honour investigation, moved by Hptm. Walz and directed against himself, as well as a transfer to his peacetime unit.
> Action: Reserve Officer Ltn d. Res. Voss of Jasta Boelcke, and Ltn von Lersner, transmit a substantiated message to his Staffelführer, Hptm Walz, that he [Walz], being worn out would be no longer fit for service as a Staffelführer.
>
> Hptm Walz did not consider this an adequate step towards preserving his interests as Staffelführer and requested Kofl. 2 on 30th May 1917 to transfer him [Voss] to another Jagdstaffel.
>
> Kogenluft 14877 pers. of 6th June 1917 decreed the transfer of Hptm Walz as Führer (leader) to Jasta 34, the punishment of Ltn d. R. Voss, the appointment of Ltn Bernert to Führer of Jasta Boelcke.
>
> Kofl., 9/17/1 pers. punished Ltn d. Res. Voss by a plain reprimand without witnesses; allowing for the extraordinary record of Ltn d. Res. Voss, appreciating the purely objective motivation and his youth.
>
> Kofl. 2 restrained himself from inflicting sterner punishment, the more so as the transfer of Ltn d. Res. Voss from Jasta Boelcke, the tradition of which is very dear to him, signifies a very harsh punishment for Ltn d. Res. Voss.

The 'plain' reprimand without witnesses is the mildest form of a formal admonishment that could be given and would not have hurt Voss as much as his posting away from his beloved Jasta B.

Oddly enough, Walz shot down a DH2 on 14 May, a machine from 32 Squadron. Had he been galvanised into being more aggressive and been lucky to gain his first kill with the Jasta, his seventh overall? Luck must have played some part in it for not only did he bring down the DH2 inside German lines but its pilot was no novice. Captain W G S Curphey had been in France with his squadron since July 1916. He had achieved six victories and won the MC and Bar, so was an experienced air fighter. He had come off second best to Jasta B earlier, on 4 February, hit in the head by a bullet fired by Erwin Böhme, and forced to land inside British lines (Böhme's 10th victory). Now another Jasta Boelcke pilot had finished him off. He got down but died of his injuries. The RFC War Diary says of this action:

Capt. Curphey and 2/Lts. Tayler and Wright, No.32 Squadron, attacked German balloons. The observers in the balloons were seen to throw out their papers and descend by parachutes, and the balloons were hauled down. The DeHavillands [were] then engaged by 6 Albatros Scouts, one of which was destroyed by 2/Lt Tayler. Capt. Curphey was driven down and his machine was seen to turn over on landing [and burnt].

Again there is no recorded loss of a German pilot of any unit this date.

With the posting of Voss on 20 May, the Jasta was left almost bereft of any really experienced air fighters, a state reflected by the fact that no more victories were achieved during May. Some new blood had arrived, Leutnant Gerhard Bassenge being one, but he had little fighter experience. From Ettlingen, this 19-year-old had gone the usual route: infantryman, two-seater pilot (Kampfstaffel 39 and Schutzstaffel 15), then fighter school and finally to Jasta 5 in April 1917, only to be moved to Jasta B on 2 May to help with numbers. He later became an ace but that was far off in the future.

Whatever his pilots thought of him, Walz would later prove an exceptional leader, so perhaps it was not so much his style of command but rather his Staffel's lack of experienced pilots. The few who had achieved several victories had all been moved away and nobody exceptional had filled the gaps. Added to this were those who did not seem to have the necessary fighting spirit or piloting skill to make a mark. That Walz was not a fighting leader such as Boelcke, or even von Richthofen, did not mean he could not command. There were several Jastas where the Staffelführer was not necessarily the best air fighter, but he was a good commander. Walz may well have fallen between these two stools, and had found that Boelcke and Kirmaier were hard acts to follow, and some of his 'young turks' missed this drive and probably felt keenly that their Jasta was no longer the front runner among fighting staffeln. The fact that one of their earlier heroes – Manfred von Richthofen – was now leading a formidable unit – Jasta 11 – no doubt made the grass seem a lot greener elsewhere.

Vizefeldwebel Fritz Rumey was another in-and-out posting, although he did last until mid-June. He achieved nothing with Jasta B but would later become a 45-victory ace with Jasta 5 alongside Josef Mai. Leutnant Albert Münz was another May arrival, in from Jastaschule on the 9th but he was killed in action on the day Voss left. He was shot down flying Albatros DIII No.790/17 in a fight with some Nieuport Scouts. Kurt Francke had been wounded in the same fight and died of his wounds on

1 June.

Münz had been in the army pre-war for his compulsory service, and once the war started was again in the infantry, winning the Iron Cross 2nd Class as early as September 1914, and was commissioned two months after that. Transferring to the Air Service he first flew as an observer, and as one received the Iron Cross 1st Class and the Würrtemberg Knight's Cross of the Military Merit Order. Learning to become a pilot he finally arrived at Jasta B but only lasted till 20 May. Jasta B were in action with 29 Squadron that day:

> While on escort duty, 2/Lt A M Wray, No.29 Squadron, attacked an Albatros which was driven down and was seen to break up in the air. 2/Lt A S Shepherd, of the same Squadron, attacked a second hostile machine, which burst into flames and fell.

Wray and Shepherd were experienced pilots. Arthur Wray would win the Military Cross and gain high rank in the RAF – MC DFC AFC. Alfred Shepherd also won the MC and later the DSO, but after gaining ten victories was killed in action on 20 July 1917.

One day earlier, the 19th, Georg Noth was reported missing in Albatros DIII 796/17, coming down inside British lines. He had been the 'victim' of Lieutenant W M Fry of 60 Squadron, for the British pilot's fourth victory. Willie Fry would survive the war with 11 victories and win the MC. In his book *Air of Battle*, Fry related:

> On May 19th our flight was about to undertake an offensive patrol which I was to lead as for some reason Bishop was not available, and we were either sitting in our lined-up machines or standing by them preparatory to our engines being started, to take off, when suddenly out of the layer of low cloud over the aerodrome at about 1,000 feet a German Albatros Scout appeared overhead. As soon as it was spotted and recognised as such there was considerable excitement with mechanics running about and pointing excitedly upwards. The pilot must have seen he was over a British aerodrome and quickly disappeared into the clouds again. Those pilots of our flight who were not already in their machines jumped in and the mechanics made haste to start their engines. One, I think it was our Scotsman, Young, forgot in the excitement to wave for the chocks to be taken away from under his wheels, and opened up his engine. Up came his tail and the machine went straight over on its back. The remainder of us took off all right and went up through the cloud individually to try and find the German machine

above it. By a piece of luck, after flying round for a time, I saw it and gave chase, firing a few bursts but too excited at first to take proper aim through the sight.

It was the ambition of every young pilot to bring down a German on our side of the lines. This particular pilot, however, with me on his tail and aware that he had stirred up a hornet's nest by appearing over the aerodrome, decided to land and did so very fast on an open space, turning over on his back.

In the excitement of following so close on his tail, I had no idea of the height we had lost and that we were so near the ground and nearly flew into it on top of him, pulling upward only just in time when I saw his machine tip up in front of me. I landed close by and shook hands with the pilot who admitted that he had lost his way. The usual crowd of soldiers appeared from nowhere and all were from a battalion of the Somerset Light Infantry in which I was commissioned and whose badges I was [still] wearing. They were in rest [briefly out of the line] nearby. The adjutant got me put through to Major Scott on the telephone and he arranged to send his motor-car out at once for the German pilot and also a salvage party to collect his machine. I flew back to the aerodrome.

The CO instructed the salvage party to dismantle and bring the German plane in as soon as possible as General Trenchard was expected on a visit the next day and he wanted to show him the machine. I seem to remember that the GOC took little interest, but the technical staff who came out later discovered that it was an improved and previously unknown type of Albatros and it was sent straight off to England for inspection.

It was the custom for RFC squadrons to entertain pilots and observers whom they had brought down alive, before handing them over to the prisoner of war cages for interrogation. The Germans did the same. So my German pilot was brought in to luncheon and plied with drink on the chance that we might get some interesting information out of him. He did not say much and gave nothing away, but we did find in his tunic pocket a ticket for Cambrai theatre for the night before. He was Leutnant Georg Noth of the Boelcke Jasta. The whole affair was no achievement on my part as it was pure luck to come across him over the clouds, there was no fight and once I got on his tail he gave up.

The photograph of Noth's Albatros being put onto a trailer clearly shows the serial number on a white tailplane and an unusual dappling paint scheme on the fuselage – 'green with yellow spots' is how Willie Fry referred to it in his combat report. Its RFC number was G39. After his meal with 60 Squadron, Noth started his stint as a prisoner, ending up in Holyport Camp, Berkshire, with personal number 1037.

Thus May ended on something of a sour note. With nothing else deemed important enough to record, Jasta B almost seemed to cease to exist. June wasn't going to be that much better.

June 1917

Pilots at the start of June:	Name	Victories
	Hptm Franz Walz	7
	Ltn Gerhard Bassenge	–
	Ltn Hans Eggers	–
	Ltn Hermann Frommherz	2
	Ltn Friedrich Kempf	1
	Ltn Rolf Fr von Lersner	–
	Vfw Fritz Rumey	–
	Vfw Thiel	–
	Ltn Johannes Wintrath	–
OzbV	Oblt Karl Bodenschatz	–

Base: Proville   Front: 1st Army

A look at this list shows a pretty sorry state of affairs as regards experience and achievement. Whether or not the row regarding Hautpmann Franz Walz's leadership was still rumbling on and in consequence the name of Jasta Boelcke was under something of a cloud is only speculation. German Jasta sizes as regards pilots can never be compared with a British scout squadron; at best a Jasta was no bigger than a large Flight. The Jasta had amassed a very respectable score of kills, numbering as it did at this time to over 140, but it had scored only about 25 in the last few weeks, and only five during May.

If anyone in authority was thinking that to transfer some experienced pilots in might give the unit some new impetus or even credibility, it did not happen quickly. Some seven pilots arrived to bolster the numbers during the month of June, but none of any real substance, and several of these soon moved on.

Fritz Rumey, who as already noted would become one of the big aces, did not open his score before he moved to Jasta 5 on 17 June, where he made his name and reputation. Leutnant Otto Hunzinger and Leutnant Franz Pernet also failed to make much of an impression. Pernet, however, was the grandson of General Erich von Ludendorff (at this time Field Marshal Paul von Hindenburg's Quartermaster-General) and it is said that he used that influence to get into combat rather than dodge it. (Perhaps he should have used it to get into von Richthofen's Jasta 11.)

Leutnant Wilhelm Prien arrived at the same time as Hunzinger and lasted a month less before he was eased out. Prien came from Hamburg and was 25. A pre-war engineer, he liked to help his ground crew maintain his Albatros. He must also have had a rather good camera for he kept an album of some superb pictures during his brief time with the Jasta.

Leutnant Wilhelm Saint-Mont's arrival date is not known, but he did not even last the month, going also to Jasta 5 on 19 June, then to Jasta 52 in 1918, where he gained his one and only victory. He was killed on 1 June 1918 baling out of his burning fighter, his parachute catching fire too as he went over the side. Leutnant Schey arrived some time in June but by the 17th he had been sent away to an Army flug-park and Leutnant Ernst Wendler, who came in on 6 June from KG3 via hospital, left for Jasta 17 less than two weeks later.

Wendler came from Ulm, so was a Würrtemberger. He was 27. In the Air Service he had flown with Kampfstaffel 14 in KG3 from January 1916, and his work there brought him his State's Gold Military Merit Medal in June. On 1 July – the first day of the Somme Offensive – he had an air fight with 32 Squadron RFC and its CO, Major L W B Rees. Rees won the Victoria Cross for his actions, and one of the machines he shot down during the battle was Wendler's LFG Roland two-seater. Wendler was wounded but got his damaged machine down safely. His observer had been shot dead. Further awards came his way; the Iron Cross 1st Class and the Knight's Cross of the Military Merit Medal. Once recovered he was posted to Jasta Boelcke.

Yet another future ace came and went in June, Vizefeldwebel Paul Bäumer. He arrived from Jastaschule I on 28 June and two days later was off to Jasta 5. Just why men like Bäumer, Rumey and Mai appeared and then disappeared at this time is strange. Had they remained with Jasta B would they have achieved the greatness that was about to come their way? For Bäumer it did not really apply, for he soon returned to find his niche.

Finally, as if the 'no smoke without fire' thoughts had at last moved up to the higher echelons, Franz Walz was posted out on the 9th. As if not to embarrass anyone he was made commander of Bavarian Jasta 34b, but for less than four weeks. Records do indicate that he had a foot problem stemming from a wound received prior to taking over Jasta B, but to what extent this played a part in his upsetting his pilots is not known. One must assume that to incur the displeasure of someone like Voss, who would have been sympathetic to a wound, it had to be more fundamental. On 7 July 1917 Walz was given command of FA304b in the Middle East.

However, in transferring to the Palestine Front Walz appears to have come into his own somewhat and flew quite a number of sorties. In fact in August 1918 he was awarded the Pour le Mérite, not for air fighting, but for accomplishing over 500 war flights. Luck was against him in September 1918. Captured by British forces he remained incarcerated till the end of 1919. Remaining in aviation he was an Oberst in the 1930s, based at Fürth, near Nürnberg, Bavaria. Back with the German Luftwaffe in WW2 he became a General-leutnant in 1941. Taken prisoner by the Russians at the end of the war, he died in captivity in Breslau, Silesia, in December 1945.

Not so certain are the movements of Leutnant Rolf Fr von Lersner. He was the co-conspirator with Werner Voss in trying to oust Walz from Jasta Boelcke, and being far less famous than Voss, was quickly moved away and back to a bomber unit, where he was killed. It does appear, however, that his move was not so rapid as it seems, for it looks as if he was with Jasta B till sometime in August. Only then did he get his posting – to KG3 – and was killed in a crash at Johannisthal, on 25 August.[4] Von Lersner is also supposed to have been the son of a ranking official in the German State Department, which is perhaps why he felt he could support Voss in the challenge to Walz.

Bernert Returns

Oberleutnant Fritz Otto Bernert returned from Jasta 6 to take command of Jasta Boelcke on 9 June. There can be little doubt that this was a popular move as far as the Jasta pilots were concerned, and most probably all the rest of the men too. Bernert, it will be remembered, had brought his personal score to 24 with five kills on 24 April. With Jasta 6 he had added three more, plus another unconfirmed, and the Jasta must have felt sure changes for the better would now begin.

Friedrich Kempf had already opened June's victory account with his own second victory on the 5th, a Sopwith Pup of 54 Squadron, and now with Bernert arriving everyone looked for improvements in scoring. And things did change. Kempf's victory was the last to be scored till mid-August!

Then Georg Zeumer was killed. On the morning of the 17th he was shot down over La Ferriere (near Honnecourt) while attacking a British RE8 two-seater. The crew of Lieutenants Douglas and E O Houghton was from 59 Squadron. Their combat report, written by Houghton, states:

> 17 June 1917, 9 am. Photo Op. East of Honnecourt, 7,000 ft.
> Albatros Scout, Nieuport type.
> Whilst taking photographs, we saw about 6 enemy aircraft above us. One EA dived and attacked us from the direction of the sun. The EA got on our tail and I opened fire on him at about 50 yards range. He immediately started firing. After I had fired he turned away and stalled, and then did a vertical nosedive. I continued firing and he burst into flames and continued to dive for about 4,000 feet and disappeared.

[4] In one of his well-received medal books, the late Neal O'Connor makes mention of a Ltn Fr von Lersner as an observer with KG1, sharing a victory over a BE with his pilot, OffStv Krause, on 17 January 1916.

Many of Zeumer's friends thought his death was a happy release. Among them was von Richthofen, who wrote in *Ein Heldenleben*:

> Yesterday, Zeumer was killed in air combat. It was perhaps the best thing that could have happened to him. He knew that he had not much longer to live. Such an excellent and noble fellow. How he would have hated to drag himself toward the inevitable end. For him it would have been tragic. As it is, he died a heroic death before the enemy. During the next few days, his body will be brought home.

Another event in June was the visit to the Jasta of pilots from the Imperial and Royal Air Service of the Austro-Hungarian Army. They were in France to study Jasta tactics and had been visiting Jasta 5 at Boistrancourt. Voss brought them over to meet Bernert and Jasta B's pilots, Hauptmann Herwan and Hauptmann Stojsaviljevic being photographed with the Boelcke pilots. Raoul Stojsaviljevic was already an ace and also spent a period with Jasta 6 on the Western Front to gain experience of how the Germans operated. On returning to his own front he brought his score to ten by the war's end.

July 1917

Pilots at the start of July:	Name	Victories
	Oblt Otto Bernert	27
	Ltn Gerhard Bassenge	–
	Ltn Hans Eggers	–
	Ltn Hermann Frommherz	2
	Ltn Otto Hunzinger	–
	Ltn Friedrich Kempf	2
	Ltn Rolf Fr von Lersner	–
	Ltn Franz Pernet	–
	Ltn Wilhelm Prien	–
	Ltn Stren	–
	Vfw Thiel	–
	Ltn Johannes Wintrath	–
OzbV	Oblt Karl Bodenschatz	–

Base: Proville   Front: 1st Army

Recording Karl Bodenschatz as adjutant is virtually academic as 1 July was his last day with the Jasta.

Jasta Boelcke's 'old boy' Manfred von Richthofen, going from strength to strength had been given command of Jagdesgeschwader Nr.I

in June, comprising four Jastas, 4, 6, 10 and 11. This was the first of the
Circuses, a permanent grouping of a number of Jagdstaffeln that could be
moved from sector to sector wherever a large group of fighters was
needed to, say, support an offensive or to help combat an enemy ground
attack. Von Richthofen was now the master of the German fighter arm
and could have virtually whatever he wanted. And he wanted Karl
Bodenschatz as his group adjutant, and of course got him. The next
morning Bodenschatz and his batman Andreas Seitz drove by car to the
Baron's airfield at Marckebecke, just outside Courtrai. It took a few
weeks for Jasta B to have a replacement arrive.

One new pilot arrived during the month, Leutnant Egon Könemann,
from Charlottenberg, who was nearing his 27th birthday – 8 August.

And that was just about the only recorded excitement for the month
except that towards the end, the Jasta received orders to move its base to
La Petrie some way north of Douai, on 1 August.

August 1917

Pilots at the start of August:	Name	Victories
	Oblt Otto Bernert	27
	Ltn Gerhard Bassenge	–
	Ltn Hans Eggers	–
	Ltn Hermann Frommherz	2
	Ltn Otto Hunzinger	–
	Ltn Friedrich Kempf	2
	Ltn Egon Könemann	–
	Ltn Rolf Fr von Lersner	–
	Ltn Franz Pernet	–
	Ltn Wilhelm Prien	–
	Ltn Stren	–
	Vfw Thiel	–
	Ltn Johannes Wintrath	–
OzbV	vacant	

Base: La Petrie   Front: 2nd Army (JGr Nord)

The move to La Petrie – Jasta 2 were the only fighter unit to fly from
there during the war – put the Jasta into a new army front – 2nd Army –
where it remained for a week, until it moved again on the 7th, this time
to Bisseghem, on the western outskirts of Courtrai (Kortrijk), Belgium. A
month previously it had housed Jasta 6. Von Richthofen's JGI was on
airfields nearby, including Marcke and Marckebecke. They were here for
an even lesser period, just five days, at which time they moved again, this
time to Ghistelles, on the 12th. Ghistelles was only about five miles south
of Ostend on the Channel coast. These latter two bases put the Jasta under
the German 4th Army.

On the 15th, Paul Bäumer came back from Jasta 5. He had opened his scoring ledger with three kills with them and he would remain with Jasta B till almost the war's end, although an injury in 1918 took him away for some three months. From Duisburg-Ruhrart, where he was born in May 1896, this former dental assistant had paid for his own flying lessons before the war. However, once war came he joined the infantry and saw service both in France and Russia, where he was wounded in the left arm.

He then reverted to his former job as a dental assistant with the Air Service, in August 1915. He followed this by applying to become a pilot, ending up as an instructor and ferry pilot. As a very junior airman, he was posted to FA7 in March 1917 as a Gefreiter (Lance Corporal), but winning both classes of the Iron Cross by May at which stage he volunteered for fighters.

* * *

Jasta Boelcke's first victory since June came on 17 August. At 08.15 that morning Leutnant Wintrath claimed his first kill by downing the first Sopwith Camel the unit had encountered. The Camel, like its sister the SE5a, would soon become the main opponent of Jasta B. Wintrath's victim appears to have been Lieutenant A M T Glover of 70 Squadron, the first RFC unit to equip with Camels. He was killed near the lines east of Ypres having taken off on an Offensive Patrol (OP) at 07.30 am that morning.

Bernert is Wounded

The next day, however, Bernert was wounded and had to be posted away.[5] The good news following this loss of Staffelführer was that his replacement was none other than Erwin Böhme, a former 'old boy'. Böhme had only added one victory to his score – now standing at 13 – since leaving to command Jasta 29. He had just recovered from a hand wound inflicted on 10 August, when he had been attacking a two-seater but was surprised by an attack from below by a British fighter plane.

On the 19th Wintrath scored again, and once again over a Camel from 70 Squadron. However, it was classified as zLgzw (zur landung gezwungen) – being forced to land inside enemy territory. It is often difficult for historians or students of the first air war to understand the difference between this sort of unconfirmed claim, and similar claims where a victory credit is given. Obviously there was a degree of perceived damage to the hostile machine, and in certain cases an Allied aircraft landing inside German lines was confirmed as destroyed following shelling by German artillery. Yet it is a fact that some German pilots, particularly some of the aces, received credit for what should really be

[5] Recovering from his wound Bernert worked with the Inspector of the Flying Service and was promoted to Oberleutnant in November. He was, however, much weakened by his war experiences and this made him vulnerable to the massive influenza outbreak in late 1918. Unable to fight the infection he died on 18 October.

termed zLg (or zLgzw). In this case, the Camel pilot, Second Lieutenant A M Epps, an Australian, did get down safely, although he had been wounded in one arm. The action had taken place east of Dunkirk, at 17.45 hours.

New Blood
Jasta Boelcke's fortunes were about to change, albeit slowly. After these early summer months in the doldrums, new pilots started to arrive during August which was to breathe new life into the unit. Böhme wrote to his fiancée:

> 18 August.
> Still something new since I wrote the letter yesterday evening. A telephone message just came from the General of the Air Service, a complete surprise to me, that I had been assigned command of Jagdstaffel Boelcke and to proceed to report immediately. I shall therefore "proceed to report" this afternoon. That is I shall simply fly to my new Staffel. It is located not too far from here, in the surroundings of Ostend, near Ghistelles.
> The assignment is honourable, but at first will also be very difficult and require much work. Naturally I am happy to return to my old Staffel which has been sanctified through his name, even if I won't find a single one of my old companions there. And it is proof of a great trust, that headquarters has handed over command of the Staffel to me, in order to bring it up again to its former heights. For its former brilliance has in recent times completely faded. There is nothing left of the old Staffel but its famous name. Now it must once again be inspired by the old Boelcke-spirit. God grant me that I shall succeed!

Leutnant Maximilian Joseph von Chelius was one of the arrivals; he had earlier seen service with FA14. Another army man, he had been with Prussian Lieb-Garde Hussar Regiment Nr.8 prior to joining the air service. He was 20-years-old and came from Karzin. Leutnant Karl Gallwitz joined on the 24th, following Böhme from Jasta 29. Sometimes the new CO was allowed to take someone from his existing unit with him upon a move. If this was the reason, Böhme was obviously keen to have Gallwitz with him in Jasta B. He was 21 (born in 1895) and came from Sigmaringen, in the principality of Hohenzollern, Baden. He had been with an artillery two-seater unit earlier in the year – FA(A)231 – then flew single-seaters with FA37 on the Eastern Front with Roland DIIIs. He had shot down two balloons on consecutive days in July 1917, and had received the Iron Cross 1st and 2nd Class. He had only been with Jasta 29 for a few days.

On the 24th Leutnant Hermann Vallendor was posted in from Jasta 26, and would remain for the duration. He was 23 and came from Offenberg, so was a Würrtemberger. A former engineering student in Mannheim he had joined the infantry in 1914, won the Iron Cross 2nd Class and was commissioned in December 1915. Transferring to aviation he ended up with FA23 in May 1917. Later in the year he moved to Jasta 26, under Bruno Loerzer, and now came to Jasta B, as yet without having scored a victory. At the end of the month a new adjutant was posted in, Leutnant Anton Stephan, who had been credited with two combat victories with an unknown unit. Things were starting to look a little brighter now that Böhme was back, and with some potentially good new pilots arriving. Only time would tell.

Chapter Five

Jasta Boelcke under Böhme

It seems fairly obvious that Böhme spent some time organising his new command and so few patrols were flown, certainly there was little combat action and no enemy aircraft shot down until the second week of September. In part this was due to bad weather, rain being most persistent during August. With the various comings and goings of pilots, it appears too that some of the existing pilots had been moved or would soon be moved out of the Jasta in order to make way for the new boys. Karl Bolle, a future leader of the Jasta, in his history of the unit recorded that:

> Their way was not easy. The pilots were young, the opponents in the Battle of Flanders battle-tested and gung-ho. The period between August and September in Ghistelles and Varssenaere was the most difficult Jagdstaffel Boelcke had ever gone through in its development. With only seven fighting members, they commenced on their way towards a fresh rise which stands as a milestone of the times when comrades fell. But in Böhme, they had a leader who was able to make their old name worthy again.

There had to be some flying nevertheless, for Egon Könemann was killed in action on the 22nd, shot down by Camels near Lombartzyde. 70 Squadron and 3 Naval Squadron both claimed Albatros fighters this date. Another pilot was posted out.

A further move of base came on the 27th, this time to Varssenaere, near Bruges, but still within 4th Army's control. The Jasta had little choice, as Böhme wrote in a letter home on 29 August, in which he also referred to his previously wounded hand, which was still giving him trouble:

> ... First, we are in the midst of transferring to another airfield (in the vicinity of Varssenaere near Bruges; the British once again drove us out of Ghistelles with artillery fire). Second, the doctors operated yesterday one more time on my wounded hand. A rich lead mine was discovered. This is very irritating. Now, at a minimum I again must quit flying, just when I had briskly returned to business.

My Staffel consists of relatively steady people and it is already becoming a going enterprise. Unfortunately, a week ago I lost two of the most capable. I am concerned about reinforcements, and hope through my acquaintances which I made at Valenciennes to obtain high quality replacements for the Staffel.

The reason British artillery was able to fire upon their airfield was due to the Third Battle of Ypres (better known as Passchendaele) which had commenced in late July, with its famous Battle for Hill 70 in mid-August. The battle would rumble on over Flanders till November.

At Varssenaere Jasta B became part of a new tactic being adopted by the German fighter arm, that of Jagdgruppen. Permanent Jagdesgeschwaderen, such as von Richthofen's JGI, remained static as far as its Jasta units were concerned and also, once formed, remained as a group till the end of the war. At this stage JGI was the only one in existence, but in 1918 two more were formed in February, another in October, and a Marine unit in September.

The group to which Jasta B now became affiliated was Jagdgruppe 4 (JGr4) also known as Jagdgruppe Nord, or Armee Jagdgruppe Nord. It was commanded by Hauptmann Otto Hartmann, leader of Jasta 28w, and comprised his unit together with Jasta B, Jasta 17, Jasta 20 and Kest 8w. Hartmann, as his own unit name suggests with the 'w' after the number, came from Würrtemberg. Born in Nassau, he was 28 years of age and had seven victories, two whilst serving with Kasta 15 (KG3), the rest with Jasta 28w.

Like all Jagdgruppen, it was a non-permanent formation. They could be formed and used for just a few days, a few weeks or a few months, and could be disbanded and reformed with other Jastas making up the unit. Generally they were put together to face an enemy offensive or to support a German one. While occasionally elements from two or even three units might join up, the group was together mainly for the sake of administration and convenience. Unlike, say, the fighter wings of WW2, the 'wing leader' (Hartmann) did not head out in front of a large force of fighters from five Jastas. It would be too unwieldy and in these days there was no inter-plane radio, so the force could not be controlled once in the air other than by hand signals or flares, and these could easily be missed.

September 1917
Pilots at the start of September:

Name	Victories
Oblt Erwin Böhme	13
Vfw Paul Bäumer	3
Ltn Gerhard Bassenge	–
Ltn Max von Chelius	–
Ltn Hans Eggers	–
Ltn Hermann Frommherz	2

Pilots at the start of September:	Name	Victories
	Ltn Karl Gallwitz	2
	Ltn Otto Hunzinger	–
	Ltn Friedrich Kempf	2
	Ltn Franz Pernet	–
	Ltn Stren	–
	Vfw Thiel	–
	Ltn Hermann Vallendor	–
	Ltn Johannes Wintrath	1
OzbV	Ltn Anton Stephan	2

Base: Varssenaere   Front: 4th Army JGr Nord

Vizefeldwebel Thiel left the Jasta on 1 September, going to Hartmann's Jasta 28w. He had flown doggedly since February – and survived – and he was far from spent. He was later commissioned and at the end of the year went to Jasta 49, surviving the war and finally getting his first combat success in October 1918.

Three other pilots joined in September. Leutnant Erich Daube had come from Valparaiso, Chile, to fight for his country; he was 26, almost 27. The other newcomers were Leutnant Richard Plange, from Ellingson, aged 24, and Leutnant Walter Lange, posted in from Jasta 40. Lange came from Richenau, and was aged 23. He had previously served with the field artillery and had been with Jasta 40 since the latter part of July 1917.

Jagdgruppe 4 lost its leader on 3 September, falling in a scrap with Bristol Fighters of 48 Squadron over the North Sea coast. His loss heralded the end of Jagdgruppe Nord. Hartmann's place as leader was taken by Hauptmann Constantin von Benthiem much later in the month, but it soon became a different formation. Von Benthiem was a leader rather than an air fighter. His main job was as Staffelführer of Jasta 8, but during the latter stages of the war he commanded (rather than led in the air), five Jagdgruppen between August 1917 and October 1918.

Two days after this loss, Jasta B lost Franz Pernet, who was shot down and fell into the sea near Westende following another combat with 48 Squadron. The BF2b crew responsible was Second Lieutenant K R Park and 2AM H Lindfield. Keith Park, a New Zealander, would rise to the rank of major in WW1 and win the MC and Bar, the DFC, and French Croix de Guerre. He would gain high rank in the RAF, commanding 11 Group of Fighter Command during the Battle of Britain, and later the RAF forces on Malta and was to become AOC Burma. He became Air Chief Marshal Sir Keith Park GCB KBE MC DFC DCL. Whether he ever discovered he had shot down von Ludendorf's grandson is not known. Vincent Orange mentions it in his biography of Park, although he notes Pernet as a stepson. He was Park's 14th victory of an eventual 20, and his body was washed up on the Dutch coast several weeks later. 48 Squadron's combat report:

5 September 1917. Noon. Bristol Fighter A7182. Escort 4 m N Ostend. Five Albatros Scout, Vee Strutters.

When returning along coast 4 miles N of Ostend the formation was attacked from rear, above and below, by five Albatros Scouts. Being rear machine 3 EA attached themselves to my tail and 2 dived. For about 4 minutes I spiralled violently 'zooming' each time. One of the EA overshot me, and I got 5 bursts at very close range in EA, and he fell apparently out of control, and I followed on his tail firing, until a second Scout got on my tail and I was unable to watch first EA any longer, as rest of hostile formation was circling round me. Three Bristol Fighters came back from our formation and EA drew away inland. Whilst trying to bait same hostile formation to dive on me and give our own formation an opportunity to close with them, a two-seater DFW passed 500 feet below me. He dived towards Middlekerke and I followed diving and firing about 150 rounds ranged from 200-100 yards. I commenced diving at 10,500', and when my front gun jammed I was at 5,000' with EA 100 yards away still diving and almost vertical.

Three Albatros Scouts approached from S Middlekerke, so I dived towards Nieuport and last saw first EA still diving steeply at about 1,000 feet over the sea. I watched but could not see this machine crash from our own lines.

2/AM Lindfield states this machine fell into the sea.

Pernet had once written home:

Mother, you cannot imagine what a heavenly feeling it is when all the day's fighting is successfully over, to lie down in bed and say to oneself before going to sleep, "Thank God! you have another twelve hours to live." The certainty of the thing is so pleasant.

Paul Bäumer claimed his fourth victory, and his first with Jasta B, on the afternoon of 9 September. He shot down an artillery-spotting RE8 of 52 Squadron in flames west of Mannekensveere, inside Allied lines. His combat report states:

9 September 1917. Albatros DV 4409/17. Location and Time: Mannekensveere, 15.25 hours.

A flight of five of the staffel's aircraft took off at 15.05 hours for a combat flight to the front. Over our positions to the south of Nieuport, I sighted several REs, one of which was being shot at by our flak. This one I attacked at 1,000 metres

high, coming down steeply from above, and I caused him to
fall at Vilette-Ferme. I followed the smoking aircraft
(apparently petrol fumes) until impact. The enemy aircraft
was completely smashed up and lies between the trenches.
Except for the Staffel, no other aircraft were nearby.

Another loss came on the 14th, Maximilian von Chelius going down to
the north of Dixmude. His death was again attributed to Keith Park of 48
Squadron, this time with Second Lieutenant H Owen in the back seat. The
Albatros DVa crashed in British lines and was coded G70. 48 Squadron's
combat report:

14 September 1917. 6.45 pm. Bristol Fighter A7227. N of
Dixmude. 1 formation. 8 Alb DIIIs [and] 2 Alb DIIIs – 10.
Whilst leading evening patrol rear machines were dived on
and attacked by 3 EA of formation of 10. Doubling back
under our machines gave my observer good shooting at one
EA which was attacking our rear machines.
    He fired one complete drum at EA which dived steeply. I
then got on his tail and following diving and fired 150
rounds at about 100 yards range.
    Hostile machine dived more steeply, side-slipped, and
was last seen going down out of control. Clouds prevented
observation lower than 6,000 feet.
    Zooming back under our patrol I saw one Bristol circling
round with Alb Scout attempting to get on his tail. I drove
this EA off own machine (of patrol) and followed, diving and
spiralling on his tail until I saw its pilot fall forward in his
seat. Continued firing at 25 yards range until cockpit of EA
burst into flames, when I zoomed up to climb under our
formation.
    My observer watched EA fall in flames and crash just our
side of the lines north of Dixmude.

Interestingly, a report concerning captured German aircraft, or in this
case, little more than the burnt out wreckage, states that the enemy pilot
had jumped from his burning Albatros DV with a parachute. The
parachute caught fire and the pilot had fallen over St. Jean Capelle, near
Dixmude. If correct, it would be one of the earliest known uses of a
parachute by a German pilot.
    Erwin Böhme went to Berlin on leave. He was due a break and his
bandaged hand still made it difficult to fly. He needed to sort out some
Jasta problems with HQ and to take the time to visit his fiancée who he
had not seen for a year – since the time he had joined Boelcke's Jasta the
previous September.
    Upon his return, Böhme, despite his bandaged hand, scored the next

victory on the 19th, another RE8, this time from 9 Squadron, flying an artillery observation sortie. This was over the preliminary bombardment heralding the next phase of Third Ypres – the battle for the Menin Road Ridge which started on the 20th. The summer was still being hampered by very bad weather, the soldiers on the ground always remembering the mud of Passchendaele, where men would literally drown in it.

Two Camels fell to Jasta B on the 20th. The first, at 12.10 pm went down to Walter Lange, but just who his victim was is unclear. Possibly a Camel of 10 Naval, but there are other claimants in the picture. The Germans were still not totally au fait with the new Allied types and it is clear that they were far from spotting the differences between Camels, SE5s, Martinsydes, DH5s and Nieuports, especially the newer Nieuport 23 and 27s. As mentioned before, when in doubt they called everything a Sopwith. Paul Bäumer was the other scorer – which was his first victory with Jasta B – and he called his Camel a Martinsyde. In fact it was a Camel from 9 Naval Squadron flown by a future British ace, Ronald Sykes. Several years ago Ron Sykes wrote to me of this combat:

> Flying in Captain Roy Brown's flight of Camels at 10,000 feet over the Belgian coast, we attacked a German two-seater and were dived on by four German Albatros Scouts. Captain Brown's guns iced up and jammed and he led the flight into climbing turns, but before I could join them I was hit and my engine stopped. Captain Brown came down to my help alone although his guns were useless. He half-rolled and stall-turned above the four Germans who left me alone and, impressed by his display of skill, they went home.
>
> The same evening Captain Brown and the rest of the flight, off duty, toured in the Squadron [Crossley] tender behind our lines and found me in a Casualty Clearing Station still under the cheerful influence of hot whisky given me by some helpful Scots troops near whose trench I had crash-landed.

Paul Bäumer's own combat report reads:

> 20 September 1917. Albatros DV 4409/17. A white (edelweiss) star on a black background with red stripes on the fuselage. Location and Time: Ramscapelle, 15.00 hours.
> I was flying with Ltn Wintrath and Ltn Plange. We were attacked by 6 enemy aircraft over the front. A Martinsyde plunged through the clouds, I followed it and shot at it at an extremely close range at 15.20 hours. He fell behind the first enemy trenches and turned over.

Ronald Sykes had force-landed near St. Pierre Capelle at 15.10 hours
(German time) inside British lines. Bäumer reported the Camel as down
at Ramscapelle, both roughly in the same locality, Ramscapelle being a
little further west, but obviously where Bäumer thought it was going
down as he flew off east. It was his fifth victory overall. It was also Jasta
Boelcke's 150th victory of the war.

Bäumer made it six the next afternoon, with another Camel downed
near Boesinghe, this time one of Jasta B's main antagonists, 70 Squadron.
The Camel pilot, wounded, managed to set his machine down inside
British lines. Bäumer's report:

> 21 September 1917. Albatros DV 4409/17. Location and
> Time: Boesinghe, 17.50 hours.
> I was flying with Ltns Wintrath, Gallwitz and Lange over the
> Ypres positions when two enemy aircraft appeared. One of
> these aircraft was taken by Ltn Wintrath, but he had to break
> off again due to a jam. Then I attacked the opponent. A hard
> banking fight developed. I got him well in my sights and shot
> him at extreme closeness. Suddenly the opponent's machine
> reared up and then went down vertically. I followed the
> Sopwith and saw it hit near Boesinghe and burst into flames.
> I circled over the crash site and saw the burning machine
> lying there.

Earlier that morning, Böhme had brought his score to 15 with an RE8 of
53 Squadron which he shot down near Warneton. The British crew had
been working with the 145th 8″ Howitzer Battery, but the artillery shoot
remained unfinished. At 10.45 British troops saw the two-seater falling
out of control following an attack by a hostile scout. Böhme wrote to his
fiancée following his return:

> 21 September.
> Since everything had gone so smoothly [his return to his
> unit], jealous fate avenged itself through the delivery of bad
> news. In Valenciennes, I heard that Wolff, exquisite and
> difficult to replace, had fallen.[1] Here in Flanders, the sad
> news awaited us that our Staffel had lost Leutnant von
> Chelius, a high-spirited individual (Hussar Guards), who had
> just recently joined our unit.
> On my first flight the next morning [19th], I quickly
> avenged his death as I shot down an English two-seater very
> close to Ypres. Today another, number 15, fell. Both times I
> had just eaten a piece of the Swedish chocolate you had

---

[1] Oblt Kurt Wolff of Jasta 11, one of von Richthofen's protégés and victor in 33 air fights
before falling to 10 Naval Squadron flying in one of the new Fokker FI Triplanes.

given me. Therefore, you should now actually be awarded a medal! My comrades were more than a little envious of my wonder drug; however, they didn't share in it this time.

These two victories were offset in part by Richard Plange being wounded before his career had really started. He was carted off to hospital and was not to return till the following month. There was another loss four days later, Johannes Wintrath being killed at 12.30 (German time) on the 25th over Westende-Bad. Wintrath had been with Jasta B since February and was one of the old hands. His Albatros went down in flames and broke up. Sopwith Pups of 54 Squadron had engaged seven Albatros Scouts over Middlekerke at 11.30 (British time, still one hour behind German time) and claimed three of them. Captain Oliver Stewart MC, a 26-year-old Londoner, sent one down into the sea for his fifth and final victory; Second Lieutenant Henry Maddocks claimed his third (of an eventual seven) down in flames, while Second Lieutenant Michael Gonne claimed his first victory – of five – seeing his victim fall to pieces in the air. Jasta B only lost one machine so one has to wonder if all three RFC airmen, in reality, saw Wintrath's Albatros (1072/17) in three different modes of fall. Perhaps it is of interest to read what each pilot wrote in his combat report.

Captain Stewart:
... while leading an Offensive Patrol noticed a formation of 7 EA over Westende going East, he immediately attacked these and shot down one which fell in the sea north of Middlekerke. This EA fell into the sea intact and went down at quite a moderate gliding angle.

2/Lt Maddocks:
During an engagement with 7 enemy scouts one broke away and dived under 2/Lieut. Maddocks, who immediately did a sharp left hand turn and dived on the top of the EA, opening fire at close range. The EA was seen to catch on fire almost immediately.
    2/Lieut. Maddocks followed the EA down to 1,000 feet, it being then about 500 feet from the ground still on fire.

2/Lt Gonne:
During engagement with 7 enemy scouts, 2/Lieut. Gonne observing an EA on another Sopwith's tail opened fire at long range. The EA turned round and 2/Lt Gonne obtaining a favourable position at close range on the EA's tail, fired a long burst. The EA turned sharply round and the right hand top wing came completely off, and the lower right hand wing folded back. The machine went down vertically emitting a cloud of smoke.

A patrol of 24 Squadron reports seeing a Sopwith Scout
shoot a machine down at this time which broke up and fell
into the sea.

This ended the short run of claims and losses for September, and Böhme
was still sorting out his pilots. There was also another move ordered for
1 October, this time to Rumbeke, on the southern outskirts of Roulers,
much nearer to the front-line and to Ypres.

It was not a perfect airfield. In fact, Paul Bäumer later recorded that it
was the worst one he had ever flown from. It had a stony, uneven surface,
and each landing and take-off was hazardous. The pilots lived in wooden
huts which quickly took on a more homely appearance as each man
decorated them to his personal choice.

Voss is Lost
News in the latter half of the month of Werner Voss being killed in a fight
with SE5s of 56 Squadron on 23 September was a huge blow to the
German air arm and to Richthofen's JGI. (Voss commanded Jasta 10
within that formation at the end of July.) He had, since leaving Jasta B,
brought his score to 48 on the very morning of his death, and had
obviously flown out on his last patrol of the day – before going on home
leave – in order to try and bring his score to a nice round 50. The
experienced air fighters of 56 Squadron ended that dream, and his life,
north of Frenzenberg, Belgium.

October 1917

Pilots at the start of October:		Name	Victories
		Oblt Erwin Böhme	15
		Vfw Paul Bäumer	6
		Ltn Gerhard Bassenge	–
		Ltn Erich Daube	–
		Ltn Hans Eggers	–
		Ltn Hermann Frommherz	2
		Ltn Karl Gallwitz	2
		Ltn Otto Hunzinger	–
		Ltn Friedrich Kempf	2
		Ltn Walter Lange	1
		Ltn Richard Plange	–
		Uffz Reichenbach (?)	–
		Ltn Hermann Vallendor	–
	OsbV	Ltn Anton Stephan	2

Base: Rumbeke   Front: 4th Army

In a letter dated 5 October to his fiancée, Böhme mentions some
happenings with his Jasta among the general talk of their relationship:

... we have moved from Varssenaere to the vicinity of Roulers. This time, however, we were not driven out by artillery fire, but simply switched locations with another fighter staffel.

For the last few days we have been at Rumbeke in the vicinity of Roulers, not very far from the front at Ypres. Today, the artillery barrages are again stupendous. They are firing towards Roulers and beyond. Up to now our location has only been hit by a couple of stray rounds. We cluster together here in very nice organised quarters. I even have an entire cottage to myself.

Unfortunately, my Staffel has been reduced to half-strength in the last few weeks through wounds, one shot down, and a big house-cleaning on my part. I miss Leutnant Wintrath who was shot down over the North Sea, and Vortmann, who received a serious hip wound, very much. Plange unfortunately is still on leave, and is at home, harvesting potatoes. I recommended that four other members seek a career other than flying. The remainder, however, are doing well. I am once again zealously seeking enlistments.

Voss could not have fallen! That is a serious loss for the flying service. He was a member of the old Boelcke Staffel, my friend, and currently Richthofen's right hand.

This morning, on an empty stomach, I wanted to and did shoot down number 16. This time it was accomplished without the help of your miracle chocolate, which has long since been eaten. I suggest that your friend Miss von Wiese who has so many contacts should return soon to Sweden and bring back more of that good and lucky chocolate.

Reference to Ludwig Vortmann is obscure, in that he is not listed as being yet with Jasta B, although he is on strength in early 1918. Either he arrived and was wounded very quickly, or he was known to Böhme and was wounded at this time with another unit, again unknown.

Who were the four pilots he recommended 'seek other careers'? Hans Eggers must have been one, who along with Otto Hunzinger, was sent to Army Flug-park 4 on 1 October. Perhaps the other two were yet to go, or had already gone. A new pilot had recently arrived, Unteroffizier Reichenbach, but it is unclear exactly when this was. He was severely injured in a crash in a landing accident on 8 October and was posted out (Albatros 2098/17). Eggers did, however, return to combat flying, and was posted to Jasta 30 in May 1918, claiming one combat victory that same month. He left in October 1918 after twice taking acting command during his Staffelführer's absence, moving to BG4 where he saw out the war.

A new pilot to arrive during the month was Leutnant Otto Löffler who came in on the 19th. He had seen service with the König Friedrich Wilhelm II Grenadier Regiment Nr.10 before transferring to the Air Service. His first unit was FA7 which he left in October 1916 to join Jasta 19. Although he was with this Staffel till June 1917 he made no combat claims. He then went to Kest 6w on home defence until October 1917, then following a week at Jastaschule I, was posted to Jasta B.

Böhme's 16th kill was a Bristol F2b north of Dadizeele on the morning of the 5th, a machine of 20 Squadron which so nearly got across the lines but in failing to do so, put its two-man crew into a prison camp.

Reichenbach's crash on the 8th, was, presumably, following a combat with a 7 Squadron RE8. On the 7th and 8th it rained almost non-stop, and this action on the latter date was the only recorded combat loss for the RFC. The RE8 had flown out to try an artillery observation sortie, taking off at 08.30. Twenty minutes later its crew gave their last wireless call, and fell south-west of Terhand, a town which is north-west of Menin. Whether Reichenbach's machine was damaged in the action, or his crash was due to pilot error or even over-exuberance following his first victory is not known.

The next day, Karl Gallwitz (in Albatros DV 4407/17) made his first claim with the Jasta, and his third overall, by downing a Sopwith Triplane. The odd thing here is that according to Jasta records it came down on the German side of the lines, but there is no Triplane loss. The Nachrichtenblatt (roughly equivalent to the RFC's Communiqués), merely lists it as a Sopwith, and at one stage the type was also noted as an RE8! The Triplane is so identifiable in the air that it seems strange he should claim one and none were lost, and nor are there any Sopwith types lost this date. There were four or five RE8s in trouble but none known to be in the time frame of Gallwitz's claim – 18.15 hours.

Böhme went on a bit of a spree now, claiming the Jasta's next three victories and his own 17th, 18th and 19th. The first of these came on the 10th, a Nieuport XXVII from 29 Squadron, one of two shot-up on an early patrol of six aircraft which were attacked by six Albatros Scouts. One got back with a pilot wounded in the hand, the other was seen to force-land near the trenches after an attack by a German fighter, its pilot having been wounded in the face. The British pilot scrambled to safety but his machine was abandoned. Böhme claimed an SE5 north of Zillebeke which went down inside British lines, but it was in fact the Nieuport Scout.

On the morning of the 13th he got a Pup of 54 Squadron south of Couckelaere. The fight had occurred over Zarren, to the east of Dixmude, and the pilot was killed. On the 14th he shot down a 'Sopwith' – again in fact a Nieuport Scout from 29 Squadron. It was another early patrol and the British pilot was killed, falling into the British lines.

Gallwitz was with his leader on this patrol and he singled out an RE8 he spotted working over the front just to the south of where Böhme was shooting down the Nieuport. With Gallwitz we do not have much luck in discovering who he was up against. There is no obvious loss, nor is it certain which side of the trenches it fell. It is also confusing because he stated his victim was a Sopwith, so we are faced with either a double claim for the same Nieuport, or if indeed it was an RE8 it too got down but without too much damage. The fact that there is also a record that his victory was over a Martinsyde helps us even less, as there were none lost this date and 27 Squadron who flew them were a little too far south now, and mainly converting to DH4s. 34 Squadron with RE8s were in the air and it had a machine shot-up and its observer wounded, but this was nothing to do with Jasta B. The RE was hit by ground fire at around 11 am (Lts G G Banting and J Duncan, RE8 No. A4263).

Böhme's Twentieth
On the morning of 16 October, Böhme would have been conscious that he was just one kill short of reaching the magic '20 victories' which should net him the Pour le Mérite. After all he had received the prerequisite Knight's Cross with Swords of the Royal Hohenzollern House Order as far back as 12 March 1917, in recognition of his 12 victories. An early call to action sent Jasta B into the air and some time after 9 am they ran into their friends of 29 Squadron. It proved to be an interesting encounter.

There were two Nieuports, out looking for a reported German wireless machine. One of the pilots was of German extraction, his parents having moved to England in the latter part of the previous century. His name was Frederick Ortweiler, who lived in north London. Although upon his return from prison camp Ortweiler made out a good report of the action, it cannot wholly be relied upon, as we shall read.

He recorded that he saw a single enemy aircraft pass below him and he dived to engage, but was blown east by a strong wind so broke away. Heading back to the lines he was attacked in turn by five Albatros Scouts. As the scrap started his gun jammed and then he stalled and spun. With German aircraft chasing him he spiralled down and then contour-chased for the lines but then his engine suddenly stopped and after zooming over some trees, he had to put down, as luck would have it, near a German Battalion Headquarters, so he was captured immediately.

From Böhme, however, we learn that no sooner had the fight started than the Nieuport pilot appeared to give up. Certainly he raised his hands above his head and so the Germans escorted him down towards their own airfield at Rumbeke, the action having taken place over Magermairie. He wrote to his fiancée about Ortweiler, whose family hailed from Frankfurt:

I recently came upon an English Nieuport single-seater at the front, in which our friend was sitting. Naturally I invited him to pay us a visit. As he did not promptly begin to descend, I became somewhat more urgent in my efforts to compel him to descend. Yet, as he continually waved at me "with his hands", I did not want to do anything to him. He then landed safe and sound at our airfield. We laughed until we were blue in the face. I never had anything like this previously happen to me.

Ortweiler had recorded that his undercarriage had been damaged and that he had been prevented from firing a flare into a pool of leaking petrol by being captured. All this is taken at face value only, for he also stated that he had got very close to the lines before being compelled, due to his engine failing, to land. One may well concede that his gun had jammed and with the odds at 5 to 1 felt it was too one-sided to continue. Be that as it may, he was obviously embarrassed to have surrendered so easily and had not wanted to say so upon his release from prison camp. Being of German parents too would have put his actions in a poor light. It has to be said, however, that he became something of a nuisance as a prisoner in Germany and for this and his escape attempts he was awarded the Military Cross. Not long after the war Ortweiler was killed in an aeroplane accident in Spain. In the same letter above, Böhme recorded:

> I am quite happy with the performance of my Staffel now that I have got rid of the duds. They are willing to follow me everywhere, and have begun to shoot down opponents. Twice this afternoon large battles between opposing fighter units occurred. In the second, over Passchendaele, my damned machine guns jammed again – and just when I really needed to fire. Right next to me I lost an able pilot, Leutnant Lange, whom I was unable to help out of his plight. The others, however, shot down three English planes.

This action, on the 20th, occurred at 12.20 pm east of Passchendaele. In fact only two British aircraft were shot down, one by Kempf for his third kill, and the other by Gerhard Bassenge, his first victory. Both were Camels.

The fight was with 70 Squadron once again and they did indeed lose two machines, with one pilot killed, the other captured. What Böhme does not record – perhaps he was not totally aware – was that the RFC aircraft were part of a massed attack upon Rumbeke airfield. Or perhaps he did not want to worry his fiancée by telling her about the raid. In total 45 aircraft from three RFC squadrons took part. The Camels, which also carried bombs, were from 70 and 28 Squadrons, with seven Spads of 23 Squadron flying protection above. The two 70 Squadron Camels were the only losses incurred, and the RFC claimed much damage to the airfield. In air fighting the RFC claimed seven victories over single-seaters. Again a little on the high side, although JGI had two pilots wounded, and Jasta 35b also had a pilot wounded. Lange was probably shot down by a 28 Squadron pilot, in fact one who was to become particularly famous,

Captain W G Barker.

Jasta Boelcke had engaged 28 Squadron, a new unit that had only arrived in France earlier in the month. Two Albatros Scouts were claimed in this action, one by Captain W G Barker MC, the other by Lieutenant J H Mitchell. Barker, who was to win the VC, DSO & Bar, MC & 2 Bars, Croix de Guerre and the Italian Medaglio d'Argento, and end the war with 50 victories (mainly on the Italian Front) gained his first on this day. His report records:

> 12.15pm. Height 10,000 ft. Locality: South of Roulers aerodrome. Albatros Scout.
> While returning from Thielt we met about 10 Albatros Scouts and dived to the attack. After a very close engagement the EA (painted green with small black crosses) went down with both wings off. I saw another machine also going down with wings off.

It was Barker's first victory, and if indeed two hostile machines went down minus their wings, then Mitchell also got his first kill – of a later total of 11 – and like Barker scored in both France and later on the Italian Front. As Jasta B appear to have lost only the one pilot and one aircraft, the thought does come to mind that both pilots were seeing the same wingless machine going down, and Barker, possibly losing sight of his victim, later picked up the falling Albatros again, and thought it to be a second one.

Gallwitz scored his fourth on 27 October. This time there is no doubt who his victim was, and indeed, it was a famous one at that. Just after the noon hour Jasta B were engaged in a fight with SE5s of 56 Squadron. The SEs were just south-west of Roulers. Spotting two Pfalz Scouts below and six Albatros DVs above, four of the British fighters dived after the Pfalz, leaving the others to take on the DVs. After a mainly indecisive action one SE was missing but nothing was thought too much about it. A further fight developed and 56 Squadron became scattered and it was not till much later they realised that the missing man was still unaccounted for and remained missing long after landing.

The man, Lieutenant Arthur P F Rhys Davids DSO MC and Bar, was the victor in 25 combats and was one month exactly past his 20th birthday. His 19th victory had been none other than Werner Voss back in September. Rhys Davids had been last seen chasing an Albatros south-west of Roulers.

Böhme was not able to see Gallwitz's triumphant return as he was away. On the 24th Ernst von Hoeppner, Commanding General of the Air Force, ordered 26 airmen, including Böhme, to attend a ceremony at the grave of Oswald Boelcke in Dessau on the 28th, the first anniversary of his death. It must have been something of a traumatic experience for Böhme, having to relive the events of a year ago, though undoubtedly something he had recalled every day since it happened.

Returning from Dessau, he called in to see his fiancée and finally got back to the Jasta early on the 31st. He wrote:

> To my relief I found everything with the Staffel to be fine. Gallwitz, who had served as commander in my absence, scored one victory while I was away. He is very proud of it. He is a very young pilot, but completely reliable. I was not able to conceal my happiness from my Staffel mates. There was great rejoicing!

Böhme brought October to a close with his 21st victory on this same day – the 31st. This time it was an SE5a south-east of Zillebeke Lake at 17.15, but again inside British lines. The fight had been with 84 Squadron. They had not been at the front that long and this day they lost two pilots, one to Jasta B, the other to a pilot in Jasta 36.

Böhme was feeling good about his unit now. Most of the pilots were to his liking, and to this list he had added one more on the 29th – Leutnant Max Müller, the former NCO pilot with Jasta B in the autumn of 1916. Müller had now achieved 29 victories and had already received his Blue Max – on 3 September. While not a man so obviously worried about personal decorations, Böhme must have been wondering if he too would soon receive the blue and gold medal for his throat following his 20th victory back in August. Müller had still been an NCO in August, but he had received a field commission to the regular army on the 21st – not the reserve – the first time this had ever happened. Müller had then received another prestigious award on 16 September, the Bavarian Gold Bravery Medal. This was an NCO's award but while it was proposed when he was still an NCO its approval had only been put through following his commission. Already the holder of the Silver Bravery Medal, he became the first and only airman to receive both, a situation that remained for the duration of the war.

There was always something of a divide between the officer class and the other ranks, but now the diminutive Bavarian had hauled himself up with the elite. No doubt Böhme was glad to have not only Müller's experience but also that link to the past as Oswald Boelcke had commanded them both. Hopefully, November would prove an even better month than October.

Chapter Six

The Lost Staffelführers

November 1917

Pilots at the start of November:	Name	Victories
	Oblt Erwin Böhme	21
	Vfw Paul Bäumer	6
	Ltn Gerhard Bassenge	–
	Ltn Erich Daube	–
	Ltn Karl Gallwitz	4
	Ltn Otto Löffler	–
	Ltn Max Müller	29
	Ltn Richard Plange	–
	Ltn Hermann Vallendor	–
	Ltn Eberhard Fr von Gudenburg	–

Base: Rumbeke   Front: 4th Army JGr Nord

Recent personnel movements included Friedrich Kempf's transfer to Jastaschule I on 17 October, but he was destined to return to Jasta B in the New Year. Hermann Frommherz left a week later, on the 24th, to become an instructor for six months with FEA3 at Gotha. For some time he was an instructor at the Fliegerschule at Lübeck. Obviously, with just two victories scored in April and nothing since, his qualities as a fighter pilot were in question, but he too would return in 1918, a very different man. While absent, he received the Hanseatic Cross from Lübeck in December.

Staffel adjutant Anton Stephan left on 8 October, his place taken on the 19th by Leutnant Eberhard Wolff Freiherr von Gudenburg. He was not a pilot but had joined Jasta 29 from Army Flug-park 1, where he had been OzbV since May 1917. He would have known Böhme during his brief period with that unit, so no surprise therefore that he received a posting to Jasta B following Stephan's move away.

Two postings during November would occur on the 2nd, with the arrival of Leutnant Paul Schröder from Kasta 30 of KG5, and on the 11th Leutnant Wilhelm Papenmeyer was posted in from Jastaschule I. He was born in Hamein, in December 1895, so was 22-years-old. Schröder had been in the Würrtemberg infantry (Grenadier Regt. 119) earlier in the war, and while with Kasta 30 had won the Würrtemberg Golden Military Merit Medal, awarded on 22 December 1916.

The Jasta would also move again, on the 17th. Before that, however, the Ypres battles rumbled on, while the second stage of the Verdun offensive was continuing down on the French front – a long way from Jasta B's area of operations.

Newcomer Otto Löffler was shot down on 5 November and made a crash-landing in front of German positions near Passchendaele. Escaping serious injury he then had to make his way from shell-hole to shell-hole away from the front, dodging bursts of machine-gun fire and rifle bullets. It took him over three hours to get back to safety.

Like so many German casualties, unless there is some injury or fatality to the pilot or crew, few records remain today to indicate pure aircraft losses. Thus the only record of Löffler's shoot-down comes from Karl Bolle's history of the Jasta. Even then he does not make it clear if he was brought down by an aircraft or from ground fire. This November day was not among the busiest in terms of air actions and in any event Bolle does not give an indication of the time of day he crash-landed. If, however, he was shot down there are only two claimants from the RFC, Captain H A Hamersley of 60 Squadron, who downed an Albatros DV shortly after the noon hour, one mile north of Westroosbeke, and Captain J C B Firth of 45 Squadron, who downed an Albatros DV over Poelcapelle at 11.50 am, although he did not see it actually crash.

Both locations are in the general area of Passchendaele and Hamersley says his victim had a yellow fuselage and he saw it crash. While the varnished plywood fuselages of many Albatros Scouts had a yellowish appearance, Löffler was later known to have yellow as the personal colour on his aircraft, which had been the distinctive colour of his former 10th Grenadier Regiment. One has to wonder if he had some kind of yellow marking on his Albatros at this time too, which was what Hamersley saw. Both British pilots were good air fighters, ending the war with 13 and 11 victories respectively.

* * *

The weather was poor, especially in the first week of the month. The battle for Passchendaele was continuing. Canadian troops finally reached the outskirts of that shattered town as October drew to a close. The weather caused three Sopwith Camels of 3 Squadron to be lost on 6 November, the day the Canadians finally pushed into Passchendaele. Strong winds and poor visibility proved to be their downfall, nothing to do with the Germans.

However, on the 6th Jasta Boelcke secured six victories, two in the morning, three more shortly before noon, and the sixth that evening. Paul Bäumer had shot down his seventh victory the day before, a Camel of 45 Squadron south of St Julien which went down inside British lines. Kurt

Wüsthoff of Jasta 4 claimed two more Camels around the same time and in the same locality, but only one Camel was lost, its pilot wounded and taken prisoner. It therefore looks as though Bäumer's opponent got away with a force-landing, for the Jasta 4 man did claim one of his victims down inside German lines.

Bäumer claimed a Spad VII at 08.25 on the 6th, east of Zonnebeke and right over the front-lines. This appears to have been a 19 Squadron machine flying a low patrol looking for ground targets. The Spad crashed near Passchendaele at 07.40 (British time) and the pilot was killed. Not long after this, Richard Plange made his first claim, an SE5a south-west of Passchendaele, inside British lines. The only recorded SE5 casualty was a 60 Squadron machine, shot-up in combat near Polygon Wood, its pilot making a safe forced-landing. The area and time are about right.

Then later in the morning Jasta B ran into a patrol of Camels of 65 Squadron. Böhme, Bäumer and Bassenge each claimed one, and indeed, 65 did lose three of its machines, with all three pilots ending up as prisoners. On his return from prison camp at the end of the war, Böhme's victim, a New Zealander by the name of W L Harrison, recorded that he had been leading a patrol over Ypres in very bad weather and in the mist he believed they had got too far over and were then attacked by a large number of German fighters. Bill Harrison's controls were shot away and he injured his back in crash-landing, but he did say he had brought down one German aircraft. All three pilots, William Harrison, Eric G S Gordon and Edward H Cutbill recorded their experiences upon returning from Germany at the end of the war.

> William Harrison:
> Leading defensive patrol over Ypres. Being very misty we got too far over lines. Attacked by a large number of Scouts and during the action my controls were disabled. Crashed badly and injured my back. Brought down one EA.

> Eric Gordon:
> Line Patrol. Drifted over enemy lines owing to thick weather and attacked by 10 scouts in clouds at about 1,500 feet. Machine shot about and crashed out of control near Staaden.

> Edward Cutbill:
> AA fire over Roulers – was not wounded – but stunned. Machine crashed into Staaden railway station which it was not possible to avoid owing to low altitude and controls being shot away. Line Patrol.

Whether Cutbill was actually brought down by AA fire, or he preferred not to admit to being defeated in combat, or he did not see his attacker and assumed it was AA fire that brought him down, is unknown.

65 Squadron had not long been in France and this was one of its first actions. The Squadron had yet to secure its first combat success. In fact Harrison may have had something of a claim in the fight, as Gerhard Bassenge was hit and wounded moments after getting his second kill. He would be out of action till the summer of 1918. Two kills in one day, then wounded.

Max Müller made his first claim since returning to Jasta B on the 7th, his 30th overall. However, the date is in question, the Nachrichtenblatt noting this victory as having been achieved on the 6th. Again it was a Spad inside British lines. Jasta records state the time as being 09.30 am, south-west of St Julien, but the only Spad noted on the 6th was some time earlier than this, claimed by Bassenge. There are no Spad losses on the 7th, but as it went down into Allied lines, there is always the doubt about the final outcome.

Bäumer claimed his ninth victory on the 7th, an RE8 observation machine south-west of Moorslede, again right over the front-lines. This was a 4 Squadron machine, both crew members being killed, although the pilot did not die until two days later. They had been operating over the 1st ANZAC Corps. Bäumer's report:

> 7 November 1917. Albatros DV 4430/17. Dark fuselage, yellow underneath with white-red-white band. Location and Time: SW of Moorslede, at 08.10 hours.
> At 08.10 in the morning, I saw, while flying along the front south-west of Moorslede, an RE under me, apparently a battle flyer. I immediately plunged down on him and surprise-attacked at a height of 200 metres and caused him to go down south-west of Moorslede. The aircraft completely crashed to pieces on the ground.

What he does not say in his report is that as he saw the observer begin to fire at him Bäumer closed his throttle and side-slipped from 350 to 300 metres, as if he had been hit. Now at the same height as the RE8, he quickly closed in and opened fire. He could see that his bullets were on target as strips of fabric ripped away from the two-seater's wings. Then a stream of white vapour came from the RE's fuel tank. He watched as the RE's dive steepened before it crashed into the trenches.

After the day's successes, came the announcement that Hermann Vallendor had been awarded the Baden Order of the Zähringen Lion – Knight 2nd Class – on this date.

Paul Bäumer made more kills on the 8th, two Camels during a late afternoon fight north of Zonnebeke. Once again the British machines were seen to go down over British lines and with no obvious RFC losses it is difficult to reconcile his claims. The nearest one can get is to suggest that rather than Camels, they were in fact SE5s of 60 Squadron, as in his report he only reported 'Sopwiths'. One of this unit's aircraft did force-land 500 yards inside Allied lines west of Poelcapelle at 16.15 hours, and although the pilot scrambled to safety his SE5 was shelled by the German artillery. The other 'Camel' appears to have survived. Nevertheless, Bäumer was credited with victories 11 and 12. In his combat report he recorded:

> 8 November 1917. Albatros DV 4430/17. Location and Time: North of Zillebeke and north of Zonnebeke, at 16.45 hours.
> Around 16.45, I was flying over the Houthulst forest at a height of 2,600 metres and saw four Sopwith single-seaters. One of these attacked me from behind, I banked towards him and let off a well-aimed burst at him from both of my machine guns at close range. Then a second Sopwith came to his assistance and attacked me from the side, whereupon I also banked towards this one and shot at close range. The rest of the enemy aircraft dived across their front in the direction of Ypres, whereupon I alternatively attacked the first two aircraft and brought them under fire. One of these Sopwiths I then saw out of control and under full power, the machine pulled up and again slipped down so that I had the impression that the pilot was dead. After that I once again turned to the second Sopwith and followed it, firing until he broke up in the crater fields north of Zonnebeke. I saw the first Sopwith still at a height of about 200 metres gliding with peculiar turns and observed how this one ran into the earth near the railway north of Zillebeke with motor full on. Other German aircraft did not participate in this aerial battle.

* * *

However keen the pilots were to score victories and achieve a 'score' it seems sometimes that their eagerness got the better of them. Occasionally they became over-enthusiastic enough to believe that what they had seen had become a victory whereas common sense should have dictated that there was an element of doubt prevailing. One often reads too in combat reports that the claimant makes mention of seeing no other friendly aircraft being involved. Often this was in order to ensure that nobody else should home in on his kill.

Böhme was not known for being a medal chaser, although as time went on he was obviously thinking more and more about the Blue Max, as a letter to his fiancée reveals on 9 November:

> You appear to be concerned that for your sake, ambition has seized me, and I am chasing the Pour le Mérite. I have already amply earned that decoration in that I conquered my Annamarie. Moreover, the award is now no longer so freely awarded as in the initial stages of the fighter Staffeln; Immelmann and Boelcke received it after their eighth

victories, and von Richthofen after his sixteenth. Besides, all decorations possess for me only the value that I can estimate for what I have done. So, for me it is actually immaterial whether I receive another medal or not. However, I would be happy to receive the Pour le Mérite because the award would constitute recognition of the valiant fighter Staffel that I command.

The Jasta appears to have become, once again, part of a Jagdgruppe, as Böhme wrote to Annamarie on the 10th:

> Presently I am functioning (not a permanent position!) as Commander of the Ypres Fighter Group. This involves the three fighter Staffeln which have been assembled in this sector of the Front and is because the senior ranking officer amongst the three fighter Staffeln is on leave. As such, I am responsible for regulating offensive patrols for the Staffeln as well as for quite a large pile of daily reports – a particular delight for me! Moreover, I am now accustomed to reading in bed, because frequently many quite important telephone calls come in the early hours of the night.

It isn't entirely clear which three Jastas were involved or the name of the Gruppe. It could have been the old Jagdgruppe Nord, now JGr4, with Jastas 8 and 20, Jasta B being attached merely because Böhme was the locally senior man, especially if von Benthiem was on leave. In Wilhelm Papenmeyer's combat report dated 18 November (see below) he recorded they were part of the Ypres Jagdgruppe, while in his report of 4 January 1918, Papenmeyer notes Jagdgruppe 4.

On the 11th Müller downed number 31 shortly after midday, again over the British lines. It was not a great day for air fighting and his claim for an SE5a in fact was some damaging hits on a DH5 of 32 Squadron. Its fuel tanks were holed in the fight and its pilot, Lieutenant A Claydon, managed a successful forced-landing. Arthur Claydon went on to become a successful air fighter although by this date he had yet to achieve his first victory. He would gain seven before his own death in action in the summer of 1918.

Jasta Move

Now came the move from Rumbeke to Bavichove, due east of Ypres and just to the north of Courtrai, but still with 4th Army. With the Allied advances on the ground, Rumbeke was too near the front-lines. Cold and fog were now the main enemies. On the 18th came two more claims, but like so many, claims that are suspect today. Bäumer attacked an RE8 at 09.20 north-east of Zillebeke Lake and saw it go down in Allied lines. At 11 am Leutnant Papenmeyer got his first chance and claimed a Spad in the front-lines north-east of Langemark. This was a Spad VII of 23 Squadron out on an interception of a wireless machine and last seen near Passchendaele at 10.20. Papenmeyer's combat report reads:

> 18 November 1917. Ypres Jagdgruppe. 1 kilometre north-east of Langemark. 11 o'clock in the morning. Albatros DV 2086/17, yellow fuselage.
> I was flying along the front in a southerly direction with two men from my Staffel, and at a height of 600 metres over Langemark met a Spad single-seater that was chasing a German C [two-seater] aircraft hard. We immediately attacked the Spad which let go of the C-plane. In the resulting dogfight, I pressured the Spad down to about 50 metres and caused it to crash from a very close distance. The aircraft went down vertically and smashed to pieces on the ground. I observed the impact. Aircraft other than those from the Staffel did not participate in this aerial battle.
> Papenmeyer, Leutnant d.R.

Paul Bäumer was in action again the next day, against another RE8 north-west of Dixmude at 16.00 hours, again sent down into Allied lines and again there is no clearly identifiable loss, either RFC or Belgian. His report seems clear enough though, and was Müller a witness?

> 19 November 1917. Albatros DV 4430/17. Location and Time: North-west of Dixmuiden, at 16.00.
> I was flying with Ltn Müller and we sighted, at a height of 1,500 metres, north of the Houthulst forest, an RE which was flying in a northward direction. Ltn Müller attacked it first, but had to break off because of a jam, whereupon I attacked it and shot at close range; after a short burst the RE broke up in the air and lies north-west of Dixmuiden.

This ended for the most part the vicious fighting that had been going on over the Flanders front for some weeks, things settling down for the winter. Not so, however, further south, as the mighty Battle of Cambrai now opened, bringing massive tank assaults to the battlefields for the first time. Jasta B, in the north, continued the daily round against the RFC along the Belgian sectors.

Erwin Böhme got his 23rd on the 20th. He attacked a Nieuport Scout over Oostkerke at 10.30 and it headed down inside Allied lines. This time, however, it was not an RFC aircraft, but a Belgian machine. His victim was 1st/Sergeant L A R Ciselet of 5e Belgian Escadrille, who crashed and was killed. Leon Ciselet – known as Robert – came from Antwerp and was 25, one of four brothers to see service, of whom only one survived. His Nieuport fell between Caeskerke and Oudecapelle, near Dixmude,

Ciselet with two bullet wounds to the head and three in his heart.

> ...I caught number 23. He was attempting to attack one of
> our observation planes. Now he has fallen into the flooded
> regions to the west of Dixmude.

Böhme was officially awarded the Pour le Mérite on 24 November. One
has to assume that someone telephoned him to this effect, although there
is no written confirmation to his fiancée that he had heard. If he had
heard, by telegram or by telephone, he probably wanted to wait until the
actual medal arrived before saying anything to anyone.

November was proving a good month for combat claims in general,
and Bäumer's name was again to the fore on the 28th, but this time his
opponent fell inside German lines. It was yet another RE8, which went
down at 2 pm north of Gheluve, a machine from 7 Squadron on a photo
op. Bäumer's report:

> 28 November 1917. Albatros DV 4430/17. Location and
> Time: 1 km north of Gheluve, at 14.00 hours.
> I was flying with 5 men from the Staffel over the crater fields
> of Ypres and sighted an RE above in the clouds in the
> direction of Zonnebeke. I attacked it immediately and
> banked with him through the clouds. After a brief exchange
> of fire, the observer disappeared from his seat. The pilot
> waved at me in a lively manner upon which I stopped
> shooting. When he, however, attempted to escape in the
> direction of Ypres, I shot at him with about 50 bullets from
> the length of an aeroplane. Aircraft totally smashed to pieces
> on the ground, it lies 1 km north of Gheluve. No other
> aircraft, besides the Staffel, participated in this aerial battle.

Böhme Falls

Böhme's last letter to his fiancée, Annamarie Brüning, serving as a nurse
in Hamburg, was started on the morning of the 29th, and was probably
meant to be finished later or simply sent as it was if he was busy:

> My love! Now just a quick affectionate morning greeting.
> The Staffel is already waiting for me. This evening I will
> write a proper letter to you. Your Erwin.

Like so many WW1 pilots, especially the aces, their loss is often
shrouded in mystery. It appears he was on his second flight of the day,
leading his men towards and over the front. There is supposed to have
been a fight with enemy aircraft, during which the Staffelführer downed
one for victory number 24. The Jasta records have this as a Sopwith
Camel. He then attacked a two-seater but was hit by return fire from the

observer and his Albatros fell to earth inside British lines and crashed.

There is no record of any Camels being lost at this time and one is left to wonder if in fact his pilots claimed a 'victory' for him, knowing that he had fallen. The fatal fight took place over Zonnebeke at around 4.10 pm according to a note dropped by the Germans requesting information on 3 December, whereas the fight with the Camels is recorded at 12.55. This of course, suggests that Böhme himself recorded a kill upon his return to the airfield, but this is by no means certain. It was then on the second flight that he was killed attacking the two-seater.

This two-seater was an Armstrong Whitworth FK8, known as a 'Big Ack', from 10 Squadron RFC, and crewed by Lieutenants J A Pattern and P W Leycester. For John Pattern and Philip Leycester it was only their second sortie together as a crew. Indeed, Leycester had only arrived on the Squadron on the 28th! Pattern had been flying Big Acks with 10 Squadron since May. The pair's first sortie was actually flown on the 28th, and they had been shot-up by a German fighter. This had obviously helped concentrate the mind of Leycester during his second sortie on the 29th. Pattern came from Leeds but had lived in Great Yarmouth, where he had been a school master, and was 25; Leycester came from Cork. Both survived the war.

Because the timing of Böhme's 'claim' and his fall were some three hours apart, it shows a later statement that claims that after he had shot down his 24th he was shot down to be ambiguous: 'Shortly after this fight he was enveloped by an enemy fighter squadron and fatally wounded over Zonnebeke.' His Albatros DVa, having fallen in British lines, was given the RFC serial G92, although there was little remaining but a wreck. Soldiers taking the body from it, and then searching through the pockets, apparently found a telegram recording that the German Kaiser had recently awarded the dead airman a decoration a few days earlier. Was this the reference to the Blue Max? There was no medal at his neck, just the Iron Cross 1st Class at his left breast, and the ribbon of the Iron Cross 2nd Class and the Hohenzollern ribbon both through a buttonhole on his jacket. The actual Pour le Mérite was in a package lying unopened on his desk back at Bavichove, awaiting his return.

Müller was credited with a DH4 at the time of Böhme's fall. Apparently it came down inside German lines but the only DH4 lost was a machine of 49 Squadron at 10.10 in the morning, near Thun St Martin, east of Cambrai, so not even in Jasta B's area. With no French or Belgian losses, this is yet another of Müller's mystery claims.

December 1917
Pilots at the start of December:

Name	Victories
Ltn Max Müller	32
Vfw Paul Bäumer	13
Ltn Erich Daube	–
Ltn Karl Gallwitz	4

Pilots at the start of December:	Name	Victories
	Ltn Otto Löffler	–
	Ltn Wilhelm Papenmeyer	1
	Ltn Richard Plange	1
	Ltn Paul Schröder	–
	Ltn Hermann Vallendor	–
OzbV & acting Staffelführer	Ltn Eberhard Fr von Gudenburg	–

Base: Bavichove   Front: 4th Army JGr 4

There was no apparent rush to send in a new Staffelführer, so von Gudenburg took the reins, at least on the ground. Müller might seem, on paper, to have been an obvious choice, but until recently he had been an NCO, and it would have gone against the officer-class grain to have him promoted to lead a Jasta so soon, whatever his record. His combat score made him stand out, but as other high-scoring fighter pilots had, and would, find out, this was no precursor to command. Werner Voss is a case in point. While he was second to none as an air fighter, he was never happy with command and was not an effective Staffel commander. After all, whatever he had achieved in the air, he was still only 20 when he commanded Jasta 10, and when he died.

Perhaps the High Command felt they wanted another Böhme and needed time to make the right choice. Karl Bolle later recorded that the search for a new leader of Jasta B was not easy due to a lack of qualified personalities. It was, therefore, almost two weeks before a successor was named, during which time von Gudenburg held temporary command.

In the end it fell to a young nobleman from a distinguished family with a sound military background. His name was Leutnant Walter von Bülow-Bothkamp, known to some as 'Jonny Bülow'. He had been born at Borby, near Eckernforde in April 1894, so was 23 years of age. He had begun to study law at Heidelberg University and by 1914 had seen much of the world.

When the war started he joined the Saxon Hussar Regiment Nr.17 – known as the Death's Head Hussars – and he saw heavy fighting in Alsace in early 1915 and quickly received a commission. Moving into the Air Service he became a pilot and served with FA22, flying twin-engined AEG CIIs, seeing action on the Champagne front from September 1915, and being credited with two victories over French aircraft in October. He received the Iron Cross 1st Class and was then sent overseas, to FA300 in Palestine. Von Bülow claimed a further three victories in the Suez area in the summer of 1916, against the RNAS, before returning to France.

His fifth victory came in January 1917, as a pilot with Jasta 18, and in May, his score having risen to 13 he was given command of Jasta 36. Over the summer and autumn of 1917 his score moved to 28, by which time he had received the Pour le Mérite. Command of Jasta Boelcke came on 13 December.

Further postings during December meant the arrival of Leutnant Theodor Cammann on the 9th. Cammann came with one victory scored with an unknown unit.

Before this took place, however, the Jasta had continued to score kills. On the 2nd Müller shot down a DH4 north-west of Menin. This time however, there is a comparable loss, a machine from 57 Squadron, its pilot wounded and taken prisoner, the observer killed.

Otto Löffler, after his long apprenticeship, scored his first victory, shooting down a Nieuport Scout on the 5th, a machine from 1 Squadron near Houthulst Forest at 10.30 German time, its pilot captured. Müller attacked and shot down an SE5a at 14.40 that same afternoon but he reported it going down over the British lines and there is no apparent loss of a machine or pilot. There are a couple of Camels shot-up but time and location are uncertain.

Müller and Bäumer both claimed Spads shortly before noon on the 7th. 19 Squadron did lose a machine, its pilot captured near Moorslede, and this appears to have been Müller's victim. The Spad pilots had been trying to engage a two-seater but were thwarted by six Albatros Scouts. In the confused fighting they claimed nothing but went home one pilot short. 23 Squadron were operating in the same general area at the time and lost a machine and pilot too, but this Spad also crashed into German lines. If this was Bäumer's claim it should have been confirmed as east of the lines. His report reads:

> 7 December 1917. Albatros DV 4430/17. Location and Time: Zonnebeke, at 11.55 hours.
> After Ltn Müller had forced a Spad from a single-seater flight to land on this side, I again attacked at a height of 1,200 metres, with a few more men of the Staffel, this same flight, and shot at a Spad from a close range. The opponent went straight down with its motor running full-out and ran into a crater field near Zonnebeke, south of the Roulers-Ypres railway line and I saw how he [it] totally smashed to pieces.

On the 8th Erich Daube was lost near Moorslede. It was a quiet day with almost no air fighting, so little is recorded about how he was killed. His was the last loss suffered by the Jasta in 1917.

In the south the Battle of Cambrai came to an end, but on the more northern Flanders front action continued, although Jasta B did not see further successful action until the 16th, by which time von Bülow had arrived. Müller and Bäumer were again the scorers, a Camel and an RE8 respectively, both timed at 14.10 hours, west of Passchendaele and north of Boesinghe – and both falling over the British side of the lines. Bäumer's RE8 may well have been a 9 Squadron aircraft on artillery observation, which survived with a wounded man on board, while

Müller's claim was probably a 70 Squadron machine, its pilot surviving but the Camel was damaged beyond repair in a forced-landing. Bäumer:

> 16 December 1917. Albatros DV 5410/17; yellow fuselage with two black rings. Location and Time: North of Boesinghe at 14.10 hours.
> I was flying with Ltn Müller and a few other men of the Staffel over the Houthulst forest, when I sighted two REs on the other side of the lines artillery spotting at a height of 2,000 metres. I attacked the one flying farthest away to the north and forced him to land on our side. After that, I flew back and saw how Ltn Müller and a few other of the Staffel's pilots found themselves in an aerial battle with the second RE which was stubbornly flying to the west and came up to me. Apparently unrecognized, I joined with him and then shot off a burst of 100 bullets, upon which the enemy machine flipped over, the observer falling out, then broke apart and shortly afterwards, at 14.00 hours, went down burning. The rubble lies between Boesinghe and Het Sas.

The odd thing here is that while his combat report seems to indicate two RE8s shot down, one landing inside German lines, the other disintegrating, with the observer thrown out, and the wreck clearly seen, he only claims one. Also it was such a quiet day in the air, that only the one 9 Squadron RE8 is listed as a casualty – which returns home with just a wounded observer! In fact there are no RFC deaths recorded for the 16th anywhere. Nor among the Belgians.

Bäumer closed the Jasta's 1917 account two days later with a Camel seen to force-land inside British lines and therefore noted as 'ZwdL' – but still recorded as his 18th victory. The action was thought to have been with 65 Squadron and involved not only Jasta B but Jasta 7, Jasta 28w and Jasta 36. The problem, however, is that while these units claimed a total of six Camels shot down, 65 only lost three, with two pilots taken prisoner and one killed. It is very difficult in the heat of battle, seeing an opponent in front starting to spin earthwards, not to assume it had crashed, and even if a pilot saw soon afterwards an Allied machine crash, he would assume it was his. The higher the number of pilots who saw such crashes, the more victory claims went in. If there were enough witnesses to confuse the issue further, credits were generally given. With aces almost desperate to increase their victory tallies, they could be forgiven if their hearts believed what their eyes failed to see. Bäumer's report:

> 18 December 1917. Albatros DV 5410/17. Location and Time: West of Becelaere, at 16.00 hours.
> I was flying alone from 15.00 to 16.30 hours. Over

Passchendaele, I sighted a Sopwith biplane which I immediately attacked and gave it around 100 bullets upon which he went down burning in the direction of Becelaere. According to [a] report, the machine lies between the lines. I myself could not observe the impact.

Jagdgruppe Nr.4

Jasta B were formally back again with a Jagdgruppe on 29 December, in company with Jastas 26, 27, 37 and 47w. It was commanded by Bruno Loerzer, leader of Jasta 26. His friend Hermann Göring commanded Jasta 27, whilst Jasta 37 was led by Ernst Udet. Jasta 47w was a new unit and its Staffelführer was Walter Kypke. Jastas 26 and 27 had moved in to Bavichove in November, Jasta 37 was at Wynghene and Jasta 47w operated from Harlebeke.

The year ended with the Jasta tally totalling 189 victories. While one can say without fear of contradiction that this was over-optimistic, especially noting some of the questionable claims already referred to, one should also keep in mind the times that a pilot may well have shot down an Allied machine, but again, in the heat of combat, had no idea he had done so, especially if he was heavily engaged with other opponents, each trying to kill him.

January 1918

Pilots at the start of January:		Name	Victories
		Ltn Walter von Bülow	28
		Vfw Paul Bäumer	18
		Ltn Theodor Cammann	1
		Ltn Karl Gallwitz	4
		Ltn Otto Löffler	1
		Ltn Max Müller	36
		Ltn Wilhelm Papenmeyer	1
		Ltn Richard Plange	1
		Ltn Paul Schröder	–
	OzbV	Ltn Eberhard Fr von Gudenburg	–

Base: Bavichove   Front: 4th Army JGr 4

Jasta Boelcke now had the makings of a good Staffel. There was both experience and the potential for a number of its young pilots to come good. On the second day of January, von Bülow had his brother Harry posted in from Jasta 36. Harry was three and a half years younger than Walter, born on the family estate in Bothkamp, Holstein, and had also been in a Saxon Hussar Regiment prior to becoming an aviator. At the end of 1916 he had started flying two-seaters, then moved to fighters, going to his brother's Jasta 36 in September. He had thus far achieved three victories.

Friedrich Kempf returned to the Jasta in January, his stint at Jastaschule I at an end and two more pilots also arrived during the month, Leutnant Erwin Klumpp, in from FA(A)284 on the 8th, and Leutnant Ludwig Vortmann. Klumpp came from Stuttgart, and was 26. He had come up through the ranks in the infantry (which he joined in 1912) and before moving to aviation had been well decorated and commissioned. He had been severely wounded in France, then served on the Eastern Front. His awards included the Iron Cross 1st Class and the Würrtemberg Friedrich Order, Knight's Cross 2nd Class with Swords. His move to aviation came in August 1916 and by May the following year he was with FA(A)284. In September he received the Würrtemberg Knight's Cross of the Military Merit Order. Vortmann came from Reckling and was approaching his 22nd birthday.

Fokker Triplanes

On New Year's Day the Jasta received a Fokker DV biplane. This was a rotary-engined training machine and was being issued to staffeln which would be receiving the Fokker Dr.I Triplanes in order for them and their ground-crews to accustom themselves to the Oberursel rotary engine. The first three examples of Triplanes arrived at Bavichove on 10 January from the 4th Army's aircraft park at Ghent. The famous Dutch designer, Anthony Fokker, also sent along gifts of walking sticks for the pilots, made from scrapped/broken propellers – a typical Fokker gesture. More Triplanes began to arrive and by mid-February Jasta B had its full complement, although it still retained some of its Albatros DV fighters.

Wilhelm Papenmeyer opened the 1918 scoring record with an SE5a shot down near Geluveld sometime after noon on 4 January. It was a 60 Squadron machine, flown by Captain F H B Selous MC. Frederick Selous was an experienced hand, having served with 19 and 45 Squadrons before becoming a flight commander with 60 Squadron, yet he was still only 19. He was the son of a famous explorer. He dived on a patrol of Jasta B machines and he may have suffered wing failure which led to his death, but German pilots were never slow in making a claim, so whatever the truth, Papenmeyer was given the credit. Papenmeyer's report:

> 4 January 1918. Jagdgruppe 4. 12.45 in the afternoon. Albatros DV 5375/17, yellow fuselage with a white band with a black 'B' on it.
> At a height of 4,000 metres at around 12.45 in the afternoon over Geluveld, I attacked an SE from a squadron of 4 enemy single-seaters that was diving on our flight. After a short attack, the opponent dived straight down. The wings broke off during the fall. German aircraft other than [those] from the Staffel did not participate in this aerial battle.
>
> Papenmeyer, Leutnant d.R.

Then disaster struck the Staffel. Walter von Bülow was shot down and killed near Ypres, to the east of Passchendaele, at 15.05 hours on the afternoon of the 6th. The British pilot who got him was the same one who had brought down Georg Noth back in May 1917 – Captain Willie Fry MC. Fry was now a flight commander with 23 Squadron, flying Spads, and like Noth had been, he brought down the Albatros DV (2080/17) inside Allied lines, being given the RFC serial number G123.

Fry and his patrol came across a battle between several Albatros Scouts and some RFC fighters, mostly Camels. Willie Fry later recorded:

> We joined in just as the fight was breaking up, with several machines in sight going down out of control and at least one in flames. My combat report states that we came across a formation of about five Albatros Scouts flying west and that I dived on one, firing a burst of about 20 rounds from behind.
>
> The enemy aircraft at once rolled over and went down in a steep spiral and crashed in a shelled area south of Passchendaele. I was given credit for the machine as destroyed. Although the CO endorsed the combat report with the words 'confirmed by AA Group', I have always since had a recollection that there was some question of a claim for the same machine made by pilots of the Camel squadron. In general mêlées that sort of thing did arise.

The other pilot who also put in a claim for the downed Albatros was Captain Francis Quigley of 70 Squadron, a Canadian ace, who ended up with 33 victories and a DSO and the MC and Bar. Unhappily he was to die in the influenza pandemic in October 1918.

Jasta B did not have to wait long this time for the announcement of a new leader. This same date Max Müller was given the job, but only as fighter leader in the air, not as Staffelführer. He had almost made it. He had risen from NCO to commissioned officer, to Acting Staffelführer of the Jasta made famous by Oswald Boelcke, a unit he had been with almost from its inception in the late summer of 1916. He must have felt great pride and that with time he might even be given full command. Although he had flown with Jasta 28 between his two Jasta B periods, he always felt happiest with the Boelcke Staffel.

His period as acting commander lasted less than three days. On 9 January he was attacking an RE8 of 21 Squadron but was hit by return fire from its observer. His Albatros caught fire and as it fell blazing, Müller jumped to avoid burning to death, preferring a less hideous but just as certain end. Many airmen in WW1 faced this moment of truth, knowing that their time was up and all that they had strived for in life was finished. Parachutes for German airmen were still some time away and for a man jumping from a doomed and burning aeroplane there was a unique finality. There is a story that Müller had been telling his pilots the best way to attack the RE8 type of machine shortly before he was killed. If true it was sad irony.

The crew who did the damage comprised Captain G F W Zimmer and Lieutenant H Somerville, at 11.50 hours, and although two SE5s from 60 Squadron joined in, the Albatros – 5405/17 – was already on its way down from Somerville's fire. George Zimmer, who later won the DFC, made out the following combat report of the action:

> While RE8 No.B5045 was taking photographs of the Corps Counter Battery Area in the district of Moorslede, it was attacked by seven EA who approached from the north. One EA got within 25 yards of the RE8's tail. The observer fired about 50 rounds into it when it turned off and burst into flames. It was last seen going down out of control and in flames between Moorslede and Dadizeele.

The confusion concerning the two SE5s was brought about by Bäumer after the war, saying to Müller's brother that he had seen the Albatros pull away probably for its pilot to clear a gun jam. At that moment he was jumped by two British fighters. However, the German authorities accepted the account of Müller's attack on the lone RE8 and his aircraft being set on fire by the observer's return fire.

For the Bavarian NCO who had reached the heights of fame and a commission, there was to be one final reward. In early 1919 a posthumous knighthood was bestowed upon him with the award of the Military Max-Joseph Order, back dated to November 1917. He thus became Leutnant Max Ritter von Müller. The number of his awards was only surpassed among German fighter pilots in WW1 by Manfred von Richthofen.

Müller's awards were: Pour le Mérite (Prussia); Military Max-Joseph Order, Knight's Cross (Bavaria); Military Merit Order, 4th Class with Swords (Bavaria); Bravery Medal in Gold (Bavaria); Bravery Medal in Silver (Bavaria); Military Merit Cross, 3rd Class with Crown and Swords (Bavaria); Royal Hohenzollern House Order, Member's Cross with Swords (Prussia); Iron Cross 1st and 2nd Class (Prussia); Military Merit Medal in Gold (Würrtemberg); Prinzregent Luitpold Medal in Bronze (Bavaria); Long Service Distinction, 3rd Class (Bavaria).

* * *

The Jasta pilots steadied themselves after this double blow and continued to engage the enemy only infrequently as they spent time in adapting to the new Triplanes. Leutnant Theodor Cammann took temporary command while the search for another new leader was made.

Karl Gallwitz had not scored since shooting down Rhys Davids back in October 1917, but on consecutive days in January, the 18th and 19th,

he accounted for two Camels, both on the German side. The first was a
65 Squadron machine north of Passchendaele, the second another 65
Squadron aircraft, both men being killed. A 65 Squadron combat report
describes the action of the 18th:

> 2/Lt A E Wylie when on patrol with two other Sopwith
> Camels was attacked by 8 Albatros scouts which dived upon
> the rear of the formation from out of the clouds. The
> formation turned to engage the EA. 2/Lt A E Wylie is since
> missing and his patrol leader reports seeing one EA go down
> and crash near Westroosbeke and also a Camel at the same
> place and time (10.30 pm). It seems extremely probable that
> 2/Lt Wylie destroyed this hostile machine a few moments
> before he himself was brought down.

Three kills came on the 22nd. The first was Plange's second claim, a
Camel at 11.40 am, seen to go down into the British lines near
Langemark. No obvious casualty but it might have been a 9 Naval
Squadron Camel whose pilot was wounded near Houthulst Forest.

Twenty-five minutes later Gallwitz and Cammann claimed Bristol
Fighters, one down inside German lines, Cammann's going down over the
lines, his first victory. 20 Squadron lost one BF2b, the crew both mortally
wounded.

The New Staffelführer

Leutnant Walter Höhne arrived on the 26th to take command. It was just
over a year since he had left Jasta B after being wounded on 10 January
1917. He had been out of action for most of 1917 but shortly after
Christmas he had been given command of Jasta 59 – its first Staffelführer
– but now the powers that be had decided that it would be a good idea if
a Jasta B 'old boy' returned to lead it.

February 1918

Pilots at the start of February:	Name	Victories
	Ltn Otto Walter Höhne	6
	Vfw Paul Bäumer	18
	Ltn H von Bülow	3
	Ltn Theodor Cammann	1
	Ltn Karl Gallwitz	7
	Ltn Friedrich Kempf	3
	Ltn Erwin Klumpp	–
	Ltn Otto Löffler	1
	Ltn Wilhelm Papenmeyer	2
	Ltn Richard Plange	2
	Ltn Paul Schröder	–
	Ltn Ludwig Vortmann	–
OzbV	Ltn Eberhard Fr von Gudenburg	–

Base: Bavichove   Front: 4th Army JGr4/JGIII

There were no new pilots arriving during the month of February, with one exception which will be mentioned shortly, but two pilots were posted out. One was Paul Schröder. Schröder, although from Alsace, had been awarded the Würrtemberg Knight's Cross of the Military Merit Order on 20 February 1918, due in part to his association with the 126th Würrtemberg Infantry Regiment. (He also had both classes of the Iron Cross, and of course, the Gold Military Merit Medal for his service with Kasta 30 in 1916.) Oddly the posting came shortly after he gained his first combat success, and he ended up as a test pilot at Schniedemühl. The other was Theodor Cammann on the 21st. He was promoted to Oberleutnant and went to Jasta 74, taking command of this unit in March. He ended the war with 12 victories, including one kill at night!

At the start of February Jagdgruppe 4 had changed. Jastas B, 26, 27 and 36 now became a permanent grouping with effect from 2 February, commanded by Bruno Loerzer – JGIII. Jasta 36, led by Heinrich Bongartz had replaced Jastas 37 and 47w. Whatever success Manfred von Richthofen's JGI had achieved since June 1917, it had led the way for two more Jagdgeschwader formations, JGII and JGIII, both formed on the same date. JGII was commanded by another former Jasta B pilot, Adolf von Tutschek, who had been leading Jasta 12. JGII comprised Jastas 12, 13, 15 and 19. Germany was planning a large offensive in the spring of 1918 and putting these two new formations into being was all part of the plan.

On the morning of the 3rd, Löffler claimed a DH4 bomber south-east of Mariakerke, at 10.40, a machine from 25 Squadron. They had been part of a bomb raid upon the railway sidings at Melle and had not made it. Both crewmen were taken prisoner. The pilot, Lieutenant E G Green, had won an MC in the spring of 1917. Returning from Germany after the Armistice, Ernest Green, from Newcastle-upon-Tyne, related:

> I left the aerodrome at Boisdinghem, near St Omer, at 8 am on Sunday 3 February, flying a DH4 with Lieutenant P C Campbell-Martin as my observer. Four other similar machines completed the formation, our orders were to drop bombs on Melle railway sidings near Ghent. After crossing the lines we were followed by six German Triplanes who attacked my machine at 15,000 ft when near Ghent. I was rear machine in the formation, observer opened fire on enemy machines whilst I flew machine in order to give him good firing positions. After ten minutes we were cut off and surrounded by Fokker Triplanes and I dropped my bombs at this point and decided to turn for our own lines.
> With my Vickers gun I attacked two enemy machines in rear. After clearing a jam in the gun and fighting again I was

Top left: Hauptmann Oswald Boelcke, the first leader of Jasta 2, August 1916.

Top right: Boelcke's Fokker DIII 352/16.

Middle left: Leutnant Wolfgang Günther in his Albatros DII, with 'G' on the fuselage.

Middle right: Herwarth Philipps, killed in action 1 October 1916.

Bottom: Jasta 2's Albatros DIIs at Lagnicourt 1916.

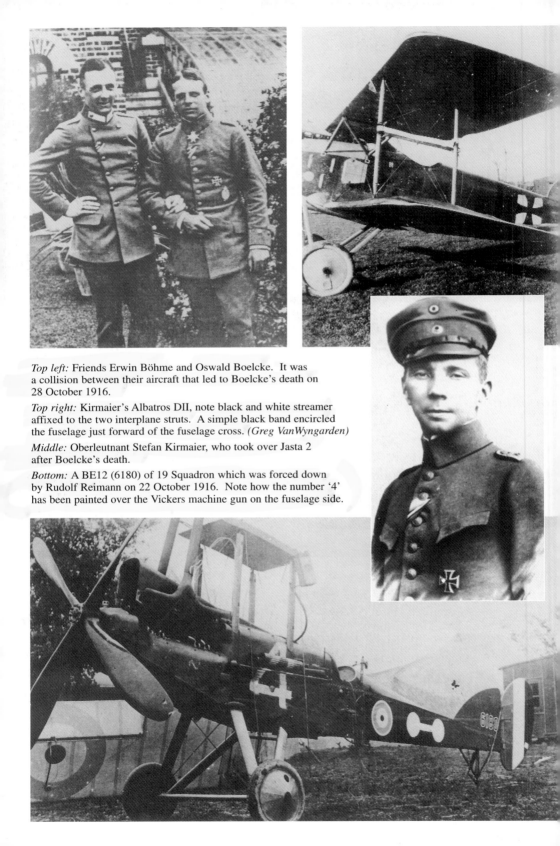

Top left: Friends Erwin Böhme and Oswald Boelcke. It was a collision between their aircraft that led to Boelcke's death on 28 October 1916.

Top right: Kirmaier's Albatros DII, note black and white streamer affixed to the two interplane struts. A simple black band encircled the fuselage just forward of the fuselage cross. *(Greg VanWyngarden)*

Middle: Oberleutnant Stefan Kirmaier, who took over Jasta 2 after Boelcke's death.

Bottom: A BE12 (6180) of 19 Squadron which was forced down by Rudolf Reimann on 22 October 1916. Note how the number '4' has been painted over the Vickers machine gun on the fuselage side.

Top: Kirmaier and his pilots. From left to right: Jürgen Sandel, Max Müller, Manfred von Richthofen, Wolfgang Günther, Kirmaier, Hans Imelmann, Erich König, Otto Höhne, Hans Wortmann and Dieter Collin.

Middle left: Kirmaier, Imelmann, von Richthofen and Wortmann in front of an Albatros DII.

Middle right: Hans Imelmann, killed in action on 23 January 1917.

Bottom: BE2c machine of 12 Squadron, Kirmaier's 5th victory, 21 October 1916. *(Bruce/Leslie collection)*

Top: Karl Büttner's Albatros DII.

Middle: Büttner's Albatros in British markings. It was captured on 16 November 1916.

Bottom left: Rudolf Reimann, an original pilot with the Jasta who died following a crash in January 1917.

Bottom centre: Dieter Collin served with Jasta B from November 1916 to February 1917. Moving to Jasta 22 and later Jasta 56, he was mortally wounded on 13 August 1918.

Bottom right: Prince Friedrich Karl of Prussia of FA(A)258 flew patrols with Jasta Boelcke and was brought down by 32 Squadron on 31 March 1917. He was mortally wounded by Australian troops as he tried to get to the German trenches.

Top left: Hauptmann Franz Walz took over Jasta Boelcke after Kirmaier's death.

Top centre: Albert Dossenbach flew with Jasta B in early 1917 before taking command of Jasta 36.

Top right: Fritz Otto Bernert became commander of Jasta B after Walz left in June 1917. He was one of a number of pilots to wear spectacles in WW1.

Bottom: The downed and captured Albatros flown by Prince Friedrich Karl on 31 March 1917. The 'death's head' insignia referred to his former Hussar Regiment badge.

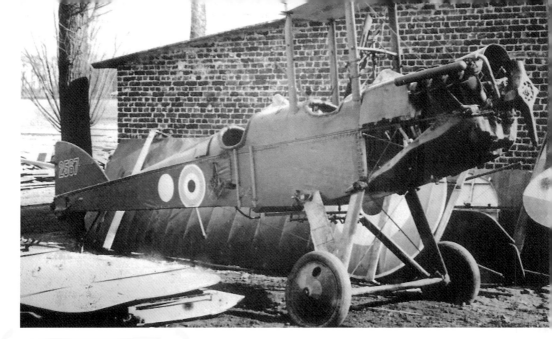

Top: An RE8 of 10 Squadron brought down by Hermann Frommherz on 14 April 1917 for his second victory.

Middle: Jasta B pilots with members of Jasta 12 at Epinoy, April 1917. From left to right: Hauptmann von Seel, Oblt von Tutschek (J/12), Vfw Schorisch (J/12), Otto Bernert, OffStv. Grigo (J/12), Hans Eggers, Vfw Robert Riessinger (J/12), Friedrich Roth (J/12).

Bottom left: Leutnant Albert Munz, centre back, killed in action 20 May 1917.

Bottom right: Werner Voss scored 28 of his 48 victories with Jasta B.

Top: Voss and his highly decorated Albatros DIII.

Middle: An FE2b of 22 Squadron, brought down by Werner Voss for his 33rd victory, 5 June 1917. *(Greg VanWyngarden)*

Bottom: Albatros DIII flown by Georg Noth. It was brought down by 60 Squadron on 19 May 1917, Noth being captured.

Top: Jasta B whilst under Bernert, taken during a visit by Austro-Hungarian pilots in June 1917. Back row, from left to right: Fritz Kempf, Hermann Frommherz, Hans Eggers, Otto Hunzinger, Georg Zeumer, Karl Bodenschatz (OzbV), Gerhard Bassenge, Wilhelm Prien, Johannes Wintrath. Middle, from left to right: Hptm Hervan von Kirchberg (KuK), Bernert, Voss (on a visit from Jasta 5), Hptm Raoul Stojsaviljevic (KuK), Ernst Wendler. Front, from left to right: Ltn Stren, Rolf Fr von Lersner, Franz Pernet.

Bottom left: Erwin Böhme, leader of Jasta B (second from right) during a visit to JGI. From left to right: Otto Brauneck, Manfred von Richthofen, Albrecht von Richthofen (the Red Baron's father), Böhme and Constantin Krefft.

Bottom right: Erwin Böhme, leader of Jasta B. The Blue Max was painted onto this picture after his death.

Top left: Vfw Paul Bäumer first joined Jasta B in June 1917, but then moved to Jasta 5. He returned to Jasta B in August 1917 where he remained for the rest of the war.

Top right: Hermann Frommherz and his 'Blau Maus' Albatros. Its pale blue fuselage had black and white diagonal bands round it and a white tail.

Middle: Gerhard Bassenge with his Albatros DIII. Personal marking was a black and white horizontal band on the varnished fuselage and a broad black band, edged in white. *(Greg VanWyngarden)*

Bottom left: Maximilian von Chelius, killed in action 14 September 1917.

Bottom centre: Max Müller was one of the original Jasta pilots but left to go to Jasta 28w in January 1917. He returned to Jasta B in October and was killed in action on January 9, 1918.

Bottom right: The new commander after Böhme's death was Walter von Bülow-Bothkamp. However, he survived less than a month.

Top: Three stalwarts of Jasta B in front of a striped Albatros DV: Gerhard Bassenge, Fritz Kempf and Hermann Vallendor. *(Greg VanWyngarden)*

Bottom: Jasta B pilots in early 1918: Von Griesheim, Otto Löffler, Karl Gallwitz, Hermann Vallendor, Karl Bolle, Fritz Kempf, Harry von Bülow, Richard Plange, Paul Schröder and Paul Bäumer. *(CCI)*

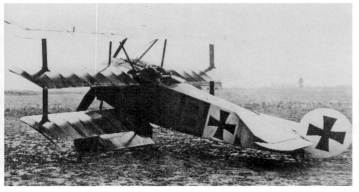

Top right: Karl Bolle, Jasta Boelcke's last wartime commander. Apart from leave he led it from February 1918 to the Armistice.

Middle left: Paul Bäumer in front of the Fokker DV that Jasta B used to convert to the Fokker Dr.I Triplane in the spring of 1918. He was on a visit to his old unit Jasta 5 at Boistrancourt.

Middle right: Fritz Kempf.

Bottom: Bäumer in front of his Fokker Triplane 209/17 which carried a red 'B' just forward of the fuselage cross; early 1918.

Top left: Otto Walter Höhne, another of the originals, returned to command Jasta B in January and February 1918 but did not remain long.

Top centre: Walter's brother Harry also served with Jasta B between January and March 1918.

1

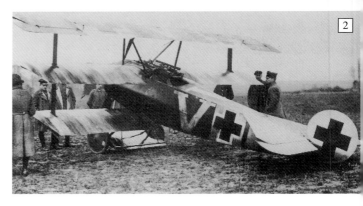

2

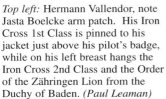

Top left: Hermann Vallendor, note Jasta Boelcke arm patch. His Iron Cross 1st Class is pinned to his jacket just above his pilot's badge, while on his left breast hangs the Iron Cross 2nd Class and the Order of the Zähringen Lion from the Duchy of Baden. *(Paul Leaman)*

Top right: Bäumer also flew Triplane 204/17, seen here in a different paint scheme and with the new Latin crosses which came in the spring of 1918. Black, white and red fuselage band and black wing tips edged in white and red. *(Greg VanWyngarden)*

Middle 1: Karl Gallwitz, with walking stick (second left), in front of his Triplane (possibly 212/17) at Bavichove. This Triplane later saw service with Jastas 36 and 15.

Middle 2: Vallendor's Fokker Triplane – 195/17. The 'V' is repeated on the centre of the top wing.

Bottom: Kempf's Triplane (493/17) with a good view of his name on the top wing and the words 'kennscht mi'noch?' The surfaces of the rear wing and elevators are divided into black and white, Jasta B's markings.

Top: After Papenmeyer's 214/17 was written off by bombing, he used 409/17, which carried a black, white and red fuselage band. He was shot down in this machine on 28 March 1918. *(Papenmeyer album via HAC/UTD)*

Middle 1: Walter Papenmeyer with his Dr.I No. 214/17, and his mechanic, Ziegler. *(Greg VanWyngarden)*

Middle 2: Jasta Boelcke line-up at Marcke, March 1918. Kempf's yellow 'K' is first. Second is Papenmeyer's, and the third machine is Karl Bolle's 413/17.

Bottom left: Bäumer's 204/17. His mechanic is helping to secure his parachute harness that he felt was not worth the while – until he was forced to use it! *(HAC/UTD via Greg VanWyngarden)*

Bottom right: Otto Löffler in front of his Triplane, 190/17, which later served with Jasta 27. *(HAC/UTD via Greg VanWyngarden)*

Top left: Kempf's 'kette'. From left to right: unknown, Papenmeyer, Vallendor, Richard Plange, Paul Schröder, and Kempf. Note the walking sticks, a present from Anthony Fokker. *(Paul Leaman)*

Top right: Paul Schröder, Jasta B.

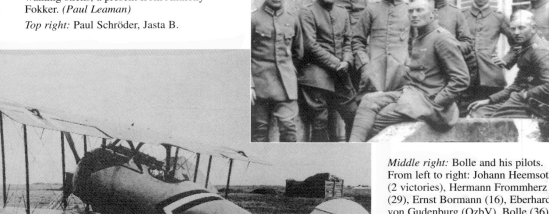

Middle right: Bolle and his pilots. From left to right: Johann Heemsoth (2 victories), Hermann Frommherz (29), Ernst Bormann (16), Eberhard von Gudenburg (OzbV), Bolle (36), Kempf (4), Gefr Mynereck, Alfred Lindenberger (11) and seated right, Hermann Bolle.

Middle left: The Pfalz DVIII which Bäumer tested under combat conditions with Jasta B in May 1918. Note it carries his personal red, white and black fuselage band.

Bottom: From left to right: Alfred Frey, Alfred Lindenberger (11), Erich Löffler (15), Wilhelm Suer, Gefr Mynereck (rear), Gerhard Bassenge (7), von Gudenburg (OzbV), Ernst Bormann (16), Karl Bolle (36), Hermann Frommherz (29), Johann Heemsoth (2).

Top left: Löffler's mechanic with his Fokker DVII. Note the white radiator, black cowling, and the white tail on the other Fokker, Jasta B's markings. *(Greg VanWyngarden)*

Top right: Kurt Jentsch served briefly with Jasta B in the summer of 1918. This picture shows him (right) while serving with FA(A)234 in 1917. He is standing with his observer, Alfred Lindenberger. They both flew together with Jasta B. *(Greg VanWyngarden)*

Middle 1: Karl Bolle's DVII which carried a yellow and white fuselage band, edged in black and white. *(Greg VanWyngarden)*

Middle 2: Karl Bolle (centre) talking to Ernst Udet, leader of Jasta 4. Left is Karl Bodenschatz, the former OzbV of Jasta B before he moved to JGI under Richthofen. *(CCI)*

Bottom: Alfred Lindenberger seated in his yellow and black striped Fokker DVII – (OAW) 4453/18. *(Greg VanWyngarden)*

Above: Jasta B on 16 August 1918. From left to right: Gefr Mynereck, Löffler (15), Fritz Heinz (2), Fritz Hoffmann (1), von Gudenburg (OzbV), Bolle (36), von Griesheim (1), Franz Klausenberg (2), Bassenge (7), Jentsch (7), Lindenberger (11). Heinz was killed in action on 27 September, Hoffmann was killed in action on 29 September, and Jentsch wounded on 4 September.

Below: Bolle in front of his DVII at Nivelles in December 1918; a later machine than depicted earlier. Note different dimensions of fuselage band. *(Greg VanWyngarden)*

Above: Fokkers pictured at the war's end, with an Albatros DVa in the foreground. Lindenberger's yellow and black machine is next in line. *(Greg VanWyngarden)*

Left: Leutnant Paul Bäumer finally received the Blue Max, an award he had worked hard for, it being awarded just days before the war ended.

hit in the side by an explosive bullet which besides fracturing my hip, cut the main petrol pipes and tail adjusting wires. Two enemy Triplanes were seen to go down out of control from the fire of my Vickers gun. The results of observer's shooting are unknown to me as he was taken away immediately we landed.

Engine stopped owing to loss of petrol and we were forced to land near Ghent. Machine was surrounded by German soldiers who lifted me out of the cockpit and a car took me to hospital where I had an operation immediately to remove bullet. Lieutenant Campbell-Martin was taken away to an officer's camp.

Green's report, like so many others who found themselves shot down and prisoners, claims shooting down some of the opposition, and undoubtedly he saw a couple of Fokkers spin away as he opened fire on them. However, Jasta Boelcke suffered no losses in this action.

Mid-afternoon saw Schröder and Vallendor in combat with Sopwith Camels east of Moorslede. Although the former's Camel is noted as coming down inside German lines, once again we have difficulty in identifying the British squadron. Camels of 54 and 65 Squadrons, and from 8, 9 and 10 Naval Squadrons were all in combat this date, but pilots of Jasta 26 appear to have better claims over those lost, so again it might be over-claiming in the heat of action where several pilots decided it was their target that came down. Two Camels were shot down and at least two others shot-up.

On this same day Erwin Klumpp was killed whilst landing on an airfield at Thielt in Belgium, clipping a small hill on his approach.

Things were obviously not going well for the Jasta under Höhne, and he was moved out on the 20th. He did not feel up to the requirements of leading such a famous unit. Yet another leader needed to be found and one must have been already earmarked for the job, as Leutnant Karl Bolle took over the same day as Höhne left. Bolle came in from Jasta 28w – his first command.

Bolle Arrives

Karl Bolle was a Berliner, born in June 1893, so he was now 24. His grandfather had been a famous and enterprising businessman. One winter he was looking at ice flowing along Berlin's Landwehr Canal, and had an idea which blossomed into the North German Ice Works. He was also the first man to ship North Sea fish into Berlin (packed in ice if not actually frozen), which in turn led to the building of the Berlin Spittal Market. Yet his most famous enterprise was a milk restaurant followed by him becoming a milk supplier to the city. By the 1930s he had over 2,600 employees supplying milk to the populace.

With the death of his grandfather, and then his own father when Karl (sometimes spelt Carl) was only 14, the family moved to Wannsee, to the south-west of the capital, on the River Havel, opposite Potsdam. Part of his education was in England, as a university student at Oxford in 1912 where he studied economics, and where his athletic prowess came to the fore too. When the war started he was with the 7th von Seydlitz Kurassier Regiment in France, then in Poland and Courland, but like so many other cavalry men, moved into aviation. By 1916 he was flying with Kamfgeschwader Nr.4, Kampfstaffel 23, where his observer had been the brother of the future Red Baron, Lothar von Richthofen. That October Bolle was badly wounded and was away from the front for the first half of 1917. Transferring to fighters he was posted to Jasta 28w in the summer and between August and January 1918 accounted for five RFC aircraft. He was well thought of, became deputy leader, and was no doubt chosen for his solid approach to air fighting and command.

Bolle had arrived four days after Jasta B had moved its base to Marcke (on the 16th), located just to the south of Courtrai. He not so much arrived as walked over, for Jasta 28 had been at this airfield since January. Werner Voss had operated there with his Jasta 10 the previous summer, although JGI collectively are more usually noted as being at Marckebeke – just over the road. When JGI operated from the Courtrai area Jastas 4 and 11 were at Marckebeke, Jasta 10 at Marcke and Jasta 6 at Bisseghem, just over the River Lys to the north.

Things seem to have taken a while to settle down for the next combat victories did not occur until the 24th and 26th of February. Papenmeyer scored victory number three on the 24th, with an RE8 claim, probably a 4 Squadron aircraft which went down on the British side with its pilot dead, the observer wounded. His report noted:

24 February 1918. Jadgdesgeschwader III. St Julien, 3.45 in the afternoon. Fokker Dr.I 214/17. White, red and black band on the fuselage.
On 24/2/18 at 3.45 in the afternoon at a height of 1,200 metres, I attacked an RE two-seater flying in the direction of Poelkapelle. After a short dogfight, the observer sank down in his seat. The aircraft went into a nosedive. Motor had stopped running. I followed him down to about 100 metres above the ground and saw him crash into a shell crater to the south of St Julien.

Papenmeyer, Leutnant d.R.

Two days later it was Richard Plange who scored, his sixth, a 19 Squadron Spad VII. The British reported that this machine was in combat with a Fokker Triplane, after which the Spad began to glide south-west from Comines. Plange noted his victory as down at Warneton – the pilot killed – both places are adjacent to each other. It is difficult to know for sure if Plange was also flying a Triplane, but his victory was certainly confirmed by the RFC's records. It was also one of the last RFC Spads lost, 19 and 23 Squadrons being in the process of exchanging Spads for the new Sopwith Dolphins.

However, the commander of Jasta 7, Josef Jacobs, also put in a claim for this British Spad, his report noting:

> Got on the tail of a Spad fighter and fired away until I left his machine smoking very heavily. I was informed, the next day, that Jasta Boelcke also had a hand in the combat and that the Spad went down burning.

Plange received credit for the kill. Whether they tossed for it, or it went to arbitration is not known, or perhaps Jacobs, already the victor in a dozen combats let the other man have it. If it was the same machine, the fact that Plange reported it down on fire and Jacobs that it was only smoking, would probably had given Plange the edge.

So ended February. Jasta Boelcke now had a new leader and new aeroplanes, of the type its famous old boy von Richthofen much preferred himself – the Fokker Dr.I Triplane. There were rumours of an offensive in the offing. Things were going to get busy soon.

Chapter Seven
The March Offensive

March 1918

Pilots at the start of March:	Name	Victories
	Ltn Karl Bolle	5
	Vfw Paul Bäumer	18
	Ltn H von Bülow	3
	Ltn Karl Gallwitz	7
	Ltn Friedrich Kempf	3
	Ltn Fritz Krafft	–
	Ltn Otto Löffler	2
	Ltn Wilhelm Papenmeyer	3
	Ltn Richard Plange	3
	Ltn Hermann Vallendor	1
	Ltn Ludwig Vortmann	–
OzbV	Ltn Eberhard Fr von Gudenburg	–

Base: Marcke   Front: 4th Army JGIII

Harry von Bülow left the Jasta on the 11th, returning to his old Jasta 36. He was to gain three more kills and win the Hohenzollern House Order, Knight's Cross with Swords. He was later taken away from the front as he was the only surviving son in order to return to the family estates. In WW2 he held commands in fighter units and is reputed to have claimed victories. He died in 1976 at Bothkamp Castle, Holstein. A pilot who joined the Jasta in either late February or early March was Leutnant Fritz Krafft.

March began drearily slow. Paul Bäumer made the month's first claim on the 9th with a Camel north of Zonnebeke at 11.10 am. He was credited with his 19th victory but again there is no combat loss that appears to fit.

> 9 March 1918. Fokker Dr.I 204/17; black-white-red band on fuselage. Location and Time: 1 km north of Zonnebeke at 11.10 hours.
> I was flying with four other men from the Staffel to the Wytschaete bend, when we saw 3 single-seater flights of 7 aircraft each flying in formation to our front. We attacked the

lower flight at a height of 2,000 metres over Becelaere. First I had a banking fight with a Sopwith from whom I had to break off again. Then I followed three Sopwith single-seaters from the same flight which were flying together. At a height of 1,500 metres I attacked one of these, whereupon he flew towards me. After a short banking fight, I, at a close distance, caused the Sopwith to crash. The Sopwith reared up and then dived down vertically. I followed the falling opponent and saw him run vertically into the ground north of the Zonnebeke-Frezenberg road. The aircraft completely smashed up.

Witnesses: 1. Ltn. Löffler, Jasta Boelcke.
2. L. O. Gruppe, Ypern.

The Camels of 65 Squadron were in a fight with Triplanes at this time and location but did not lose anyone. Captain G M Cox claimed a Fokker, which he said he shot down into a spin, one of its wings folded and then it crashed. This was probably Leutnant Max Naujock of Jasta 36, who died of his injuries in a field hospital, but was the falling Triplane mistaken by Bäumer as 'his' victim? Captain Cox's combat report:

Whilst on offensive patrol between Becelaere and Dadizeele the formation was attacked by several Fokker Triplanes. I saw one of them on the tail of one of our machines. I got into a good position and put a burst of about 50 rounds into him at about 100 yards. The Triplane turned over on its side, stalled and went down in a spin. I watched him spin for about 1,500 feet when one of his planes folded up. Time 10.10 am.

Bäumer's victory was his first since the previous December and it is strange that a prolific scorer should go through such a lean period. It has been suggested that being a non-commissioned officer and the highest living scorer (18 kills) in the Jasta, that he was not allowed to fly as it should not be that an NCO be the highest scorer. This seems ridiculous, but if true, extraordinary. And if indeed true, common sense soon prevailed and he was once more back on the battle roster.

He had, nevertheless, fallen in love with the new Triplane fighter. His Dr.I at this time carried additional iron crosses on the top surfaces of the lower wing and on the upper surface of the rear fuselage and wing. This is supposed to be because Bäumer feared that his machine might be mistaken for a Sopwith Triplane and shot down by another German airman. While this sounds quite feasible it should be remembered that the Sopwith Triplane had been out of front-line service since the end of October 1917 – five months earlier!

Karl Bolle called the pilots to his office on the 12th and informed them that the Staffel was being transferred to the vicinity of the 17th Army area in a couple of days. The next day, the 13th, the airfield was raided by the RFC as if bidding them a fond farewell. Bombers made attacks on a number of German airfields, Jasta B having some Triplanes damaged and Wilhelm Papenmeyer's 214/17 had to be written off. In all six aircraft were casualties while five personnel were killed and 11 others wounded. Those who died are named as:

> Flieger Vinzent Starzynsky from Posen, aged 30.
> Unteroffizier August Schmidt from Königshütte, aged 24.
> Gefreiter Ferdinand Niemann from Minden, aged 22.
> Flieger Georg Kabus from Haselhorst, aged 20.
> Flieger Arnold Nieraad from Gütersloh, aged 18.

* * *

JGIII moved south on the 15th in readiness for the battle ahead. Jasta B moved to Erchin, south-east of Douai, along with Jastas 26 and 36 (Jasta 27 remaining at Marckebecke). They were now operating on the German 17th Army Front but were told not to engage in dogfights so as to conserve strength for the coming battle.

The big German offensive began on 21 March – Operation Michael. This was also known by the Germans as the Great Battle, the 'Kaiserschlacht'. While it had been expected by the Allies to happen sometime and somewhere, it caught them by surprise and before they had a chance to check the assault, the Allied line had been pushed back severely; in fact the biggest loss of ground since the early days of the war.

Aircraft of the Royal Flying Corps and Royal Naval Air Service were constantly in the air, attempting to stem the tide of German field-grey uniformed troops that appeared unstoppable. The main thrust centred along a front south from Arras in the north to La Fère in the south. By the 23rd the centre of the advance line had reached Péronne and Ham and three days later it had passed Albert, Thiepval, Lihons and Roye. Then south of the Somme it moved to Moreuil, Grivesnes and Montdidier on the French front, while at the centre, Amiens was under direct threat.

The British and French retreated. Allied airfields were hastily abandoned yet all the while the RFC and RNAS maintained an almost round the clock attack on ground targets over the whole front.

Bäumer scored again on the 23rd, another Camel, right on the front-line south-east of St Léger at 13.30. 46 Squadron were in a fight and one Camel came down near Lagnicourt while another returned shot-up but did not fall. Bongartz of Jasta 36 had the better claim. In the afternoon, Bäumer returned with two more claims, both RE8 observation machines, one down north of Tilloy at 15.45, the second north of Beugnâtre half an hour later. Bäumer's combat reports:

23 March 1918. Fokker Dr.I. Location and Time: South-east St Léger around 13.00 hours.

I took off with my Staffel and got separated from them during an aerial battle. Then I sighted Staffel 36 flying in the direction of Arras, with which I joined up. Then we turned towards the south and sighted 5 Sopwith single-seaters which the flight leader of Staffel 36, as the first, attacked. I the second one, attacked a Sopwith at 2,000 metres height, and had a banking fight down to 1,000 metres. At this height, a Triplane from 36 came vertically underneath and mixed itself into the fight. After two further bursts from both MGs, the opponent went down vertically and dashed to pieces on the ground south-east of St Léger.

Location and Time: North of Tilloy at 15.45 hours and north of Beugnâtre at 16.15 hours.

I took off 15 minutes later than my Staffel because of a defective motor and flew in the direction of Arras. In the haze beneath me I suddenly sighted at 800 metres height an enemy working [Corps] aeroplane RE[8]. I attacked the RE, coming from out of the sun and placed myself under his tail. The opponent did not give me the chance to shoot at him and attempted to escape in the direction of Arras. I kept behind him and shot at him from a short distance. The aeroplane flew smoking, its left wing hit the ground and [the RE] completely smashed up.

Then I flew, being heavily shot at by flak, in a south-easterly direction and looked for my Staffel. Over Bapaume I spotted a second RE and attacked it at a height of 1,000 metres. When he saw me, he banked towards me, shooting, upon which I flew under him and placed myself behind him. After a few shots, the opponent went down burning. I saw the wreckage hit the ground, still burning, to the north of Beugnâtre. No other German aircraft participated in this aerial battle.

There were plenty of observation craft over the battle areas, on artillery observation missions, contact patrols and even photographic sorties. Several were shot-up and returned with damage and or wounded crew members, but one 5 Squadron machine was shot about over Bois Vilain which was probably one of the German ace's targets, but they got back unwounded, although damaged. This NCO was certainly having a charmed life as far as claiming victories was concerned – and having them confirmed. It did not hurt his reputation to receive a telegram from von Hoeppner a few days later, congratulating him on his three kills on the 23rd. His score had now reached 22. It is also recorded that these actions brought Jasta Boelcke's total victories to 200, although a study of its claims puts the 200 total a month earlier. Nevertheless, it was still a substantial total.

200 Victories
Despite the reference to Bäumer having achieved the Jasta's 200th kill at this time, it appears that this total was actually reached at the end of February, or certainly by 9 March. Possible confirmation of this comes from a letter by Bolle to Boelcke's father dated 10 March. While this does not specifically refer to the Jasta's total, there was obviously some kind of celebration at this time, and something of a party, with several distinguished guests invited. The letter read:

Airfield, 10.III.18

Esteemed Professor,
Today, the special day of Jagdstaffel Boelcke, we remember especially the parents of our most distinguished Master, and promise again to follow his example and to hold his name in high esteem.

Bolle,
Leutnant and Leader of
Jagdstaffel Boelcke.

The letter was also signed by several pilots and guests, including Kempf, Plange, Vallendor, Papenmeyer, Bäumer, Höhne, Harry von Bülow, Gallwitz, Schröder, and guests such as von Richthofen, Helmut Dilthey of Jasta 27, Heinrich Bongartz of Jasta 36, and Prince Rupprecht.

* * *

On the 26th Richard Plange shot down a Dolphin of 19 Squadron, caught while its pilot was ground strafing. Unused to seeing the new Sopwith design German pilots began calling them 'Martinsydes', although the Martinsyde machines had long disappeared from the front. They were also apt to confuse Dolphins with Bristol F2b Fighters, simply because both machines had twin bays of wing struts, forgetting the fact that one was a single-seater, the other a two-seater. The Red Baron fell into that trap on 27 March, claiming a Bristol which in fact was a Dolphin.

Plange was getting into his stride now, gaining two more victories the next day, while Gallwitz got his eighth. Gallwitz sent down a Bristol Fighter south of Albert over the front-line. There was a good deal of confused fighting this day, and claims were far from clear cut. However, there seems little doubt that Gallwitz brought down the Bristol crewed by Captain K R Kirkham MC and Captain J H Hedley CdeG, who both ended their busy morning by travelling to a prison camp.

Plange reported shooting down an RE8 and an SE5a in the same general area during the afternoon. The RE came from 16 Squadron on what was described as a 'Special Mission' which could have been anything but was more than likely a contact patrol. In other words, find the extent of the German advance by finding their soldiers – and expect to be fired upon!

The combat with the SE5s was against 56 Squadron. Only one was lost but Hermann Vallendor was also in the fight and claimed an SE5 too. No doubt Jasta B got the one lost, but which pilot? 56 had been attacked by seven Triplanes and the lost SE had gone down in flames almost immediately. The British fighters scattered and had a brief scrap but they suffered no further loss nor made any claims against the German machines.

Leutnant Papenmeyer claimed his fourth victory on 28 March, an RE8 down at Arleux-en-Gohelle, just on the German side. The ground fighting was still severe with the German First and Third Armies launching a fresh series of assaults. British observation machines were out in force and Papenmeyer probably got the one lost by 5 Squadron mid-morning. However, he failed to return, lost in Fokker Dr.I 409/17 near Acheville.

His attack upon the RE8 occurred at 10.20 am, at 800 metres, in the vicinity of Thelus-Bailleul. The two-seater broke up in the air before it crashed. It appears, however, that the observer got in a telling burst in his last moments and hit Papenmeyer. If it was the 5 Squadron RE8, its crew were Second Lieutenant P W Woodhouse and Lieutenant S Collier MC.

Several days later, von Gudenburg was sent forward to pick up Papenmeyer's body. Apparently he had managed to get his Triplane down in the front-lines despite his wound. He got clear of the machine and dived into a shell-hole or a trench where he bled to death. German troops discovered his body a couple of days later. He had a brother Fritz, also a pilot, and there was a move to have him transferred to Jasta B, but for some time efforts failed.

April 1918

Pilots at the start of April:		Name	Victories
		Ltn Karl Bolle	5
		Vfw Paul Bäumer	22
		Ltn Karl Gallwitz	8
		Ltn Friedrich Kempf	3
		Ltn Fritz Krafft	–
		Ltn Richard Plange	5
		Ltn Hermann Vallendor	2
		Ltn Ludwig Vortmann	–
	OzbV	Ltn Eberhard Fr von Gudenburg	–

Base: Erchin   Front: 17th Army JGIII

The Jasta was now down to just eight pilots and further victories eluded the unit for the first three weeks of April. Paul Bäumer was commissioned on the 10th, and on the 15th, JGIII moved back to the 4th Army Front, Jasta B operating from Halluin-Ost on the south-east side of Menin, together with the rest of the Jagdgeschwader.

The German air service would now be fighting the Royal Air Force, the Royal Flying Corps and the Royal Naval Air Service, as they had merged on 1 April. Not that it would make any great difference for either side. Certainly the former RNAS boys tried to continue much as they had done previously and only time gradually changed that.

On 21 April Gallwitz shot down a Camel west of Bailleul, inside German lines. Two Camels of 54 Squadron were lost this date but these were claimed by Jasta 7, although a good two hours earlier. The time favours the Gallwitz combat claim, but nobody else in Jasta B claimed the other Camel. However, one has to wonder if his opponent had not been the Australian ace, Captain R A 'Bob' Little DSO and Bar, DSC and Bar, of 203 Squadron. He was forced down west of Bailleul at 16.30 British time and while there is a slight time difference the locality checks out. By this time Little had nearly 40 victories flying with the RNAS, mainly with 8 Naval. He was to die of wounds following a night encounter with a Gotha bomber in May.

The big news of the day however, was the loss of Germany's premier fighter ace, Manfred von Richthofen. During a combat with Camels of 209 Squadron he chased one Camel too far and too long behind the Allied lines, with one gun jammed and the other firing only intermittently. By the time he realised he was not acting in his usual rational way, it was too late and he was hit low down by machine-gun fire and, mortally wounded, force-landed on top of the Morlancourt Ridge, east of Amiens. Moments after coming down he succumbed to his wound. Jasta Boelcke mourned the loss of their most famous old boy who had exactly doubled the score achieved by the old master Boelcke himself.

Four days later Bolle secured his first kill since joining Jasta B. He downed a Camel of 73 Squadron south-east of Wulverghem, on the German side, for his sixth victory. The Camels had been engaged by Triplanes east of Messines. This was above the fighting – the renewed fighting – for nearby Kemmel Ridge, a key position on this sector of the front. It was being held by mainly French troops but thirteen German divisions captured the position that afternoon.

The Jasta's third and last victory of the month came on the 29th, Richard Plange claiming a Spad during the evening, which he saw go down into the Allied lines over Westoutre. There were in fact no RAF Spad losses simply because there were none in France, the two British Spad units having changed their equipment to Dolphins. Therefore, if it was indeed a Spad it must have been a French-flown machine – possibly the loss reported by Escadrille Spa 68.

A loss which occurred on the 29th involved Ludwig Vortmann who was shot down during a combat with SE5s north-west of Kemmel Ridge.

This appears to have been a fight with 74 Squadron south of Dickebusch Lake shortly before midday. Captain C B Glynn saw a Triplane approaching him from behind and trying to stay above, but Glynn zoomed upwards, turned towards the German and opened up with a long burst from his Vickers gun and a short burst from his wing-mounted Lewis gun. Moments later, Captain E Mannock and Lieutenant H E Dolan saw the Fokker dive vertically into the ground. In this scrap were fighters of Jasta 36 and its leader Heinrich Bongartz was hit and wounded in the left arm (Dr.I 575/17). Mannock and Dolan each claimed enemy aircraft shot down. Bongartz, who had achieved 33 victories, had been slightly wounded twice before in recent weeks, but this injury which included a damaged left eye – which he later lost – put him out of the war. Of interest are the three combat reports made out by the pilots of 74 Squadron:

> Capt E Mannock. 29 April 1918. 11.40 am. 5,000 ft. Line Patrol. S of Dickebusch Lake.
> Strange type single-seater. Very long fuselage, swept back wing tips, very pronounced mackerel shaped tail.
> Engaged formation of approx 10 EA south of Dickebusch Lake. Fired approx 40 rounds at close range from front, when EA burst into flames and was destroyed.
> This EA was observed to flame and descend in pieces by Captain Glynn and Lt Dolan.

> Captain C B Glynn. 29 April 1918. Triplane – silver and green.
> I was flying on Captain Mannock's left when I saw EA approaching from my left rear, trying to get height on me. I zoomed upwards and turned towards him, flying straight at EA which flew end on at me. Fired a good burst from Vickers and short burst from Lewis Gun.
> This Triplane was seen a few seconds afterwards by Captain Mannock and Lt Dolan to dive almost vertically into the ground just south of the scene of engagement.

> Lieutenant H E Dolan. 29 April 1918. Albatros Scout, green and silver markings.
> Dived on EA patrol of about 10 machines with Patrol Leader and engaged Albatros Scout.
> Fired about 50 rounds at him from directly behind at a range of about 20 yards, when EA was seen to break to pieces and fall to earth.
> This machine was observed to break up in the air by Captains Mannock MC and Glynn, who were in the same patrol.

Mannock appears to have shot down Vortmann, who, considering Mannock's description of the aeroplane, must have been flying Jasta B's Fokker DV conversion machine, but just why he was flying this operationally is unclear, unless the Jasta was low on serviceable machines. Bongartz of Jasta 36 was in a Triplane (575/17) so Glynn got him. It was his first victory, but he would claim seven more before the war ended. Who or what Dolan shot down is also unclear and one has to wonder if his claim was confused with Mannock's Fokker DV as the DV was a biplane while the other machines were Triplanes, the difference being obvious.

The loss of Bongartz led to a change within Jasta 36, for his place as acting Staffelführer was taken by Richard Plange on the 30th. He continued as acting leader until 16 May, the date his appointment was confirmed. Three days later, on the 19th, he was killed attacking an AWFK8 of 10 Squadron, the same unit that had shot down Erwin Böhme back in November. This time the crew was Lieutenants W Hughes and F C Peacock, Plange's Fokker Triplane (203/17) falling near Zillebeke, in Allied lines.[1] The crashed machine was given the RAF serial G/2Bde/10. British serial numbers had now changed, with the advent of the Royal Air Force, from a straightforward numerical number prefixed with 'G'. The new numbering identified the RAF Brigade area in which the aircraft fell. Plange's crashed Dr.I was now referred to as the tenth German aircraft to fall in Allied lines in the area covered by 2 Brigade RAF. He had not improved on his score of seven before his death. Also out of the war this month was Karl Gallwitz, injured in a crash.

May 1918

Pilots at the start of May:	Name	Victories
	Ltn Karl Bolle	6
	Ltn Paul Bäumer	22
	Ltn Friedrich Kempf	3
	Ltn Fritz Krafft	–
	Ltn Hermann Vallendor	2
OzbV	Ltn Eberhard Fr von Gudenburg	–

Base: Halluin   Front: 4th Army JGIII

The Jasta obviously needed some replacement pilots, and these started to arrive during May. Hermann Frommherz returned from his training post on the 18th and his experience and his recent period away galvanised him into achieving great things in the days ahead, although not all with Jasta

---

[1] The serial number of this Dr.I has been variously given as 546/17 and 453/17 but Paul Leaman, a specialist on everything to do with the Fokker Triplane, confirms it as being 203/17. 546/17 was a Jasta 4 machine, brought down on 16 May, while 453/17 was confused with the engine number – 2453.

B. There was also a new ribbon on his chest for on Christmas Eve 1917, the Senate of the City of Lübeck had awarded Frommherz its Hanseatic Cross, as mentioned earlier.

Leutnants Johann Heemsoth and Wilhelm Suer were posted in – both as far as is known – fresh from Jastaschule. Leutnant Ernst Bormann was posted in from Jasta 12 after a very brief stay there. Bormann came from Kirchbreck, near Holzminden, and was born in November 1897. In 1915 he had become an officer cadet with a reserve infantry regiment but by 1917 he had transferred to aviation. At the start of 1918 he was sent to FA42 but on 4 May he got his wish to fly fighters, being sent to Jasta B. He would make his mark.

The fourth arrival, on the 9th, was Leutnant Alfred Lindenberger, an experienced aviator who had achieved three victories over French Spads as an observer with FA234 in 1917. For two of his claims he had had as his pilot Vizefeldwebel Kurt Jentsch who we shall meet briefly in a future chapter. In the infantry, Lindenberger had won the Würrtemberg Silver Military Merit Medal in 1915, and for his work with FA(A)234, he received the Gold Military Merit Medal on 4 January 1918. Lindenberger came from Stuttgart, born on 22 April 1897, so was just past his 21st birthday.

If Bolle had been biding his time, he certainly ended a lean period for himself and his unit in May. On the 3rd he claimed a double, a Camel and a DH9 bomber. The Camel came from 73 Squadron at 13.45 German time, its pilot being captured, followed at 14.10 by the bomber – from 98 Squadron. The DeHavilland began to tear apart as it fell then burst into flames, the observer being seen to jump or fall from the burning wreckage.

On the 8th Bolle scored another double, an SE5a in the morning, then he and Kempf claimed a Camel each in the afternoon. The SE came from 1 Squadron, its wounded pilot ending up a prisoner. The Camels were from 43 Squadron although they only recorded one loss. Both Germans claimed west of Steenwerck but Bolle's may have been the only one seen to come down inside German lines, otherwise it was the usual story of two pilots seeing the same opponent go down and crash.

Bolle got his eleventh victory on the 19th, another DH9, this time from 206 Squadron, south-west of Zonnebeke, at 08.20 am. 206 were to lose four bombers during this day, two in this morning raid, two in a late afternoon attack. Bolle in his history of Jasta B recorded an action against RAF bombers which is of interest and may have referred to this day:

> Daily, and even several times during the same day, the Englishmen had become used to attacking Kortrijk [Courtrai] with bombs. These were the new DeHavilland 9 biplanes which, especially in speed, were superior to our Fokker Triplanes. Just such a squadron of nine aircraft were caught within the Ypres Salient one morning as they were on

their return flight by seven aircraft from my Staffel, who were approaching the opponents from the side, but now flew into the squadron from behind. I had targeted the leader's aircraft, flying ahead and in the middle but I, however, left my course upon my Staffel's attack towards the front.

The opponent, flying cleverly, let me go ahead and plunge into the wedge of his formation and had me completely surrounded before my comrades could be there. The concentrated fire from 18 machine guns totally covered my machine so that I had to bid farewell downwards – after I could only get off a brief burst at the enemy lead aircraft – with a shot-up tank, a shot-up engine and a quite shredded aircraft. I believe, though, that I noticed this aircraft – at the moment in which I let myself spin – had begun to smoke. At the same time, the Staffel's dogfight against the English squadron began.

A short time after [I had landed at base] (I had, in the meantime, counted 42 hits on my machine), they also landed smoothly. From the reports, it turned out that several English aircraft must have raced off hotly along with the lead aircraft, a further two others had recognisably 'indicated' – i.e.: showed signs of damage/smoking – another one had passed by burning as well. Investigations by ground-based observers provided no clear picture. It was indeed a dogfight and it was observed from far away as well that the aircraft which we attacked had smoked heavily, but a crash was not able to be determined. Thus our efforts were apparently in vain. Ours was the firm intention to do everything better the next time and that was the end of the matter.

A few days later a single DH9 was shot down by flak south of Kemmel and its unwounded crew captured. During questioning, they asked about a universally feared German Triplane Staffel whose markings they exactly described, and reported that an English squadron to which this (captured) crew had belonged had withstood a hard aerial engagement with these Triplanes a few days earlier on a return flight from Kortrijk. The nine aircraft from this squadron had in fact just reached the lines above their own territory but had lost five of them with their crews in crash-landings, some of them dead, some of them badly wounded. Thus our work of a few days previously was indeed not totally in vain, even though these opponents' losses could not be counted among the Staffel's number of victories.

The French Front

Jasta Boelcke moved bases yet again on the 21st, it and JGIII heading for the 7th Army Front, with everyone crowding onto Vivaise airfield north-west of Laon, on the French Front. This was the first time Jasta B had been opposite the French and the 'Circus' had moved south in order to help support the German offensive on the Aisne, due to commence on the 27th (actually the third Battle of the Aisne). It would last until the first week of June.

Bolle bagged a French Spad on the 29th, two days into the battle. It is believed the pilot was Caporal Clarence Shoninger of Escadrille Spa 99, who was brought down and taken prisoner near Fismes. This day also saw Paul Bäumer injuring himself in a crash, whilst returning to the airfield late in the evening. It would take him away from the fighting till September. He had gone off the boil somewhat, not having added to his 22 victories for two months.

What happened to Bäumer was just a simple accident caused by an error of judgement. Today it would be termed pilot error. He had flown out to make the most of the remaining hour of daylight to help familiarise himself with the new front they were to operate over. At around 22.30 he returned by which time it was nearly dark and coming into land on a new and unfamiliar landing area he failed to judge his height correctly in the gloom and also came in too fast. He crashed. As his comrades reached him they found him still alive but with a complicated fracture of the lower jaw. He was rushed to Feld-Lazarett Nr.602 and on 12 June he was moved to a hospital in Düsseldorf. He would not return until mid-September.

On the last day of the month, Lindenberger claimed his first kill as a fighter pilot, he and newcomer Ernst Bormann both knocked down Bréguet XIV bombers, although the latter pilot's claim was not upheld as it had landed just behind the front-lines and was not seen to be destroyed. Even Lindenberger's claim was not immediately confirmed, and by the time it was he had secured another victory.[2] As can be imagined, the air over the battle zone was full of aeroplanes and the French suffered heavy casualties, so it is impossible to be certain of who got who. A number of Bréguet bombers were shot down during the day, but there is also the question of positive identification. Bréguets could easily be mistaken for Salmson 2A2 aircraft, as well as Spad S11 two-seaters. Later, after the Americans began to arrive and support the French, they used Salmsons too, as well as borrowed DH4s, which also added to the confusion with two-seater claims on occasions.

---

[2] In this particular case, Lindenberger's 4th victory was actually recorded as his 5th due to a late confirmation, whereas his next claim on 1 June (his 5th in date order) actually became his 4th.

June 1918

Pilots at the start of June:	Name	Victories
	Ltn Karl Bolle	11
	Ltn Ernst Bormann	–
	Ltn Hermann Frommherz	2
	Ltn Johann Heemsoth	–
	Ltn Friedrich Kempf	4
	Ltn Alfred Lindenberger	4
	Ltn Otto Löffler	2
	Ltn Wilhelm Suer	–
	Ltn Hermann Vallendor	2
OzbV	Ltn Eberhard Fr von Gudenburg	–

Base: Vivaise   Front: 7th Army JGIII

The only personnel movement in June was the arrival of Leutnant Alfred Frey. His stay was short, as he was posted out in July.

While on the French Front, Bolle was later to record that the Gruppe found themselves opposed in the air by mainly second-class French escadrilles that exhibited a decidedly less aggressive posture; a sort of live-and-let-live attitude. However, this changed in the second half of June with the arrival of more forceful escadrilles on their sectors, including the elite Division Aérienne (Escadre de Combat No.1 and Escadre de Combat No.2) as well as some veteran RAF squadrons. It was followed early in July by the arrival of the four aero squadrons of the US 1st Pursuit Group.

Alfred Lindenberger bagged his second kill with the Jasta on the first day of June, another Bréguet XIV, inside German lines at Priez. Again the losses were numerous so it is not possible to surmise which unit it came from. Leutnant Heemsoth claimed his first victory the next day, another Bréguet, again in German lines.

Bolle and Frommherz shot down Spads on the third. This was Frommherz's third victory and he was surely thankful to add to his score. His victories had been way back in April 1917. Bolle got the next two, a Bréguet on the 4th, followed by a Spad on the 9th, and in the same action Frommherz got another for his fourth.

By the 9th, however, the Gruppe had moved again, this time to Mont de Soissons Ferme three days earlier (7th Army), located just to the east of Soissons itself. Having settled in, Bolle made his total 15 on 14 June with another Bréguet. Two days later, on the 16th, the Jasta claimed three DH9 bombers, although on the face of it there appears to be a distance problem with this.

Being based just east of Soissons, it is difficult to reconcile the action and the locations, for the claims were recorded down south of Roye and at Bus-la-Mésière. These areas are 50 kilometres or so from the airfield, but indications are that they engaged DeHavilland bombers from 27

Squadron mid-morning. Three were certainly shot down, one in flames, and a fourth scraped home with a wounded pilot and a dead observer. Pilots of Jasta 5 and Jasta 15 also appear to have edged into the action and made claims too. As the time of the action as far as Jasta B is concerned has not been confirmed, there is also the possibility that two DH9s of 103 Squadron may have been involved during a raid on Roye, one crew being brought down and captured, another lost with its crew, but this might have been caused by AA fire. Nevertheless, Bolle had his 16th victory while Heemsoth and Suer were credited with their second and first kills.

The Jasta also began to attack ground targets. On the 18th it strafed American troops which as Bolle described were 'halted and dashed apart.'

Bolle finished up the month with two more victories, a Bréguet on the 24th, and a Spad in the front-lines on the 28th. Also in June, on the 7th, Otto Löffler received the Baden Order of the Zähringen Lion.

July 1918

Pilots at the start of July:

	Name	Victories
	Ltn Karl Bolle	18
	Ltn Ernst Bormann	–
	Ltn Alfred Frey	–
	Ltn Hermann Frommherz	4
	Ltn Friedrich Kempf	4
	Ltn Alfred Lindenberger	5
	Ltn Otto Löffler	2
	Ltn Wilhelm Suer	1
	Ltn Hermann Vallendor	2
OzbV	Ltn Eberhard Fr von Gudenburg	–

Base: Mont de Soissons Ferme   Front: 7th Army JGIII

Movements this month were the return of Gerhard Bassenge having recovered from his wound of the previous November, and the arrival of Leutnant Hermann Bolle, younger brother of Karl. Hermann Frommherz was posted to Jasta 27 on the 29th to take command.

JGIII still consisted of Jastas B, 26, 27 and 36, and Frommherz was moved across to Jasta 27 following the promotion of its former Staffelführer, Hermann Göring, to take command of JGI. Wilhelm Reinhard had taken over leadership of JGI after von Richthofen's death, but he had been killed testing a new fighter aircraft in Berlin. It was a requirement that only non-reserve officers could command a Jagdgeschwader, and Göring was a regular army officer.

Hermann Frommherz, after his delayed start in the scoring stakes, was about to blossom. He would leave Jasta B with a score standing at ten, the last six being scored during this month of July.

Ernst Bormann finally got his first confirmed victory on 3 July, a Spad down at Noroy on the German side. It is understood his victim was

Lieutenant Comte Sanche de Gramont de Coigny, commanding officer of Escadrille N471/Camp Retranche de Paris (Paris Defence Group). Bolle and Frommherz claimed two Nieuports on the 5th, both falling in a combat above Courchamps. Both were American-flown machines.

These latter two kills were the first recorded by Jasta B against the American Expeditionary Force. They were Nieuport 28 single-seaters, the only Nieuport type not used by the French, but instead given to the new American fighter squadrons which had started to arrive earlier in the year without aircraft. These two came from the US 95th Aero Squadron, both pilots being brought down inside German territory, one killed and one taken into captivity. Their names were First Lieutenants Sidney P Thompson, from Ithaca, New York, and Carlyle Rhodes, from Indiana, operating under the control of the French VI° Armée. In his semi-official history of the 95th Aero, Harold Buckley (himself an ace with the 95th) wrote in his book *Squadron 95*:

> On the fifth of July we began our active work again and immediately discovered that we had landed in a hornet's nest of Fokkers with death-dealing stings of lead. First to test the mettle of our new opponents were Mitchell, Heinrichs, Rhodes and Thompson, who hopped off early in the morning and ran into a bunch of red-nosed single-seaters just back of Château-Thierry. Poor Thompson was making his first patrol and didn't have a chance. He went down in flames with the first burst of the enemy guns. The other three put up a terrible fight against odds of two to one. Rhodes went down and Mitchell and Heinrichs brought down one of the Germans which was seen to crash and was confirmed that very day. By breakfast time they were back at the airdrome with their ships looking like sieves and a lurid tale for the rest of us.
>
> One dead German, Sid Thompson down in flames, Rhodes gone, all before breakfast on the morning of our first day – disquieting was not the word.

Jasta Boelcke did not suffer a casualty in this action, so in the heat of combat the other two Americans had undoubtedly seen one of their comrades hitting the ground, a far from rare occurrence.

Ten days later, the 15th, the final German offensive on the River Marne began – which was also the last offensive by the German army in the war. It broke against the French army around Reims, with the RAF providing air support and co-operation, with its airmen edging down towards the south over the more northerly French sectors. Jasta B was also flying in support for the German army, Bolle and Frommherz again scoring a victory each.

Frommherz scored first with another Nieuport 28 near Château-

Thierry although it fell into the French lines. Bolle's victory was over a Sopwith Camel, timed at 14.30 pm inside German territory at Dormans. Frommherz's target was again from the 95th Aero, First Lieutenant John L Mitchell being severely shot-up, but he got down. Harold Buckley again:

> Mitchell, Wooley and Richards had a run-in with three Fokker Triplanes, the last we ever saw. This was most fortunate according to Wooley who said they could climb like a rocket and turn inside of a dime. Mitchell's ship was so badly shot-up in this fracas that it had to be condemned.

Bolle might have shot down a 43 Squadron machine but witnesses who saw the fight reported the RAF pilot in action with five Pfalz Scouts. 54 Squadron on the other hand lost two Camels, one of which fell to JGIII's Jasta 36, which suggests 54 Squadron were more involved with Jasta B.

Two DH9 bombers were claimed on the 16th, one each to Bolle and Bormann, one over Soilly and the other north-east of Soilly. They are noted as down in German territory but it is difficult to see which units they came from. Records are lacking in times, which does not help either. There were several DH9 squadrons operating which suffered casualties, but the only ones which failed to return were one from 49 Squadron during an attack on a bridge across the Marne, and a 98 Squadron aircraft seen attacked by enemy fighters south of Soilly which went down in a spin at 16.40 British time. It doesn't help either that Jasta records say its pilots downed three DH9s on the 17th, but there were no actions against DeHavilland aircraft on the 17th.

Frommherz is noted as claiming the third DH9 on the 17th, or was his a lone claim, of a type unknown? Unless of course all three victories were over DH9s on the 16th, and Frommherz got the date wrong, and one of the lost bombers either did not come down inside German territory, or was so close to the front-line as to suggest it did. It looks favourite to say the actions were against a variety of DH9s on the 16th and three were believed to have come down, two at least well inside German territory.

To Vauxcère

Jagdesgeschwader Nr.III began to move to Vauxcère on the 18th, Jasta B moving first followed by the other three Jastas the next day. Vauxcère was just a few kilometres to the east, just north-west of Fismes, situated midway between Soissons to the west and Reims to the east. Unlike actions further north, on the British sectors, where German airmen found the lines to the west, JGIII generally flew due south towards the French lines.

Whether it was before or after the move is not certain, but Jasta B netted two more victories on the 18th, both by Bolle, a Bréguet and a Spad. The French air service were certainly taking a beating during this offensive and any number of Bréguets were being brought down, shot-up, or returning with wounded men aboard. Bolle's Spad victim looks like Lieutenant Pierre Daire of Spa 159 who went missing this date. This day saw Bolle's brother Hermann wounded whilst he was attacking a Bréguet, and put out of the war.

Bolle scored again on the 22nd, at 19.10 in the evening, this time a Camel over Coincy on the German side. The fight was with 73 Squadron, Bolle knocking down Lieutenant W S G Kidder, who was wounded and made a prisoner.

The air war was becoming desperate. The sky seemed full of British, French and American aircraft and kills rarely came in large clumps. Frommherz got his eighth victory on the 24th, a Spad XIII down at Acy, a machine from Escadrille Spa 83, flown by Maréchal-des-Logis (Sgt) André Conraux, who became a prisoner.

However, on the evening of the 25th, the Jasta shot down three Sopwith Camels in a single action above Fère-en-Tardenois, well to the south-east of Soissons. The luckless unit was 43 Squadron RAF. When the battle ended, Bolle had secured his 26th victory, Frommherz his ninth and Bassenge his third. 43 Squadron's Record Book gives us the story from their viewpoint:

> Offensive Patrol led by Captain C F King MC DFC; 5.45 – 7.55 pm. Six Camels – King, Lieutenants N Wilson, F S Coghill, R E Meredith, R S Rucker and H M Jacques.
> Visibility good. Clouds from 6,000 to 10,000 feet. Patrol co-operated with bombers. When near objective, patrol saw returning bombers escorted by Camels followed and being attacked by about 20 Fokker biplanes. Patrol dived on EA. Lt Rucker fired a few rounds into one and just at that moment he saw four or five of the EA climb in order to get over the bombers. He also went up and joined two other Camels (not 43 Squadron). All three were then attacked by Huns overhead. Lt Rucker's guns having jammed previously (extractor top broken) he was obliged to make off west alone. He fired 40 rounds in all. Captain C F King reports that he dived on a number of Fokker biplanes firing 20 rounds when his gun jammed, and having then rectified it, he, along with Lt Jacques, dived on three Fokker biplanes which were attacking a Camel. Three other EA came down and joined forces with the others and as soon as they came down, Captain King fired on the leader and the other two separated. Captain King then continued going down on the first three, and considers that the Camel got away. Subsequent to this he had a long fight with a Fokker biplane, which came down suddenly on his tail.
> Finally, after firing some shots at Captain King, EA zoomed up. Captain King fired 140 rounds in all. In the

neighbourhood of Fère-en-Tardenois, Captain King observed one machine in flames and two machines broken up in the air.

Unfortunately, all three of these aircraft were from King's patrol. Wilson and Coghill were both made prisoners, while Meredith was dead. 73 Squadron had been the other Camel unit and had also lost three machines, one being claimed by Lothar von Richthofen of Jasta 11 – his 30th victory.

Two kills were made on the 28th, giving Bolle his 27th victory, and Frommherz his tenth. Both were American-flown Salmson 2A2 aircraft of the US 12th Aero Squadron. Bolle's came down on the German side, at Villers-sur-Fère, Frommherz's came down at Sergy, on the French side. Of the four Americans one pilot was wounded, the other taken prisoner, and both observers were killed. Both locations were just to the south of Fère-en-Tardenois, right on the trench line. Most significant was that one of these was deemed to be Jasta Boelcke's 250th victory.

Hermann Frommherz left Jasta B on the 29th, promoted to acting commander of Jasta 27. Its former leader for over a year had been Hermann Göring, but he had left in early July to take over JGI (Richthofen). Frommherz would be confirmed as its Staffelführer on 7 August. He would lead it till the war's end by which time his victory score had risen to 32. Although eligible for the Pour le Mérite, and indeed he was recommended for it, the war ended before the Kaiser had signed its authorisation. As can be imagined, Frommherz was not happy to be denied this high honour, and was often seen wearing a Blue Max 'medal' after the war.

Chambry

On the 30th the Gruppe moved yet again, this time to Chambry, just to the north of Laon, but still in the 7th Army area. No sooner had they started unpacking, than Karl Bolle bagged his 28th – a Spad XIII – over Courtemain on the 31st. Without knowing the time of Bolle's action it is difficult to be sure who he brought down, but it is possible it could have been one of two Americans: 1st Lieutenant Gilford C Davidson, killed with Spa 100, or 1st Lieutenant Paul H Montague, captured whilst flying with the 95th Aero Squadron, which had changed over to Spads. All we know from Harold Buckley's book is that Montague had struggled to catch up with his patrol which had got off before him, and ended up a prisoner. Whether he was picked off by Karl Bolle we don't know.

However, July had come to an end with the Jasta's score now standing at 252 victories. The Germans were aware that there was something of a build-up on the other side of the lines, and were therefore expecting some sort of major offensive to break any time soon. That offensive came in early August, and was to herald the end of the war.

Chapter Eight

The Beginning of the End

August 1918

Pilots at the start of August:	Name	Victories
	Oblt Karl Bolle	28
	Ltn Gerhard Bassenge	3
	Ltn Ernst Bormann	2
	Ltn Johann Heemsoth	2
	Ltn Friedrich Kempf	4
	Ltn Alfred Lindenberger	5
	Ltn Otto Löffler	2
	Ltn Hermann Vallendor	2
OzbV	Ltn Eberhard Fr von Gudenburg	–

Base: Chambry   Front: 7th Army JGIII

There were to be several new pilots joining during the month, which was just as well with the Jasta down to just eight pilots, although all of them had become experienced air fighters. Those arriving were Oberleutnant Kurt von Griesheim, Leutnant Fritz Heinz, a 24-year-old from Brebach, Leutnant Fritz Paul Hoffmann, another 24-year-old from Dronecken, Leutnant Franz Klausenberg, and Gefrieter Mynereck.

Von Griesheim came from Hildersheim, was born in October 1895 and had seen service with the Garde-Grenadier 'Kaiser Franz' Regiment Nr.2. Hoffmann was only 150 cm tall (4 foot, 11 inches) and his Fokker had to be modified to take his small frame. None of these pilots had any combat victories as far as is known, and in all probability their combat experience was poor. However, one pilot to join in August did have considerable experience – Vizefeldwebel Karl Friedrich Kurt Jentsch who arrived on 13 August.

Kurt Jentsch had seen much action with FA66 and FA30 in Macedonia in 1916, returning from that front with three confirmed and five unconfirmed victories. In France in 1917 he served with Jasta 1, gaining another confirmed kill and one more which appears to be unconfirmed. Moving to FA234 in August 1917 he brought his score to seven. After a brief stint with Jasta 5 at the start of January 1918, he then went to Jasta 61 (scoring another unconfirmed victory) and now had turned up at Jasta B. He had a friend in the Jasta. Alfred Lindenberger had been his observer in FA234 as related earlier, and they had gained two kills together. In fact it was Lindenberger who managed to get Jentsch into Jasta B. In his book *Flieger im Feuer (Fliers under Fire)*, Jentsch relates how he first came into contact with the Boelcke Staffel:

Today, shortly before lunch, I was called on the telephone. My old observer, Leutnant Lindenberger, was on the line. Upon his invitation, I flew to Chambry. Immediately after landing I was introduced to the pilots of 'Jagdstaffel Boelcke', which Lindenberger is a part of.

Jagdstaffel Boelcke is led by Leutnant Bolle and belongs to Jagdesgeschwader III, whose commander is Oberleutnant Loerzer, a Knight of the Pour le Mérite. Under his energetic leadership the Geschwader has developed splendidly. It holds, thanks to the number of its victories, a prominent position in the army.

Leutnant Lindenberger took me to the mess for coffee. The rectangular room made an impression of picture perfect cleanliness. Tablecloths as white as blossoms, uniform coffee service and flowers in vases, cleverly spread about, gave the tables a friendly look. Staffelführer Bolle sits at the head of the table.

Next to his place stands the telephone, which is indispensable to a successful air service. On the walls hang pictures of the fallen. First was Hauptmann Boelcke and Oberleutnant Kirmaier, then came Leutnant Voss, Oberleutnant Bernert, Leutnant Ritter Max von Müller, Leutnant Walter von Bülow and many others.

At one time our most important combat pilots began their careers in this Jagdstaffel; they absorbed Hauptmann Boelcke's teachings which brought about their unforeseen blossoming. Rittmeister Manfred Freiherr von Richthofen greatly exceeded his teacher and master through his exemplary number of victories. I have to think of all of these things because they immediately come involuntarily to mind when one is a guest here.

It was mentioned that two shot down enemy aircraft were in possession of the Staffel, a Spad and a Sopwith. If I wanted to, I could take them up, said Leutnant Bolle. I accepted this opportunity with joy; firstly, one would not be the dumber for it and secondly, it excited me, just for military reasons, to put these two enemy machines through the motions.

The Spad was taken out of the tent and made ready for take-off. A mechanic quickly explained the interior furnishings. The instruments were not so clearly arranged as in German military aeroplanes. The looping-belt (shoulder harness) provided the pilot with more freedom of movement than the ones used by us. The engine, a Hispano-Suiza, has to be swung on; the Frenchmen apparently do not know of starters. After several unsuccessful ignitions, I took off. The engine revs – 2,400 per minute – were higher than with our engines.

The Spad sat in the air wonderfully and responded to the slightest touch of the controls. In addition, the engine ran without knocking because of its fine 'V' form. This is why these craft sit quietly in the air, there is not any swinging back and forth as with our aircraft, which is caused by the type of construction of the stationary German motors. Material does not play a role with the allied enemy states, as the entire world is open to them for obtaining raw and industrial material. With such a foundation, one can bring out the very best performance in aircraft construction. In wing performance, the Spad towers over our aircraft. The loops and banks flown by me confirmed my assumptions in the end. A light went on in my head, why the first attack by a Spad is always so dangerous: they can hardly miss with the smooth conditions of the aircraft and the marvellous field of fire. Our combat pilots at the controls of their Spads would virtually mean the end of the enemy air forces.

Landing was, beyond my expectations, good. As a result of the landing skid which stands vertically, I had to make a landing by wheel. The Spad requires a comparatively long taxi; however the Chambry airfield offered no difficulties in this regard.

Then I went to the Sopwith, which has a Clerget rotary engine. The wiring of this aircraft was apparently not in order. The Clerget's singing, which is so characteristic for this type of motor, rang in my ears for a long time afterwards.

Lindenberger informed me, as we bade farewell, that Leutnant Bolle would apply for my transfer to Jagdstaffel Boelcke. I was very happy about this. Hopefully, Jagdstaffel 61 will not cross out the request.

* * *

One of two pilots to leave the Jasta in August was Leutnant Wilhelm Suer, who had not improved on his one victory scored back in June. The other was Fritz Kempf. Kempf had spent a total of almost 15 months with Jasta B, in two periods, April to October 1917, and January to 18 August 1918. His modest score of just four victories did not reflect either his experience or his leadership qualities, having been a ketten (section) leader for some time. He left to return to Jastaschule I as an instructor where he remained till the war's end. Photos of his well-known Fokker Triplane showed the phrase: 'kennscht mi nocht?', which translates to 'remember me still?' or perhaps 'remember me?' If this was for Allied airmen on his tail to read, why was it not in French or certainly English?? It was painted on his middle wings, while his name – KEMPF – was marked on the upper wing across the centre section.

His work had been recognised by several awards including the Iron Cross 1st and 2nd Class, the Bulgarian Military Merit Cross 5th Class with War Ribbon and the Baden Knight's Cross 2nd Class with Swords to the Order of the Zähringen Lion.

August began slowly enough on the more northern sectors, but further south the French and Americans were hit hard on 1 August. Despite the air activity, there were no great moments recorded by Jasta Boelcke, or JGIII. Bruno Loerzer was still leader of the Gruppe, while Jasta 26 was headed by Leutnant Franz Brandt now – and had been since 2 July. Jasta 27 had had Hermann Frommherz as leader since the end of July, and Jasta 36 was led by Harry von Bülow, although at this time he was on leave and would not return. On 15 August, Leutnant Theodor Quandt took over and led the Jasta till the Armistice.

Most of the Gruppe now flew Fokker DVII biplanes, although it is just possible the odd Triplane remained. The four Jastas, by the beginning of August, could boast high scores. Jasta B's tally was 252, Jasta 26 had 126, Jasta 27's score stood at 65 and Jasta 36 had reached 103. There now appeared to be something of a lull in the air which in fact was that 'quiet before the storm' period just prior to a major offensive being unleashed.

The Amiens Offensive

The Allies had dusted themselves off after the retreats of March and April and were now about to hit back with a vengeance. The Americans were helping to bolster the French sectors of the line and the British were again preparing for a try at moving east.

The date for the strike was set for 8 August, beginning with a massive attack by the British 4th Army and the French 1st Army along the Amiens front. After the activity of the 1st, the next few days were comparatively quiet but all that changed on the 8th. For some days the British had been trying to keep German attention away from the area planned for the assault, so there was renewed activity over Flanders. Meanwhile, as the preparations further south moved along, the RAF were given specific tasks once the offensive started, as described for us in the RAF's Official History:

(i) At daybreak [on the 8th] the bomber squadrons were to attack aerodromes on the 4th Army front, with the fighter

squadrons giving their support. These were at St Christ, Ennemain, Bray Station and Moislains.
(ii) The fighter squadrons afterwards were to stand by ready to operate on the 4th Army front if enemy activity became important (namely, offensive patrolling in protection of low flying aircraft), and
(iii) The day bomber squadrons were to attack in the evening, with the help of the fighter squadrons, the railway stations at Péronne and Chaulnes, Marchelpot, Villers Carbonnel and Etricourt.

The attack opened on the 8th with a massive artillery barrage from more than 2,000 guns at 04.20 am. While large, this was nothing particularly new. It had all been tried before and failed. Would this time be different?

Soon afterwards the troops went 'over the top' supported by tanks, along a 20-mile front between Morlancourt (the nearby ridge is where Manfred von Richthofen had fallen in April) and La Neuville on the River Avre. A heavy ground mist aided the initial assault and the Germans were somewhat taken by surprise. Before they knew what was happening, the Germans had been forced back seven or eight miles in some places. RAF bombers went for bridges across the Somme to hinder German reinforcements, some squadrons flying more than one sortie.

JGIII were in action on the 8th but while Jastas 26, 27 and 36 all scored kills, Jasta B did not. They fared better on the 9th, the day the battle edged further eastwards and the RAF bombers continued bombing bridges across the Somme.

Over any offensive battle front the main targets for German fighters would be the Corps aircraft – aircraft flying artillery observation duties, contact patrols or supporting ground troops with ground attack missions. Interspersed with these would be fighters – mainly Sopwith Camels – that would swoop down to bomb and strafe German troops and strong-points. Above this maelstrom would be the SE5s, the Dolphins and the Bristol Fighters, whose job it was to engage the Fokkers and the Albatros Scouts in order to keep them away from the more vulnerable aircraft operating at lower levels.

Karl Bolle and Otto Löffler were the scorers on the 9th, an RE8 for the former, a 'Big Ack' (AFWK8) to the latter. Bolle's kill was a machine from 6 Squadron, shot down near Rosières mid-afternoon, while Löffler appears to have downed a 35 Squadron machine in the early evening, putting its two-man crew into a prison camp. However, the main talking point that evening was about Jasta 2's attack on ground targets and troops as Bolle recorded:

English infantry, along with Americans, attacked the village of Rosières with ground attack aircraft and tanks. The tanks, covered [hidden] by a range of hills, led against the village, were not observed by the German artillery and thus were not fired upon. After the ground attack aircraft retreated before our German Staffel, we dived as a unit into the tanks and attacked with machine guns. After the third attack, the artillery, which had in the meantime obviously become aware of the tanks because of the continual dives being made by our aircraft, laid down a destructive fire in the area concerned. After a short time, three tanks were burning, two others remained motionless and the rest had turned round.

On the 11th Bolle downed a Spad two-seater over Villesavage, actually a Salmson 2A2 machine from the 88th US Aero Squadron, killing both crewmen. The 88th were on a photo-reconnaissance mission to Fismes, and a second Salmson was lost with another shot-up with one crewman wounded. They reported being attacked by 11 Fokker DVIIs. Nobody appears to have claimed the second lost Salmson, although a pilot in Jasta 26 did claim a Bréguet this date. Bolle had now secured his 30th victory, making him more than eligible for the Pour le Mérite. He had already received the Knight's Cross with Swords of the Hohenzollern House Order (exact date unknown) as well as the Military Merit Cross 2nd Class from the Grand Duchy of Mecklenburg-Schwerin. Somewhere in the bureaucratic pipeline was his recommendation for the Blue Max.

Kurt Jentsch arrived on the 13th, met the Geschwader commander, Bruno Loerzer, then reported to Oberleutnant Dahlmann, his adjutant. That afternoon he made a front flight near Soissons with Lindenberger, meeting anti-aircraft fire but nothing else. Jentsch was given his own Fokker DVII, not a new machine but airworthy. He and his ground crew made the necessary adjustments, and that evening he flew another front-line sortie but again saw no action.

A week was to pass before the next claims, when on the 18th, Bormann and Lindenberger each shot down French two-seaters. Bormann claimed an AR2 over Nouvron, Lindenberger a Bréguet XIV at Moulin-sous-Touvent. The AR2 was a machine of Escadrille Ar268. Two days later Lindenberger bagged an AR2 west of Champs. As mentioned earlier, German fighter pilots often confused Bréguets, Salmsons, Spad XIs and AR2s. And of course, with air battles over a fluid battleground, it became more difficult to inspect the wreckage of downed aircraft which would help verify the actual type. Another problem with air battles fought over a battle area is that it becomes impossible to ascertain which side an Allied machine fell of the moving troop lines. If an Allied machine in fact got down behind its own forward troops, the crew and sometimes the aircraft would be saved but it would then become difficult for the historian to try and identify it in relation to a German claim. On this day there were no obvious AR2 losses, so we are left with either a misidentification, or an AR2 was forced down but its crew saved and the machine possibly salvaged. Whatever the result in this case, Alfred Lindenberger had secured his seventh victory.

Otto Löffler brought down a Bréguet in exactly the same area on the 21st for his fourth victory although again we have only one possible French Bréguet crew as a casualty, a machine from Escadrille Br 131, both men being wounded but presumably safe on their side of the lines. He obviously had a problem with confirmation for this claim for by the time he received it he had scored two more kills. Bormann got his fourth victory on the 22nd, a Spad XIII fighter, south of Neufheuse.

Back to the British Front

JGIII and Jasta Boelcke were on the move again on the 25th, this time going to the airfield at Emerchicourt, some dozen kilometres south-east of Douai, and just to the south of Aniche. The Gruppe now came under the control of the 17th Army.

The day before, Jentsch was asked to fly the unit's DFW two-seater to Aulnoye carrying some of the pilot's baggage in the rear cockpit, with other bags strapped to the lower wings. The baggage was put on a train at Aulnoye to be taken to a new base at Emerchicourt.

The Geschwader flew north on the 25th. Jentsch described the move:

> The new day breaks. It is raining and thick mist lies over the earth. With the others, Jagdstaffel Boelcke waits for the order to take off. All the aircraft engines bubble in neutral and from a retarded position. Oberleutnant Loerzer gives the order to take off and, as the first one, he roars away and then it is our turn, under the leadership of Leutnant Bolle. One aircraft after another attaches itself. In this misty air it is difficult to keep contact. Like a shadow, Leutnant Lindenberger's Fokker lifts up, flying to the right of me. At tree level the Geschwader races ahead, flying over roads and villages. Of the other machines, only now and then we see their wheels, when they drop down out of the fog; propeller back wash from those flying in front of us causes movement and forces us to wrestle with our control sticks.
>
> It becomes light over St Quentin. Shortly afterwards the foggy region is behind us and sunshine surges around our aircraft. The Geschwader flies superbly together; no Staffel lags behind. Even fog and rain are not capable of loosening the discipline of the Geschwader.
>
> [We] reach Emerchicourt [located between Arras and Lens, 10 km to the south-east of Douai]; one Staffel after the other lands. The airfield is broad and lies favourably; one can take off and land from all corners of the sky. In the southern part of Aniche – a small town and the intersection of several railway lines – we take up our pilots' quarters.

The move came just as the Allied advance was about to spill over into the

Battle of the Scarpe, the British 1st Army moving east from Arras. Hoffmann arrived on the 25th, Jentsch mentioning him in his book:

> A new pilot, Leutnant Hoffmann has joined today; he was an infantryman and now comes to the front for the first time as a pilot. The chief mechanic has grief with him because he cannot reach the controls. When one is hardly 150 centimetres tall, such things are somewhat difficult. With the aid of a welded steel pipe frame, the controls are to be lengthened for the small Leutnant.
>
> After dinner Hoffmann sat down at the piano which stands in our mess' winter garden. It is a joy to hear him play; music diverts and relaxes [us].

Jasta B were in action the next day (26th), Bolle and the newcomer Fritz Heinz both shot down Sopwith Camels on the German side, Bolle's falling near the famed Bourlon Wood, the other west of Beugny. JGIII had run into the American 17th Aero Squadron, one of two American-manned Camel outfits attached to the RAF's 65th Wing. Flying on an offensive patrol in the late afternoon between Péronne and Cambrai they were hit by JGIII and lost six of their number to Bruno Loerzer and his pilots in Jasta B and Jasta 27. Loerzer claimed one for his 31st victory, equalling the score of Bolle. Hermann Frommherz leading Jasta 27 claimed no less than three, and with Rudolf Klimke shooting down one more this made it a total of seven claims – one more than actually lost. One of those shot down was Lieutenant Robert M Todd, who later recorded in his 1978 book *Sopwith Camel Fighter Ace*:

> Our flight on August 26th, which ended in disaster, was unscheduled. All flights had been cancelled because the weather was cloudy and raining. About 3 o'clock in the afternoon it cleared up and we were advised by the Wing that there were a number of enemy planes flying, and we were ordered to get as many aircraft as possible into the air on offensive patrol immediately. We left with ten planes. [W D] Tipton was the leader and I was flying on his right wing as deputy flight leader.
>
> When we reached the lines at Bapaume, we saw five Huns attacking what we thought was one of our observation planes. To try to save him we went over the lines after the Huns. Just as we reached them, thirty or forty Huns came down on us from out of the clouds. They were a mixture of several groups, the checkerboards, the yellow noses, etc; all Fokker DVII biplanes. They were equal to anything we could do, so when we turned to attack them, I knew we were in for a big fight.

I lost Tipton almost immediately and started firing
steadily for there were Huns everywhere I flew. I dove on
one Hun who was on the tail of a Camel and got him out of
control. He went over on his back, then went down nose first
out of sight. I continued to fire and take evasive action – we
could turn sharper than the Fokker but they could outclimb
and out-dive us. Our best defensive action was to go into a
tight turn and hold it.

Someone finally got me as my motor quit and down I
went. Looking back I saw white smoke (fumes) coming out
of my tail, and I flinched, thinking I was on fire. It finally
dawned on me that I was seeing petrol fumes, so I switched
over to my gravity tank, the motor started up and I headed
towards the sun and the lines on my way home. I knew I
could do nothing more in the dogfight as you cannot throw
your plane around on gravity as the motor will cut out as
soon as the petrol stops flowing. While I was flying at about
500 feet elevation heading west, two Huns followed me
down and started taking turns in shooting at me. I took as
many evasive turns as my motor would stand to keep them
from lining up on me. They turned back when I reached the
lines but the ground troops continued to fire at me. I could
see them standing up firing at me. Finally my motor quit and
down I had to go.

Bob Todd became a prisoner as did Tipton and 1st Lieutenant H B Frost.
2nd Lieutenant H H Jackson Jr, and 1st Lieutenant L C Roberts were both
killed, while 2nd Lieutenant H P Bittinger died of wounds after crashing
inside the German lines. This 'seventh' Camel was most likely a machine
of the 148th Aero, the other American squadron flying with the 65th
Wing. It was probably this machine that was initially seen being attacked
by some Fokkers, and in fact was the first kill by Frommherz. Its pilot,
1st Lieutenant G V Siebold, was killed.

As if in celebration of his Staffel's success, this day came the
announcement of the award of the Blue Max to Oberleutnant Karl Bolle.
Everyone congratulated him on attaining this ultimate German decoration
for bravery, he being only the second person to win it while with Jasta B.
Boelcke, Dossenbach, von Richthofen, Bernert, Müller and von Bülow
had all received their award while with other units.

Kurt Jentsch was also in action. The date is unclear but he recorded in
his book:

... we were lucky enough to jump an English squadron. The
white threads from the phosphorus ammunition criss-crossed
the sky. I had fixed myself on a DeHavilland 9 that was

trying to escape to his lines. At a distance of 400 metres I opened fire to force him to bank. Because I was a bit lower, I had to get closer by using all means available to me. Forced by my long-distance shooting, the Tommy flew zig-zagging banks and finally I was successful in sneaking up on him. Due to the many banks, he lost height so that in the end I was flying somewhat higher than my opponent.

The enemy observer fired at my machine but did not hit it. His shots were too high; I saw this from the tracer's threads. For this, a burst from my machine guns got him. He fell back into his seat like a sack. This could not be a feint. At a distance of 100 metres I got a jam in both guns. I worked like crazy to bring my weapons back into order but nothing happened.

The Tommy continued flying zig-zags, rolled from the left to the right wing and endeavoured to maintain course to Arras. A few minutes later I was over him and could look into his crate. The observer had collapsed and lay lifeless on his seat. The coupled [twin] machine guns stared forlornly up at me. The pilot must also have been wounded; he hung helplessly to the right, flying with his left hand... I could not bring him down with a few shots, but... with these two useless things [in front of me] I had to let the Tommy fly away.

Lindenberger made the last claim of the month on the 31st, an RE8 over Haynecourt on the German side. Four RE8s were shot about this date but only one came down on the German side, and two German pilots had claimed for REs on the German side, so it is unclear which one Lindenberger scored over. Obviously one of the others that was hit came down so close to the front-line in order for the crew to scramble to safety but it was viewed as down behind the German lines.

At the conclusion of the month a party was held to celebrate Bolle's Blue Max. Several dignitaries were invited, among them Hermann Göring, leader of JGI, Bruno Loerzer, JGIII, Hauptmann Martin Zander, commander of Jastaschule I, Hauptmann Zahn from headquarters, Dahlmann, JGIII's adjutant, Hermann Frommherz, leader of Jasta 27, Emil Thuy, leader of Jasta 28w, Leutnant Helmuth Lange, leader of Jasta 26, Leutnant Hupfer, adjutant of Jasta 26, Leutnant Erich Weiss, adjutant of Jasta 28w, who had just in the last month received the Würrtemberg Friedrich Order, and finally, Leutnant Aristides Müller, adjutant of Jasta 36.

According to Kurt Jentsch the evening went well with more than enough to eat and drink, cigarettes and cigars aplenty, and an accompaniment of string music. For a couple of hours the war was forgotten.

September 1918

Pilots at the start of September:	Name	Victories
	Oblt Karl Bolle	31
	Ltn Gerhard Bassenge	3
	Ltn Ernst Bormann	4
	Oblt Kurt von Griesheim	–
	Ltn Fritz Heinz	1
	Ltn Fritz Hoffmann	–
	Vfw Kurt Jentsch	7
	Ltn Franz Klausenberg	–
	Ltn Alfred Lindenberger	8
	Ltn Otto Löffler	4
	Gefr Mynereck	–
	Ltn Hermann Vallendor	2
OzbV	Ltn Eberhard Fr von Gudenburg	–

Base: Emerchicourt   Front: 17th Army JGIII

There were some posting movements during September. On the 4th Paul Bäumer returned having recovered from his crash at the back end of May, and a new NCO pilot arrived, Unteroffizier Karl Fervers. Vizefeldwebel Paul Keusen, from Ohligs, between Düsseldorf and Cologne, was another new arrival. This month would see him celebrate his 22nd – and last – birthday. Another pilot to mention was Leutnant von Becker. So little is known of this man, not even when he arrived or when he left, that all that can be said about him is that at some stage in 1918 he was with the Jasta, probably only briefly.

Posted out was Franz Klausenberg on the 24th. He went to Jasta 53 where he saw out the war, gaining two victories in October.

The month would see a massive increase in air actions, resulting in Jasta B pilots claiming 46 victories. This was the highest score the Jasta had ever achieved in a month, and the best since it had accounted for 30 Allied aircraft way back in October 1916. It eclipsed even the 21 it scored during Bloody April 1917.

The Americans Take Another Beating

It began on the first day of the month, with Bormann knocking down a Bristol Fighter of 62 Squadron in the early afternoon. Another BF2b was shot by the Jasta and its observer was wounded, but it got back to make a crash landing at base. The next day came another massacre of American-flown Sopwith Camels.

The Germans were forced to retreat to prepared positions east of Bapaume and the RAF were thick in the air covering the advance as the Canadian Corps broke through the long established Drocourt-Quéant Line. JGIII were in full evidence, Loerzer and his adjutant scoring victories, Jasta 26 scoring victories, Jasta 27 (including Frommherz) scoring victories, while Theodor Quant of Jasta 36 added two to his personal tally. In all the Jagdesgeschwader claimed 27 victories during the day, but the day's biggest single coup was against the American 148th Aero Squadron.

In Burke Davis' evocative biography of Elliott White Springs, he lets Springs' own words tell the story of 2 September 1918. Springs was the leader of the Squadron's B Flight and was by this time an experienced aviator. He had flown with 85 Squadron RAF before moving to the 148th, and by this date had scored ten combat victories and won the British DFC. The leader of the Squadron's A Flight was yet another experienced air fighter, Field Kindley, who had also flown with the RAF before joining the 148th, and had thus far scored four kills. Springs hailed from Lancaster, South Carolina, Kindley from Gravette, Arkansas. Both men were 22-years-old.

On this blustery day the 148th had flown over the front to aid and protect observation machines, but JGIII literally fell on them. Springs wrote:

> The Huns meant business and so did we. As soon as I would get on the tail of one, another would get me and as soon as I would shake him off there would be another. My lower left wing buckled. I went into a spin. I thought the machine was falling to pieces and reflected with pleasure that I had forgotten my pocketbook. I thought of Mac and of how glad he would be to see me.[1] But my plane held together... and I got out of the spin in time to hop a Hun. I don't know how many Huns we got out of it. I'm the only one of my flight who returned.

The 148th lost four pilots, two were killed, and two made prisoners of war. Field Kindley and his flight had tried to help but Kindley himself was shot-up and was lucky to get back across the lines, and so was Jesse Creech who had to make a crash-landing inside Allied lines. Jasta Boelcke claimed seven Camels, three by Löffler, three by Bormann and one by Heinz.

The next afternoon Löffler shot down a DH9 of 98 Squadron at Epehy that had been bombing Cambrai-Ville railway junction, while Lindenberger netted a Bristol Fighter near the hamlet of Combles. He was fighting Brisfits of 20 Squadron and while this unit did lose one, two other German pilots claimed it. 20 Squadron also had another machine damaged and its observer killed. The latter was most probably Lindenberger's claim as it is recorded as going down on the British side.

---

[1] Reference to Mac concerned his dead friend John McGiven Grider, whom he thought he would soon be meeting in the afterlife.

It is uncertain if Bolle was in the air on these last two days. If he had been one might have thought he would have scored. However, he had his leave pass in his pocket for the 4th and may well have thought it prudent not to tempt fate. He left to go home, leaving Otto Löffler as acting commander. Löffler was an interesting choice, considering there were other pilots with longer service with Jasta B than him, he having joined in October 1917. Gerhard Bassenge had been with the unit since May 1917, although he had been away in hospital for some months from late 1917 till July 1918. Hermann Vallendor had been with the Jasta since August 1917, and then of course there was Paul Bäumer. He had been with the Jasta, on and off, since June 1917 and had been credited with over 20 victories, but obviously he, like Max Müller earlier, had not been considered for command. And of course, Bäumer had come up from the ranks rather than through the officer corps. In any event, Bäumer only arrived back on the day Bolle left.

In the late morning of the 4th, Bormann shot down an SE5 fighter at Pelves. This appears to be a loss sustained by 64 Squadron who were not having a good day. On an early patrol they had lost one fighter following a mid-air collision (the other SE5 managed to fly home) and another pilot was wounded. On the next patrol which took off just after 8 am, Second Lieutenant V Harley failed to return, ending up as a guest of the Germans.

The only serious casualty of the month occurred on this day, Kurt Jentsch being wounded. It may have been an attack by 64 Squadron, for Captain Dudley Lloyd-Evans MC claimed a Fokker DVII 'out of control' at 07.30 near Brebières. Lloyd-Evans was an experienced fighter pilot and in his combat report he says:

> Whilst leading top formation of Offensive Patrol, and during general engagement with 12 Fokker biplanes, observed one EA diving on an SE5. Fired about 100 rounds from about 60/100 yards range. EA turned right over on to its back and fell down 'flopping' from one side to the other, obviously out of control. Confirmed by two other pilots.

Jentsch managed to pull out of his spinning nosedive and returned to Emerchicourt to make a fair landing. It was Lloyd-Evans' fifth victory out of a total of eight. He had been awarded his Military Cross in the army, and for his RAF service he would receive the DFC, and after the war a Bar for operations in Mesopotamia. Jentsch said in his book:

> With the sun at our back, another English squadron, of the Sopwith Dolphin type, showed itself behind us; they had come from the direction of Bapaume. Above Barelle, they were behind us. If they had dived down they would have immediately had me – as the one flying highest in the Staffel – by the scruff of my neck. And perhaps some of us were

going to get it because they were three times as strong as we, and were higher up.

A few seconds later, there was a rattling behind me. The first shots struck my Fokker and one of these hit my left side. Immediately banking, I saw the tracer threads spraying about me. In spite of this I did not leave my post.

The Tommies did not dive after me; it seems to be a questionable thing for them to get mixed up in a fight with our Staffel. Blood was running down my left leg; I felt its warmth here and there. It was now 08.35; the bullet wound was beginning to hurt and because of this I had to fly back. Twenty minutes later our airfield at Emerchicourt came into view. I landed smoothly despite the fact that I could hardly move. In front of my [hangar] I turned off the petrol and ignition. My mechanics lifted me out of the seat. My left leg had nearly gone stiff; it could hardly move, and the parachute upon which I had been sitting had been shredded by several hits. A hand's length to the right and my backbone would have got it!

Despite the fact that Jentsch noted Dolphins up above, no Dolphin pilots made any claims on this day. It is of course, possible that a Dolphin pilot did not put in a claim, but it could still have been an unseen SE5 that actually got in the fatal burst.

Paul Bäumer claimed a Bristol Fighter the next day. The war had come to a temporary stop on the 5th, in order for the Allied soldiers to consolidate their recent gains, and RAF aircraft were over the front in order to prevent German ground attack aircraft from interfering with trench-digging and wire-fixing. Bäumer noted his combat as being south of Douai at 18.40 pm German time but the nearest one can get to finding out who he was fighting is looking at an action by 22 Squadron. Just after 17.00 hours – the German time was one hour ahead – 22 Squadron had a scrap with Fokker DVIIs and one crew claimed a Fokker out of control but suffered no losses. This is not the first time Bäumer's claims were suspect, and at best perhaps a 22 Squadron Bristol headed down over the lines damaged, but its crew unharmed. This could also be true of 88 Squadron.

Nevertheless, most of Bäumer's claims can be substantiated. There is no doubt he was an excellent pilot, and an aggressive one. He was able to combine his piloting ability with a keen shooting eye and like many successful aces, had learnt to get in close. He once advised Karl Degelow, another successful fighter ace and later leader of Jasta 40, that once he thought he was close and on target he should take his finger off the trigger, get in closer, then closer still, before firing. Only then, said Bäumer, will you be close enough and the enemy must fall.

Bäumer went after another BF2b the next day, but this time the claim was better, in fact he and Löffler both succeeded and brought down two

Bristols of 11 Squadron inside German lines, one north of Bourlon Wood, the other west of Cantaing. The flight of Bristols were chased back over Cambrai towards the lines by several German fighters near the end of the reconnaissance patrol. All four RAF crewmen were killed. Later that afternoon Bormann downed a Camel north-west of Bourlon Wood, inside German lines, while Lindenberger sent one down over the trenches near Lagnicourt. 208 Squadron were the opposition, losing one machine in a fight above the Canal du Nord, but the other claim was on the British side and this machine obviously escaped but was possibly damaged.

Bäumer Shot Down

On an unrecorded date during September, Paul Bäumer's fighter was set on fire and he took to his parachute. In some post-war recollections, he recorded the incident but did not give a date and unfortunately Jasta records do not enlighten us on the exact day it happened. All we do know is that he was in a fight with Bristol Fighters and claimed one down in flames. During September 1918 he claimed Bristols on the 6th, 16th and 29th. It might have been somewhere about his 29th victory, which occurred on the 21st, the day he claimed three bombers, but this does not seem to fit the circumstances of which he wrote.

The day in question Bäumer recorded that he had gone up after an artillery machine and had ended up attacking a Bristol (not normally associated with art obs sorties) and in the encounter the German noted the enemy machine had several strips of fabric shot from its wings before it finally caught fire and went down. He was then surprised from behind by another RAF aircraft and within seconds his Fokker was starting to burn. The Fokker slipped so steeply he was thrown from the cockpit and for some seconds he hung between it and the ground before starting to fall away. Although he was wearing a parachute harness he had not had much confidence in the apparatus, and in those seconds he saw both his Fokker and the Bristol going down in a mass of flames, the latter smashing into the ground below him.

Suddenly he felt a jerk as the static line pulled the silken parachute canopy from its container and broke away. Somewhat surprised, yet relieved, he found himself suspended below his parachute, and drifting down to the ground. He was near the lines but the wind was sending him further east and away from the deadly trenches. Looking down he saw that his boots were smouldering and he took some moments to try and beat out the flames that now began to flicker but unable to do so, finally managed to jettison the footwear altogether.

As the ground raced towards him he heard someone call out his name but then he hit the ground. Sitting up, glad and still surprised about his survival, he came face to face with an old school chum, now a soldier, who had recognised him as he neared the ground. The friend had reached him first and helped him to extricate himself from his harness and from some muddy ground into which he had fallen. The experience taught him

not to disregard the parachute in future, for he and some of the others sometimes felt it was more trouble than it was worth to keep buckling it on.

In another undated story, Bäumer related how on one occasion he had
out-fought a twin-engined machine and eventually forced it to head for a
German airfield. While he was shepherding his victim down, a novice
pilot from another Jasta had spotted the enemy machine, attacked it and
shot it down, much to Bäumer's anger and frustration.

*   *   *

Victories dried up until the 14th, Bäumer claiming an RE8 over Cantaing
but there is no corresponding RAF loss, the only RE8 downed this date
was by Jasta 7 up on the Ypres front. There was even more confusion over
claims on the 16th. Jasta records seem to indicate four DH4 bombers and
a Bristol Fighter shot down, two at least on the German side, one north-
east of Hénin-Liétard, the other at Haveluy; one bomber on the British
side, and the Bristol down south-west of Cambrai. The first two were
credited to Bäumer and Löffler, the third also to Löffler, and the fourth to
Fritz Hoffmann.

British and German times now became the same, and would continue
so until 7 October. On the 16th German observation aircraft tried
desperately to reconnoitre the battle area of the British 3rd Army, and
with RAF bombers out in force, air fighting was much in evidence. Jasta
records give no indication of times of claims which makes it difficult, but
JGIII's Jasta 26 was in a fight with Bristols of 11 Squadron at 08.45 in the
Cambrai-Le Cateau area, losing two to them and having another damaged
and crash-land. 22 Squadron also had aircraft shot-up over the front but
suffered no losses. DH9 bombers of 98 Squadron were in a fight heading
back from a raid on Valenciennes railway station during the morning and
had one crew brought down south-west of Douai and another DH shot
about but it got home. Also in the frame are DH4s of 57 Squadron that
had one of their aircraft shot down in flames east of Marcoing, with
another aircraft damaged and its pilot wounded.

Karl Bolle returned from home leave on 18 September to resume his
leadership, proudly wearing the gold and blue enamelled Pour le Mérite
at his throat. No doubt he was happy to find his Staffel intact, only
Jentsch having been wounded in his absence. He returned just as the
Allies were starting their assault on the outskirts of the German positions
on the Hindenburg Line, supported by tanks and aircraft.

Bäumer's Run

On the afternoon of the 20th Paul Bäumer claimed his 27th victory by
shooting down a Sopwith Camel east of Rumaucourt, on the German side.
Elements of JGIII got in amongst Camels of 203 Squadron in which they
lost two to Fokker biplanes. Jasta 26 claimed two in addition to Bäumer's
but we can assume with the latter's noted as inside German lines, his was

one of the two crashed Camels. Always assuming, of course, that he wasn't seeing one of Jasta 26's victories hit the ground! One of Jasta 26's 'victories' was in fact due to a collision with Vizefeldwebel Otto Frühner, but whereas the British pilot was killed, Frühner was able to parachute to safety. He had thus achieved his 27th victory, but he did not see further combat.

This was the start of a run of victories for Bäumer, and although some of his claims appear suspect, there is no mistaking his achievements on 21 September. Or is there? Jasta records note him as downing three DH4 bombers, although again a lack of the actual time does not help with their identification. On the face of it it looks as though the bombers were from 57 Squadron, but they only lost one – in flames east of Bourlon Wood – in the early evening. This tallies nicely with Bäumer's claim – east of Bourlon Wood, on the German side. His next two claims were located east of Lagnicourt and east of Morchies. One was probably a DH4 of 205 Squadron, attacked by 12 Fokker DVIIs over Le Catelet, which then broke up. Both victories are timed at 18.45, and as another 205 Squadron aircraft appeared to be going down over the lines – with one crew member wounded – this may have been the third 'claim'. One problem, however, is that Offizierstellvertreter Josef Mai of Jasta 5 also claimed one of 205's losses on the German side. Le Catelet, of course, is some way to the south-east of the action, which doesn't help, unless the crew(s) managed to struggle north-west before coming down. One of these was Bäumer's 30th victory.

Then on the 24th Bäumer claimed a double – a Camel and a DH9. The Sopwith fell over Sailly (Cambrai), the bomber south-west of Clary, which was way over on the German side, south-east of Cambrai. The bomber was from 49 Squadron, on a bomb raid against Aulnoye Junction, east of the Forêt de Mormal, soon after dawn. He had chased it some way south-east before it came down, with a mortally wounded pilot.

The Camel is more of a problem. Sailly as a name does not help as there are several, but it must be assumed this is the Sailly just west of Cambrai. Only two Camels were among the RAF casualties, and both were too far north to be anything to do with our Jasta B man, one being up near Lille, the other further north still, near to the Channel coast.

The 24th also saw Löffler down his twelfth victory, a DH9 to the west of Cambrai. This must have been the same action in which 49 Squadron were involved, as in total they lost three bombers. Both were last seen in combat with fighters west of the Forêt de Mormal.

Ernst Bormann got his eleventh victory on the 26th, a Camel, north of Cambrai. 203 Squadron were on a Special Mission – which could mean anything – but in this case it was a low attack upon the German airfield at Lieu St Amand, by 14 Camels of 203, 11 SE5s of 40 Squadron, with escort by BF2bs of 22 Squadron. Second Lieutenant W H Coghill, last seen in combat with Fokker VIIs and making a landing near Cambrai, was taken prisoner. Two other Camels failed to return but both pilots had flopped down in the front-lines, and managed to run to safety.

To Lieu St Amand, then Spultier

After the raid on Lieu St Amand by 40, 203 and 22 Squadrons on the 26th, perhaps it was a case of believing lightning never strikes twice, for on the very next day – the 27th – Jasta Boelcke moved from Emerchicourt to this airfield. It was situated north-east of Cambrai, just south-west of Denain. In the event, they were only there three days. On the 30th the Gruppe moved again, Jasta B to Spultier, while Jastas 26, 27 and 36 went to Saultain, all on the southern outskirts of Valenciennes.

This same day Jasta B claimed nine victories, a day noted as being the start of the Battle of the Canal du Nord. This commenced with the attack on the mighty German Hindenburg (Defence) Line, the British 1st and 3rd Armies advancing towards Cambrai along a 13-mile front between Ecourt St Quentin to Gouzencourt. The canal was a natural barrier and was virtually impossible to pass en masse, so the British, led by Canadian troops, attacked at Moeuvres where a crossing might be accomplished. Supported by large numbers of Allied aircraft, the assault went well and by the early evening the canal had been crossed at the point of attack.

Again we have a lack of timings for the Jasta's claims, but the Jasta lists Bäumer with two SE5s for his 33rd and 34th victories, both west of Cambrai, on the German side, and a DH4 south-east of Oisy-le-Verger – recorded as his 35th. As mentioned before, air battles over a battle zone made it more difficult to confirm individual victories, and while some aircraft would come down behind the German front-line infantry, few would linger around to make notes of crashed aircraft numbers or the names of dead or wounded airmen with a battle raging about them, so the fighter pilot's usual information about downed opponents was lacking. There were several SE5s lost as well as a couple of DH4s, but which ones Bäumer was responsible for is far from clear. It is possible one fight was with 56 Squadron who lost a pilot.

Hermann Vallendor was credited with two Camels, one near Marquion, the other certainly on the German side, north of Bourlon Wood, while Bormann also bagged two Camels, one east of Epinoy, the other north of Ecourt St Quentin. Unteroffizier Fervers gained his first victory with another Camel over Aubencheul, and Gerhard Bassenge claimed an SE5a over Noyelles, timed at 17.35.

Vallendor's might have been a 73 Squadron Camel lost over Bourlon Wood, last seen going down in flames on a morning sortie, while he and Bormann may have been in action against 54 Squadron shortly after midday.

Jasta B lost one pilot on this day, the first loss since July! Leutnant Fritz Heinz was killed in an air fight over Awoingt, south-east of Cambrai, during the period the Jasta was engaged with 56 Squadron. A Jasta B old boy was lost on the 27th too, Fritz Rumey, who had served for a short period in May/June 1917 before going on to Jasta 5. Rumey had amassed a score of 45 victories and won the Blue Max but this day his Fokker DVII was severely damaged and he elected to use his parachute. Unfortunately it failed to deploy and Rumey fell to his death.

Significant as Jasta B's seven victories were, it should also be noted that at the end of the day, the unit's score of claims reached the 300 mark!

Three more kills came the next day, the 28th. Löffler brought his tally to 13 with a victory at Epinoy. Bassenge got his fifth with another kill at Ham-Langelet – at 08.35 – while Fervers made it two in two days with a Camel also over Epinoy. Bassenge's victim may have been a 203 Squadron machine, after a low-bombing attack, but identification of crashed aircraft continued to plague those seeking confirmations, as they do historians all these years later.

This steady scoring rate continued on the 29th, with a total of five more kills. One fell to Karl Fervers, whose eye was most definitely in, one to new boy Paul Keusen – breaking his duck – and three to Bäumer! Fervers and Keusen were in combat with Bristol Fighters of 22 Squadron mid-morning, but this unit only lost one machine. Bäumer is shown as claiming an RE8 although there is a suggestion that he too was engaged with the Bristols. One might think, however, that someone with his experience would have been able to recognise the difference. Whether it was a BF2b or an RE8, neither is readily identifiable in the casualty records, but in any event, Bäumer's score had reached 36. The lost Bristol was flown by an ace crew, Lieutenants C W M Thompson and L R James, who were taken prisoner.

Before the day ended, Paul Bäumer had claimed two Camels, thought to have been casualties suffered by 46 Squadron, who had two pilots brought down and taken prisoner. The Jasta lost its third pilot of the month, Leutnant Fritz Hoffmann being shot down over Cambrai, in a fight with SE5s of 64 Squadron. Captain C W Cudemore claimed a Fokker DVII north-west of Cambrai at 11.15, with another out of control. These were his 12th and 13th victories. Charles Cudemore was an experienced fighter pilot having served with 40 and 29 Squadrons in 1917, before becoming a flight commander with 64 Squadron. He added two more victories to his score and received the DFC by the war's end. His combat report for the 29th reads:

Offensive Patrol. 11.15 am. 8,000 to 1,000 feet. NE Cambrai. Leader of patrol; observed formation of Fokker biplanes NE of Cambrai, guarding balloons. Climbed and attacked, got in a long burst at close range on one EA which went down completely out of control (confirmed by Lt Francis). After being attacked, had three indecisive combats, and diving low saw a Fokker attack a Camel (Machine 'D' of 148 American

Sqn). Attacked, EA crashed into ground north-west of Sailly (about 2,000 yards west of lines) and burst into flames.

On the last day of the month came yet another move of airfield, this time to Spultier as mentioned earlier. This brought September to a close. Total victories now amounted to 309, and although the outcome of the war was becoming to look a little desperate for the Germans, Jasta Boelcke had not finished yet.

Chapter Nine

Undefeated to the End

October 1918

Pilots at the start of October:	Name	Victories
	Oblt Karl Bolle	31
	Ltn Paul Bäumer	38
	Ltn Gerhard Bassenge	5
	Ltn Ernst Bormann	13
	Uffz Karl Fervers	3
	Oblt Kurt von Griesheim	–
	Ltn Johann Heemsoth	2
	Vfw Paul Keusen	1
	Ltn Alfred Lindenberger	10
	Ltn Otto Löffler	13
	Gfr Mynereck	–
	Ltn Fritz Papenmeyer	–
	Ltn Ludwig Schmid	2
	Ltn Hermann Vallendor	4
OzbV	Ltn Eberhard Fr von Gudenburg	–

Base: Spultier   Front: 17th Army JGIII

The above list shows a familiar name, that of Papenmeyer. This was Wilhelm Papenmeyer's brother Fritz. It is understood that following Wilhelm's death, Jasta B endeavoured to get Fritz posted to them and finally succeeded, Fritz arriving at Jasta B on 30 September. He had passed through Jastaschule I in mid-June 1918 and had been posted to Jasta 51. He was only with this unit for about three weeks before being sent off to Army Flug-park 4, from where he received his new posting to his brother's former Jagdstaffel.

Two pilots joined Jasta B during October, Leutnant Paul Blunck and Leutnant Schlack. Blunck had been a pilot with Jasta 29 in the summer of 1917 but had then been posted to Army-flug Park 4. His next operational posting was to Kest 1b, a Home Defence Staffel, in May 1918, where he had scored a single kill against the Independent Force, a DH4 bomber of 55 Squadron during a raid on Karlsruhe. He had just been awarded the

170

Baden Knight's Cross 2nd Class of the Order of the Zähringen Lion, on 18 September.

During the month – on the 9th – Leutnant Ludwig Schmid would be transferred to command Jasta 78b, and be promoted to Oberleutnant.

Paul Bäumer got his 39th victory on the third day of October – a Bristol Fighter. This is noted as down at Rumilly on the German side at 14.30, but there are no BF2b losses. The nearest one can guess is that this was a Big-Ack (AWFK8) of 35 Squadron, but the time is a bit early, the location a bit further south, and it was thought to be brought down by AA fire. With so many of Bäumer's claims just a little suspect, one has to wonder if he was so busy chasing his Pour le Mérite that desire had become the mother of invention!

Next day he claimed another Bristol Fighter near Cambrai, again inside German lines, but the only BF2b lost was near Ingelmünster at 18.30, which is far too north, being east of Roulers. It might have been a 25 Squadron DH4 which failed to return from a raid on Maubeuge, which is situated east of Cambrai, so let's be charitable and say it was. The DH4's pilot, Lieutenant Leslie Young, was buried near Cambrai along with his NCO observer, Sergeant H E Whitehead.

Bäumer and Bassenge then claimed an SE5a each, the former's certainly noted as inside German lines. These would appear to be aircraft from 85 Squadron who lost three pilots killed around noon time. Jasta B put in two claims as noted, and a Jasta 36 pilot made it three, all in the area south-west of Busigny. Bäumer by this time must have been wondering just what he must do to win the Blue Max. Even if the score of 20+ victories had been raised to an arbitrary 30, he had now been officially credited with 40! Another thorn in his side must have been the fact that he had not yet received (nor did he) the Hohenzollern House Order, which normally gave a strong hint that the top award was at least on its way. In fact he had been nominated for the Blue Max after his 30th victory but it was still bogged down somewhere in the bureaucratic pipeline.

Bassenge got another fighter the next day, this time a Camel, over Crevecoeur south of Cambrai, for his seventh and final victory. There is no corresponding Allied loss, although a few SE5s failed to return with which his claim may have been confused.

On the 8th Bäumer and Karl Fervers both claimed Sopwith Camels as the Second Battle of Le Cateau began. There are no obvious losses, and lack of recorded timings does not help. The battle, headed by the British 3rd and 4th Armies, was along a 17-mile front south of Cambrai, supported by the 1st French Army to their right. A few miles were punched into the German line, and Jasta B was again in action the next day.

This time Bäumer shot down a Bristol Fighter, one of two lost by 62 Squadron. This Squadron were escorting bombers on an early raid and were engaged by German fighters over the Forêt de Mormal. Fighters other than those from Jasta B were involved in the air battle, and one of the Bristols which came down was being flown by Captain Lynn Campbell, a Canadian from Hamilton, Ontario, who had achieved nine victories. He and his observer were both killed. This was Bäumer's 43rd and final victory.

In the afternoon, during a combat with DH9s at 14.40 pm Vallendor and Löffler each crashed a bomber inside German lines. These were losses sustained by 107 Squadron attacking the rail station at Mons and were Vallendor's fifth and Löffler's 14th victories.

A Move to Lens
Jasta Boelcke packed its bags and transported itself to Lens on the 10th. Lens was situated around 10-12 kilometres north-west of Mons, in Belgium, which, although some way north of JGIII's previous sector of operations, was still within the retreating area covered by the 17th Army.

The Germans were now in virtual full retreat, and although the Air Service continued to be a very dangerous opponent despite the overwhelming numbers of Allied aircraft put up against it, its staffeln were having trouble with fuel supplies, as well as replacement pilots. Certainly good and experienced pilots were at a premium. The training schools were still churning new ones out but the quality was no longer there.

Paul Bäumer left the Jasta (on the 12th), going back to Germany to take part in the final fighter trials being held at Adlersdorf, Berlin. Officially his posting was to Idflieg – Inspektion der Fliegertruppe. These fighter trials had been held at fairly regular intervals throughout the later years of the war. Experienced and successful fighter aces were gathered together to fly and test the latest fighter types and from their reports came the decisions to produce the best one(s) in numbers. If readers have seen the film *The Blue Max* they would have seen the final scenes where George Peppard had been allowed by James Mason to fly an unstable new aircraft which led to a crash and Peppard's character's death. The scenario was scripted around a fighter trial in Berlin. Other aces that attended this last fighter trial alongside Bäumer included Franz Buchner, leader of Jasta 13 (40 victories), Oskar Fr von Boenigk, leader of JGII (22 victories), Josef Veltjens, leader of Jasta 15 (35 victories), Bruno Loerzer, leader of JGIII (44 victories), Hans-Joachim Rolfes, Jasta 45 and leader of Jagdgruppe Ost (17 victories), Ernst Udet, leader of Jasta 4 (62 victories), but still recovering from an earlier wound, Josef Jacobs, leader of Jasta 7 (48 victories), who still preferred to fly the Fokker Triplane rather than the Fokker DVII, and Hermann Göring, leader of JGI (22 victories). As it turned out, none of these pilots scored further combat victories before the war ended. It is also a fact that with the exception of Rolfes, Bäumer, while the leading ace of Jasta B, was the only one who had never commanded a Jasta.

It was during these trials, which began in late October, that three pilots received their Pour le Mérite's – Büchner, von Boenigk, and (at last) Paul Bäumer. Franz Büchner had only recently scored his 40th and last victory (22 October) while von Boenigk's final victory, his 26th, had been achieved back in September.

There must have been some parties in celebration, but for Bäumer there still appeared to be the final indignity of waiting, for both Büchner and von Boenigk had their awards announced on 25 October, while Bäumer's did not come through till 2 November. With his two comrades in arms having achieved only 40 and 26 kills respectively and he with a total of 43, he must have been on tenterhooks till finally the announcement came.

As mentioned previously, Bäumer for some reason did not receive the Knight's Cross of the Hohenzollern House Order, the normal prerequisite before the Pour le Mérite was promulgated. In some post-war photographs Bäumer is seen wearing both the Blue Max **and** the Hohenzollern, as if to say, I earned it, deserved it, so I shall wear it! This was, as mentioned earlier, much like former Jasta Boelcke pilot Hermann Frommherz who narrowly failed to receive the Pour le Mérite due to the Kaiser's abdication before the recommendation could be signed and approved, but he too is seen in uniform after the war wearing the Blue Max at his throat.

According to one list, there were well over 20 or so German fighter pilots who were awarded or recommended for the Pour le Mérite but did not receive it. Some were killed before the decoration was presented, while others, like Frommherz, were thwarted by the collapse of Germany and the abdication of Kaiser Wilhelm, without whose approving signature on the documentation the decoration could not be given. It occurred to this author that while Hermann Göring was building his new Luftwaffe in the 1930s, he might have brushed aside this technicality and had someone (Hitler perhaps?) approve the awards. Quite probably this was not possible because Germany no longer had a 'Kaiser', but it is a thought. On the other hand one could say that people like Göring would have preferred to be amongst a smaller elite band of Blue Max winners, rather than expand its membership. The fact that he received his after only 18 victories, at a time when it took more than 20-25 is another interesting facet.

Whether it had been the intention for Bäumer to return to Jasta Boelcke is not known for certain, but in any event the war came to an end before he completed his task for Idflieg, so he does not appear on the final pilot rosta at the Armistice.

The Final Days
While all this was going on back in Germany, Jasta B, in a little bit of a backwater at Lens, did not achieve a single victory between the 9th and 29th of October 1918. Then on the 29th, Bormann and Blunck each claimed a Camel near Valenciennes.

The final battles over Flanders had begun on the 14th, along a front from Dixmude to the Lys, and then the British 4th and French 1st Armies resumed assaults in front of Le Cateau (further south) followed on the 26th by the British 1st and 3rd Armies north of Le Cateau.

A main feature of all British offensives over many months had been harassment of German ground troops by low flying aircraft, particularly Sopwith Camels. They made life even more difficult for the German soldiery by swooping in low and fast, spitting .303 bullets from their twin Browning machine guns, and/or dropping deadly 20lb Cooper bombs, four of which they carried beneath the fuselage. Jasta B caught two 3 Squadron Camels engaged in this work during the morning of the 29th and two young second lieutenants paid with their lives.

As if to prove the German fighter force was still very much a dangerous foe even now, on the 30th Jasta Boelcke claimed six British aircraft shot down. Three of these were shot down by aces, three by novice pilots, two of whom gained their first kills. On this day occurred the heaviest day of air fighting of the entire war!

German time had again increased over Allied time by one hour from 6 October, and noted as around 09.20 am British time, SE5s of 32 Squadron ran into Jasta Boelcke over Ghislain, east of Mons, and suffered heavily. Chased south-east by Jasta B, Lindenberger, Bormann and von Griesheim each claimed one SE5 shot down, and 32 Squadron did indeed lose three pilots, two of whom were aces! Captain A A Callender and Lieutenant R W Farquhar were both killed, while Second Lieutenant W Amory was brought down and made a prisoner.

The fight really developed south-east of Valenciennes and all three SE5s came down at Harchies, north of Neuville (sur Escaut) and Fresnes. Alvin Callender was a 25-year-old American from New Orleans, who had enlisted into the RFC in Canada in 1917. He had been with 32 Squadron since May 1918 and had achieved eight victories. It is believed he survived being shot down but died of his wounds soon afterwards. He is buried in Valenciennes. Robert Farquhar was a 20-year-old lad from East Dulwich, London, who despite his age, was an experienced aviator. He had flown FE2s in 1916-17 with 18 Squadron, then Spads with 23 Squadron in 1917 before beginning a third period in France in late 1918 with 32 Squadron. He had been credited with seven victories and had survived being brought down by Manfred von Richthofen on 23 June 1917 – the German's 54th victory.[1] He is buried in Auberchicourt Cemetery, between Valenciennes and Douai.

---

[1] For many years the identity of von Richthofen's 54th victory was a mystery until this author, in researching his co-authored book *Under the Guns of the Red Baron* unearthed information which showed it to be Lt R W Farquhar of 23 Squadron, whose Spad was hit and damaged by the German ace, but bullets only holed the machine's radiator. This caused the 'smoke' seen by von Richthofen as the Spad headed down into Allied territory. Farquhar was flying again the following day.

The action report of 32 Squadron states:

> 09.20 am. Offensive Patrol, 13,000 feet. Ghislain.
> Patrol on escort duty attacked a formation of 25 Fokker biplanes who were making to attack bombers. Lt H R Carson, 1 out of control, confirmed by Lt B Rogers, [but not allowed].
>
> Captain C L Veitch 1 destroyed, spinning and trailing smoke and observed to crash between canal and railway station at Ghislain. Lt E C Spicer 1 out of control confirmed by Captain E L Zink. 62 Squadron [BF2bs] reported seeing 1 EA in flames which crashed 3 miles NW of Mons at 09.10.

Ironically 32 Squadron had just moved into Jasta B's old airfield at Pronville. Bogart Rogers, who saw Carson send down a Fokker, although this claim was not allowed, wrote home about the action, as recorded in a book entitled *A Yankee Ace in the RAF* (his letters edited by J H Morrow Jr and E Rogers). Rogers was an American from Los Angeles, who would end the war with six victories and a DFC.

> ... We had a bad day today. Got into a terrible mess this morning bringing the bombers home. They all got back, but we got properly into the soup driving Huns away from them and had to stay and fight more than twice our number. There were Huns everywhere, above, below, and on both sides. Every time you'd look around there would be more of them coming up. I had two of 'em worry me almost to tears, one above and one below. The one above kept coming down and taking the odd shot, and the one below got rid of some spare ammunition too. I couldn't go down on the bottom one for fear of the top one and there were seven more coming up behind. Everyone else had their hands full. We have a man or so missing and another chap down in a CCS full of holes.
>
> We did another show this afternoon, but didn't see anything, thank heaven. One large party a day is plenty.

Despite what Rogers says about bomber losses, the other three victories were all DH9 bombers, downed by Löffler (his 15th victory), Blunck (his 3rd) and Schlack (his 1st). Again all three came down inside German lines, the locations given as north of Quievrain, Fayet and Blaton. Perhaps Rogers was helping to protect another group of two-seaters. There were several air actions with DH9 bombers this date, and again the lack of exact times of Jasta B's combats does not make it easy to identify which bombers were being fought. 98 Squadron attacked Mons railway station late morning and suffered heavy losses – five shot down, and one force-landed just inside British lines and then shelled to destruction.

Sopwith Dolphins that were escorting the DeHavillands also suffered losses – five shot down with another pilot returning wounded.

Three units of JGIII were in this fight, Jasta B, Jasta 26 and Jasta 27, the latter unit claiming four Dolphins. Jasta 26 claimed two bombers and two Dolphins. Hermann Frommherz, still leader of Jasta 27, claimed one of the Dolphins for his 30th victory.

November 1918

Pilots at the start of November:	Name	Victories
	Oblt Karl Bolle	31
	Ltn Gerhard Bassenge	7
	Ltn Paul Blunck	3
	Ltn Ernst Bormann	15
	Uffz Karl Fervers	4
	Oblt Kurt von Griesheim	1
	Ltn Johann Heemsoth	2
	Vfw Paul Keusen	1
	Ltn Alfred Lindenberger	11
	Ltn Otto Löffler	15
	Gfr Mynereck	–
	Ltn Fritz Papenmeyer	–
	Ltn Schlack	1
	Ltn Hermann Vallendor	5
OzbV	Ltn Eberhard Fr von Gudenburg	–

Base: Lens   Front: 17th Army JGIII

As the war entered its final month, Jasta Boelcke, despite the increasingly bad weather, stood ready as always to do its part in repelling the ever-increasing Allied air forces. Fuel continued to be a problem and although most Germans could clearly read the writing on the wall, there was no immediate sign that the war was about to end.

For reasons not apparent, Karl Bolle had not scored a single victory since his return from leave in mid-September, but on the first day of November, leading his pilots in an engagement with SE5s, he downed his 32nd hostile aircraft and Lindenberger and Vallendor scored too. Again it was the luckless 32 Squadron RAF that met the wrath of Jasta B east of Valenciennes, losing two pilots and having a third shot-up although its pilot, Captain C L Veitch, managed to reach the lines.

The Jasta had its final successes on the 4th, achieving six kills. This day saw the last great air battles of WW1 fought. On the ground the British 4th, 3rd and 1st Armies continued their surge forward along a 30-mile front, pushing on from the taking of Valenciennes on the 2nd. To the south the French also pushed forward. Resistance was strong in some places but on the other hand the will to halt the Allied advances was growing thin in others.

Vizefeldwebel Keusen shot down a Bristol Fighter near Villerau for his second victory, possibly one of the three losses sustained by 62 Squadron. Then came the last massed dogfight. There was a new fighter in France by this time, a successor to the supreme Sopwith Camel, that looked slightly bigger than its older brother and more pugnacious. It was called the Sopwith Snipe. Had the war continued into 1919 more Snipes would have arrived in France to re-equip existing Camel equipment, but as yet only two Allied squadrons had been re-equipped with them: 43 Squadron and 4 Squadron, Australian Flying Corps. In the morning and then later during the afternoon of the 4th Jasta B met the Australians and were soundly thrashed by the Fokker pilots.

The Australian squadron was part of Colonel Louis Strange's 80th Wing and they had already seen some action on the morning of the 4th. Perhaps quoting the Official History of the Australian Flying Corps we will get a better flavour of what occurred in the early afternoon, the time 4 AFC tangled with Jasta Boelcke. First the morning action, at around 10.15 British time:

> . . . [Lt E A] Cato, leading four Snipes from No.4 Squadron, saw seven Fokkers a little above him at 10,000 feet north-east of Tournai. Joining four British SE5s, he climbed towards the enemy. The SE5s manoeuvred to the north, and the Snipes to the south of the enemy, and, having made their height, dived on the Fokkers from 15,000 feet. Cato shot one down out of control, but two of the Snipes were lost in the scrimmage; Lieutenant E J Goodman, hit by an anti-aircraft shell, crashed in the canal at Tournai, and Lieutenant C W Rhodes, a newly-joined pilot, shot down in combat. Both were taken prisoner.

The Australian Official History continues with the early afternoon action:

> At noon the whole Wing took the air to harass the German retreat on the Leuze-Ath road and to raid the aerodrome at Chapelle-à-Wattines just north of it, east of Leuze. The full squadron of Snipes formed the escort. Every machine of No.2 Squadron [2 Sqn AFC flew SE5s] was loaded up with bombs for the low-flying attack, as were also the heavier British bombers of the DH9 squadron [27 Sqn RAF]. The SE5s were about to descend and bomb the aerodrome at Wattines, when the leading machines were attacked by five Fokkers, at 4,000 feet from the north-east. A number of other Fokkers appeared above these five. The Australians released their bombs in a shower at the aerodrome and at once joined combat with the enemy. Colonel Strange (flying a Sopwith Camel) and the DH9s proceeded to a more leisurely bombing

run, and saw four hangars burning, one fired by No.2
Squadron's bombs. Strange then flew in a northerly circle
and with machine-gun fire stampeded horse-transport and
troops at Grandmetz and at Leuze station.

Meanwhile the first five Fokkers were all shot down after
a furious encounter – two by Davies, and one each by
Blaxland, Stone and Simonson. The ground was hidden by a
thick carpet of cloud, and into this the Fokkers fell spinning,
one by one; beyond it they could not be watched. Of the
upper Fokkers only three or four came down to fight, but
these, on sighting the Snipes, sheered off.

King, leading the Snipes, escorted the bombers back
across the lines and then, seeing twelve Fokkers following
his formation, turned back, climbed, and dived on the
enemy's leader. He fired 150 rounds into this machine,
which stalled, fell on its side, and dropped earthwards on its
back. A general scrimmage ensued. King fastened on to
another Fokker which was shooting on the tail of a Snipe,
and sent it down in flames after four rapid bursts of fire at
100-feet range. G Jones attacked the rearmost German of the
formation, overran it during his opening fusillade, and sped
on to another, which was attacking H A Wilkinson. This
Fokker also fell in flames. Wilkinson, delivered from it,
dropped with a quick turn on two more Fokkers behind and
below him, fired a close-range burst into the nearer one, and
saw it fall out of control. Such is the vignette of a short and
willing encounter preserved in the laconic narratives of the
Australian pilots. The fight lasted but two or three minutes
and died out in the usual way, with machines spread over a
wide area and making to regain formation. When the Snipes
had re-formed it was found that three splendid pilots had
been lost in the action – Baker (a flight commander), and
Lieutenants Palliser and P W Symons.

In this action Bolle scored again – twice – making it four kills in one day,
to bring his final wartime victory tally to 36. The fifth Snipe fell to Ernst
Bormann, his 16th and final kill.

It wouldn't be the first time that Allied pilots reported seeing an
aircraft break-up in the air and assume – and report – that it had been
(apparently) hit by AA fire, nor would it be something new for a pilot to
claim two victories if he saw two go down and crash, especially if nobody
else was making a claim for them. So if in fact Goodman had been struck
by a shell during the action in which Bolle was fighting them, Bolle
probably wouldn't be slow in coming forward to report it must have been
hit by his fire.

It is unclear from which action Jasta B suffered its last casualty of the war, but suffer one it did. Vizefeldwebel Paul Keuson was shot down in one of these actions, and one might conclude it was in the second one. As the Jasta (and JGIII for that matter) only lost one pilot killed this date, the two claims by Captain E R 'Bo' King and Lieutenant George Jones look suspiciously similar in nature. Both attacked a Fokker on the tail of a Snipe and both saw their victim fall in flames. It is not difficult to imagine that both shot down Keuson and each man, in good faith, claimed a victory. It is also interesting to speculate that if King had actually fired at the 'leader' of the Fokker formation, and this had been Bolle, then Bolle quickly recovered from it by putting his machine into an inverted dive, and had climbed back and knocked down two of the assailing Snipes.

As a matter of interest it is believed that the original claims by Bolle were for two SE5s, but none were lost in these actions, and it may be safe to assume Bolle was slightly confused by encountering Snipes for the first time, and by the fact that SE5s were seen in the initial contact. What, however, is not in doubt is that 4 AFC lost five Snipes on the 4th, with three pilots killed and two taken prisoner. Two of the three dead Australians were aces – 21-year-old T C R Baker DFC MM (12 victories), and A J Palliser, aged 28 (7 victories). Bo King and George Jones were also aces, ending the war with 26 and 7 victories respectively.

The Final Move

Whilst celebrating this spectacular victory, Bolle and his pilots did not know this action represented their final acts against the Allied air forces. It brought the Jasta's total of claimed victories to a massive 336 (333 aircraft and three kite balloons). This was only second to Manfred von Richthofen's famous Jasta 11, which scored 350.

It had suffered 31 pilots killed, nine wounded, two taken prisoner and two fatalities in crashes.

Despite a few more sorties, no further actions of note are recorded, and then on 9 November the unit moved to Aniche, midway between Douai and Valenciennes, and still under 17th Army. Here it heard of the Armistice and the defeat of Germany two days later. The remnants left for the Fatherland on the 14th.

The initial instruction was for the Jasta to surrender its Fokker DVIIs to the British. This did not go down well, but it was carried out, although with one final act of defiance as Bolle recorded:

> [After the 4th] the fighting activities of Jadgstaffel Boelcke came to an end. In the following days till the ceasefire, it no longer appeared over the battlefields due to rain and because it was on the move. It could be proud of the results of the first four days [of November], with nine aerial victories. According to the conditions of the ceasefire, its aircraft were to be given up to the Englishmen. It was not easy to convince the Staffel that this order was to be complied with. Yet it had

to be carried out. The handover followed; each aircraft carried the glorious name of its pilot and the number of his victories. Thus they gave witness to the deeds which were accomplished by them.

* * *

Victory Claims by Month

Month	1916	1917	1918
January	–	3	6
February	–	14	5
March	–	15	10
April	–	21	3
May	–	5	8
June	–	1	13
July	–	–	18
August	–	1	11
September	21	6	46
October	30	11	18
November	25	18	9
December	10	8	–
Totals	**86**	**103**	**147 = 336**

* * *

Aftermath
Pilots at the Armistice:

	Name	Victories
	Oblt Karl Bolle	36
	Ltn Gerhard Bassenge	7
	Ltn Paul Blunck	3
	Ltn Ernst Bormann	16
	Uffz Karl Fervers	4
	Oblt Kurt von Griesheim	1
	Ltn Johann Heemsoth	2
	Ltn Alfred Lindenberger	12
	Ltn Otto Löffler	15
	Gfr Mynereck	–
	Ltn Schlack	–
	Ltn Hermann Vallendor	6
OsbV	Ltn Eberhard Fr von Gudenburg	–

One decoration Karl Bolle received which has not been mentioned thus far was the Military Merit Cross 2nd Class, which he received from the Grand Duchy of Mecklenburg-Schwerin. This is mainly because the date it was given is not known although he is seen wearing the ribbon in May

1918, along with his Knight's Cross 2nd Class with Swords of the Württemberg Friedrich Order. After the Armistice Bolle served as a platoon leader of a cavalry regiment of the Reichswehr, then became a liaison officer with the inter-Allied Aviation Monitoring Commission, ending his military service with the rank of Rittmeister. He then went into engineering, helping to construct a heavy oil motor at the Charlottenburg Technical University. He also remained active in sport aviation and in 1926 he was appointed a Director of the German Transportation Flying School. Within ten years he was in charge of all pilot training in Germany. With the coming of the Luftwaffe he was chosen by Hermann Göring to be special advisor within the service. He lived until 1955, passing away on 9 October in Berlin, the city of his birth, in his 62nd year.

Gerhard Bassenge returned to his army roots post-war and studied engineering. He was promoted to Hauptmann in early 1932 and then Major in 1935. By April 1937 he was an Oberstleutnant (Lt-Colonel) as commander of the German parachute school at Strendal, becoming a full colonel in May 1939. With the coming of the Second World War, Bassenge was Chief of Staff to a special mission to Rumania between October 1940 to June 1941. Later he was put in charge of aerodromes in North Africa. In February 1942 his work was rewarded with the Deutchescross in Gold, and by early 1943 he was a Major-General as Officer Commanding the 19th Luftwaffe Field Division. In the last days of the fighting in the Tunisian peninsular he commanded forces between February and May. He was captured by the Allies on 10 May 1943 and remained a prisoner until 1947. He died in Lübeck on 13 March 1977 aged 79.

Ernst Bormann became a flying instructor. Between August 1925 and the end of September 1930 he was an instructor at Lipizk, in Russia, and again back in Germany after 1930. In 1934 he joined the Luftwaffe as a Hauptmann and between April 1935 and May 1938 he was a staffelkapitän with Kampfgeschwader 154 'Boelcke' – Jasta B having become a bomber unit and the first unit to operate with the Heinkel 111 bomber. Between June and October 1938 Bormann commanded the third Gruppe of JG2 'Richthofen', followed by commanding 1st Gruppe of LG1 till July 1940. After commanding KG76 he became Fliegerführer 'Crimea' for most of the first half of 1943 with the rank of Major-General. On 5 October 1941 he had been awarded the Knight's Cross of the Iron Cross, followed by the Oak Leaves on 3 September 1942. Shortly after the end of WW2 he was captured by the Russians and remained incarcerated until October 1955. He received a doctorate post-WW2 and died in Düsseldorf on 1 August 1960, at the age of 62.

Alfred Lindenberger also joined the Luftwaffe prior to the Second World War and with the rank of Major in 1944 again saw action as a fighter pilot. In June 1944 he was with Jagdgeschwader 3 and between October 1944 and February 1945 commanded II Gruppe of JG300 on Home Defence sorties. He had lost none of his fighting expertise in the intervening years, for in late 1944 he shot down four American aircraft, one P51 Mustang, one B.17 Flying Fortress and two B.24 Liberators. The fighter and the Fortress occurred in one action in September, the two Libs in one action in December. Not bad for an 'old timer' well into his forties. This brought his total victories in two wars to 15 (although it is not clear if he added any others to his tally in early 1945 – possibly not – before he left the unit at the end of January). He died on 30 June 1973, aged 76, in the town of Nürtingen.

Otto Löffler survived the war but little is known of his career afterwards. What is known is that his son Kurt became a fighter pilot during World War Two and of his 26 victories, 15 were claimed whilst serving with I Gruppe JG51 'Mölders'.

Former Jasta B pilot Hermann Frommherz ended the war with 32 victories. Although he did not, through various circumstances, receive the Blue Max, he was awarded, in October 1918, the Knight's Cross of the Military Karl Friedrich Merit Order, by the Grand Duke of Baden, becoming only the eighth (and last) airman to receive this high honour. He too remained closely associated with flying, firstly with the German Aviation Police then with the Deutsche-Luftreederie, flying mail-planes, an organisation which later became Lufthansa. In the 1920s he worked as technical officer at the new airfield at Lorrach, but with increasing restrictions imposed on Germany's flying services, he went to Russia in 1925, and six years later worked for over a year in China, teaching fighter tactics to General Chiang Kai-shek's new air force. Back in Germany he joined the new Luftwaffe and during WW2 he commanded I Gruppe of JG134. Later still he rose to the rank of Major-General, his last assignment being in charge of fighter aircraft operating from the areas of Schliessheim, Dortmund and Danzig. After the second war Frommherz returned to civic affairs in his home town of Waldshut where he died from a heart attack on 30 December 1964, aged 71.

Hermann Vallendor had received both Classes of the Iron Cross, the 1st Class in March 1918. His Baden Ritterkreuz 2nd Class had been awarded in December 1917.

Three of the famous former Jasta Boelcke pilots went on to gain real fame during WW1 but were all destined to fall before it ended. First of course was Manfred von Richthofen. Given command of Jasta 11 in early 1917, he then commanded the first Jagdgeschwader – Nr I – in June of that year, and before his death to ground fire on 21 April 1918, had amassed 80 victories. Werner Voss served under von Richthofen as leader of Jasta 10 within JGI and ran his score to 48 before falling in combat with SE5s of 56 Squadron on 23 September 1917. His victor, Lieutenant A P F Rhys Davids DSO MC was himself shot down and killed on 27 October 1917 by a Jasta B member, Karl Gallwitz.

Third was Adolf von Tutschek. After commanding Jasta 12 he led JGII and brought his score to 27 by March 1918. However, he was hit a glancing blow to the temple in a fight with SE5s of 24 Squadron on 15

March, and although he managed to get down safely, died beside his black-tailed Triplane soon afterwards.

Paul Bäumer, Pour le Mérite not withstanding, had to find work in the Hamburg dockyards immediately after the war, getting a job with the Blohm und Voss ship and aeroplane builders. However, he then returned to his studies, passing his examinations to become a professional dentist. He remained interested in flying, starting as a display aerobatic pilot and then, by forming his own Bäumer Aero GmbH Company in Hamburg in 1922, building aeroplanes. This company was formed with an old wartime friend, Harry von Bülow-Bothkamp. Harry, it will be recalled, had been in Jasta Boelcke briefly, and his brother Walter had died whilst commanding it in January 1918. In early July 1927 Bäumer broke two altitude and speed records in his all-red 'Sausewind' machine. Only days afterwards, he flew to Copenhagen where he displayed his latest B.IV version of the Sausewind, on 15 July. After completing his flying display, he was asked to fly the Rofix model produced by the Rohrbach company in order to show it off to a group of Turkish Army officials. The pilot who was supposed to fly it had not arrived, so Bäumer agreed to take it up. He took off at 19.30 that evening. The flight was routine until he initiated a spin at around 6,500 feet, from which he failed to recover. The Rofix fell in front of the observers, crashing into the waters of the Oersund sound, between Denmark and Sweden, two kilometres from the coast. He died instantly; he was 31. Bäumer was buried at Ohlsdorf, near Hamburg, on the afternoon of the 21st. His company continued in business until 1932, his Sausewind design becoming synonymous with the later Heinkel high-speed aircraft designs, due to Ernst Heinkel employing Bäumer's brilliant designer twins, Walter and Siegfried Guenter.

Later a memorial was unveiled at Hamburg Airport, while opposite Fuhlsbüttel airfield a street junction was named 'Paul Bäumer Platz'. In his home-town of Duisberg a street was named after him while a street near Berlin's Tempelhof Airport also carried his name.

Former leader and Staffel pilot Otto Höhne was another who joined the Luftwaffe – in 1937 – and flew bombers. Commanding I Gruppe of KG54 from March of that year to June 1940, he then became Kommodore of the whole Geschwader with the rank of Colonel (Oberst). He was awarded the Knight's Cross of the Iron Cross on 5 September 1940. On 15 August the following year he was severely injured in a take-off accident at Ohlau, flying in a Heinkel 111 and did not return to front-line service, and in 1944 he commanded the Air War School at Furstenfeldbrück. He died on 22 November 1969.

Fritz Kempf survived the war too and returned to Freiburg. In addition to both Classes of the Iron Cross his war service brought him the Bulgarian Military Merit Cross 5th Class with War Decoration (June 1917), and the Wound Badge in August 1918. He died in August 1966.

The Jasta had flown all the major fighter aircraft used by the German Jastas in WW1, starting with the early Halberstadt and Albatros DI and DII machines, then progressing to the Albatros DIII, DV and DVa types, as well as a few Pfalz DIIIs. It also equipped with the Fokker Dr I Triplanes and finally the Fokker DVIIs, and especially the BMW-engine powered DVIIs from September 1918. These looked exactly the same as those DVIIs which had the standard Mercedes 130 hp engine but with 20+ more horsepower which gave them a significantly better performance. As these BMW-engined DVIIs became available, it was policy to equip the elite Circus Jagdstaffeln with them first. Bäumer had also test-flown the Pfalz DVIII.

Since the Jastas were first formed in the late summer of 1916, in good part the inspirational idea of Oswald Boelcke, these fighting units had wreaked havoc on British, French and American air forces alike. After the successes by Jasta 11 and Jasta B, Jasta 5 scored over 250 victories, and another 14 had achieved more than 100 kills, ranging from 101 to 196.

The tactics used by the Germans generally heralded success, but the mainly defensive posture due to small numbers – despite Allied pilots reporting to be massively out-numbered on many occasions – ultimately gave the aggressive stance and the upper hand to the Allies. However, it allowed the German fighter pilots the chance to select the time and place of battle, and to choose whether to engage or not, depending on whether they had a tactical advantage in doing so. It also enabled them to have many of their claims confirmed because the majority of Allied aircraft shot down fell on the German side of the trenches.

The main tactic used by the Germans was to allow a leader and/or a successful fighter pilot the chance to strike first whilst being protected from behind by his Staffel. By the start of World War Two the German fighter arm had got this tactic down to a fine art by using the 'Schwarm' – an element of four aircraft – which comprised two Rotten, each with a leader and wingman. This two-man formation of leader and wingman was even more effective due to the advent of inter-aircraft radio. There was a reason this tactic developed, in part by Werner Mölders, arguably the Oswald Boelcke of WW2. Due to limited numbers of Messerschmitt 109 fighters available during the Spanish Civil War they were used sparingly and in order to protect the numbers they began operating in pairs. The Schwarm of four fighters, flying in two pairs, could easily cover each other's blind spots and once action commenced, each pair could operate on its own, the leader to attack, the wingman to watch and protect. It took the RAF more than a year to start operating in sections of four, rather than in antiquated vics of three, where the two wingmen spent most of their time making sure they didn't ram their leader.

As the skies over France fell silent and the whirl of Mercêdes, Le Rhône, Hispano-Suiza, and Clerget engines was heard no more, the airmen of all sides – those who had survived the first Great War in the air – returned to their homes and families. Much had been learnt about air warfare – warfare in the third dimension – and the development of aeroplanes and engines had progressed massively since 1914. In the few short years since countries like Germany, France and England had first decided to create air forces, the men and machines of 1918 bore little resemblance to those which started out when war began.

This has been the story of just one German fighter unit, but it is similar to the histories of others, except that a few of the top Jagdstaffeln men, men of a very special breed, had 'pushed the envelope' to use a modern phrase, and had taken time to study what they were doing rather than just blindly doing it, had improved it, and taught others if a tactic proved successful. And the name of the one man who had thought about things the most lives on, not in the memories of comrades now long dead, but in the history of military aviation. That man was Oswald Boelcke.

Appendix A

Staffelführers

Hauptmann Oswald Boelcke	27 Aug – 22 Sep 1916
Oberleutnant Günther Viehweger (acting)	22 Sep – 23 Sep 1916
Hauptmann Oswald Boelcke	23 Sep – 28 Oct 1916
Oberleutnant Stefan Kirmaier	30 Oct – 22 Nov 1916
Oberleutnant Karl Bodenschatz (acting)	22 Nov – 29 Nov 1916
Hauptmann Franz Josef Walz	29 Nov – 9 Jun 1917
Oberleutnant Fritz Otto Bernert	9 Jun – 28 Jun 1917
Leutnant Otto Hunzinger (acting)	28 Jun – 29 Jun 1917
Oberleutnant Fritz Otto Bernert	29 Jun – 18 Aug 1917
Leutnant Erwin Böhme	18 Aug – 29 Nov 1917
Leutnant Eberhard Fr von Gudenburg (acting)	29 Nov – 13 Dec 1917
Leutnant Walter von Bülow-Bothkamp	13 Dec – 6 Jan 1918
Leutnant Max Ritter von Müller (acting)	6 Jan – 9 Jan 1918
Leutnant Theodor Cammann (acting)	9 Jan – 26 Jan 1918
Leutnant Otto Walter Höhne	26 Jan – 20 Feb 1918
Leutnant Karl Bolle	20 Feb – 4 Sep 1918
Leutnant Otto Löffler (acting)	4 Sep – 18 Sep 1918
Oberleutnant Karl Bolle	18 Sep – Disbandment

Appendix B
Bases

Location	Dates	Army	JG
1916			
Bertincourt, E Bapaume	10 Aug – 19 Aug	1st	–
Velu, E Bapaume	19 Aug – 27 Aug	1st	–
Bertincourt, E Bapaume	27 Aug – 24 Sep	1st	–
Lagnicourt, NE Bapaume	24 Sep – 5 Dec	1st	–
Pronville, Nr Quéant	5 Dec – 14 Mar	1st	–
1917			
Eswars, N Cambrai	14 Mar – 23 Mar	1st	–
Proville, Nr Cambrai	23 Mar – 1 Aug	1st/2nd	–
La Petrie, N Douai	1 Aug – 7 Aug	2nd	–
Bisseghem, Courtrai	7 Aug – 12 Aug	4th	–
Ghistelles, S Ostend	12 Aug – 27 Aug	4th	–
Varssenaere, Nr Bruges	27 Aug – 1 Oct	4th	JGr 'Nord'
Rumbeke, S Roulers	1 Oct – 13 Nov	4th	,, ,,
Bavichove, E Ypres	13 Nov – 16 Feb	4th	JGr 4
1918			
Marke, Nr Courtrai	16 Feb – 15 Mar	4th	JGIII
Erchin, SE Douai	15 Mar – 15 Apr	17th	,,
Halluin, SE Menin	15 Apr – 21 May	4th	,,
Vivaise, NW Laon	21 May – 6 Jun	7th	,,
Mont Soissons Farm	6 Jun – 18 Jul	7th	,,
Vauxcère, NW Fismes	18 Jul – 30 Jul	7th	,,
Chambry, N Laon	30 Jul – 25 Aug	7th	,,
Emerchicourt, SE Douai	25 Aug – 27 Sep	17th	,,
Lieu St Amand, Cambrai	27 Sep – 30 Sep	17th	,,
Spultier, Valenciennes	30 Sep – 10 Oct	17th	,,
Lens, NW Mons	10 Oct – 9 Nov	17th	,,
Aniche, E Douai	9 Nov – 14 Nov	17th	,,
Neuville	14 Nov – 16 Nov	17th	–
Lüttich	16 Nov – 19 Nov	17th	–
Weiden, Aachen	19 Nov – 22 Nov	17th	–
Stolberg, RR transport	22 Nov – 24 Nov	–	–
Demobilized at Braunschweig	24 Nov	–	–

Losses

1916	Name	Location	Cause
22 Sep	Ltn Winard Grafe – KIA	Bapaume	19 Sqn RFC
23 Sep	Ltn Hans Reimann – KIA	Noreuil	27 Sqn RFC
30 Sep	Ltn Ernst Diener – KIA	Bapaume	Esc Spa 3
1 Oct	Ltn Herwarth Philipps – KIA	Beaulincourt	AA fire
22 Oct	OffStv Leopold Reimann – WIA	St Catherine	FE2s
28 Oct	Hptm Oswald Boelcke – KIA	Grevillers	collision
13 Nov	Ltn Bodo Fr von Lyncker – inj	?	accident
16 Nov	Ltn Karl Büttner – PoW	Arras	8 Sqn RFC
22 Nov	Oblt Stefan Kirmaier – KIA	Flers	24 Sqn RFC
1 Dec	Ltn Amann – PoW	?	?
1917			
10 Jan	Ltn Otto Höhne – WIA	?	Sopwith 2/S
23 Jan	Ltn Hans Imelmann – KIA	Miraumont	4 Sqn RFC
23 Jan	Vfw Paul Ostrop – KIA	Miraumont	24 Sqn RFC
24 Jan	Vfw Leopold Reimann – KIFA	Valenciennes	crash
25 Jan	Flgm Gustav Kinkel – KIA	Moislains	24 Sqn RFC
4 Feb	Ltn Franz von Scheele – KIA	Le Mesnil	24 Sqn RFC
5 Feb	Vfw Thiel – WIA	?	?
11 Feb	Ltn Erwin Böhme – WIA	?	Sopwith 2/S
2 Apr	Ltn Erich König – KIA	Wancourt	57 Sqn RFC
2 Apr	Ltn Hans Wortmann – KIA	Vitry-en-Artois	57 Sqn RFC
19 May	Ltn Georg Noth – PoW	Gouy-en-Artois	60 Sqn RFC
20 May	Ltn Albert Münz – KIA	St Quentin	Nieuports
20 May	Ltn Kurt Franke – DoW	St Quentin	Nieuports
17 Jun	Oblt Georg Zeumer – KIA	Haynecourt	59 Sqn RFC
18 Aug	Oblt Otto Bernert – WIA	?	?
22 Aug	Ltn Egon Könemann – KIA	Lombartzyde	70 Sqn RFC/3(N)
5 Sep	Ltn Franz Pernet – KIA	off Westende	48 Sqn RFC
14 Sep	Ltn Maximilian von Chelius – KIA	Dixmude	48 Sqn RFC
21 Sep	Ltn Richard Plange – WIA	?	?
25 Sep	Ltn Johannes Wintrath – KIA	Westende	54 Sqn
8 Oct	Vfw Reichenbach – inj	Rumbeke	crash

Date	Name	Location	Cause
20 Oct	Ltn Walter Lange – KIA	Passchendaele	28 Sqn RFC
6 Nov	Ltn Gerhard Bassenge – WIA	Staden area	65 Sqn RFC
29 Nov	Ltn Erwin Böhme – KIA	Zonnebeke	10 Sqn RFC
8 Dec	Ltn Erich Daube – KIA	Moorslede	?
1918			
6 Jan	Ltn Walter von Bülow – KIA	St Julien	23 Sqn RFC
9 Jan	Ltn Max Müller – KIA	Moorslede	21 Sqn RFC
3 Feb	Ltn Erwin Klumpp – KIFA	Thielt	crash
28 Mar	Ltn Wilhelm Papenmeyer – KIA	Acheville	?
29 Apr	Ltn Ludwig Vortmann – KIA	Kemmel Ridge	74 Sqn RAF
? Apr	Ltn Karl Gallwitz – inj	?	crash
29 May	Ltn Paul Bäumer – inj	Vivaise	crash
18 Jul	Ltn Hermann Bolle – WIA	?	?
4 Sep	Vfw Kurt Jentsch – WIA	Emerchicourt	64 Sqn RAF
27 Sep	Ltn Fritz Heinz – KIA	Awoingt	56 Sqn RAF
29 Sep	Ltn Fritz Hoffmann – KIA	Cambrai	64 Sqn RAF
4 Nov	Vfw Paul Keusen – KIA	Monbray	4 Sqn AFC

Known Aeroplanes used by Jasta Boelcke

Fokker DIII

350/16	
352/16	Boelcke claimed victories 20 to 26 in this machine

Halberstadt D

Albatros DI

390/16	Höhne's aircraft; marked 'Hö' on fuselage
391/16	Büttner PoW in this aircraft 16 Nov 1916; marked 'Bü'
410/16	Prince Friedrich Karl; skull & crossbones on fuselage
426/16	First aircraft with Jasta 2; marked initially with a 'G' on the rear fuselage, later an 'R'
427/16	von Tutschek
434/16	
438/16	von Tutschek

Albatros DII

386/16	Boelcke's aircraft; killed 28 Oct 1916
47?/16	Kirmaier lost in this aircraft 22 Nov 1916
491/16	von Richthofen's aircraft
497/16	
1708/16	
1994/16	

Albatros DIII

751/17	Hunzinger's aircraft; two 'H's on a white fuselage band
789/17	von Richthofen's aircraft
790/17	Münz KIA in this aircraft 20 May 1917
796/17	Noth PoW in this aircraft 19 May 1917
1982/16	Kinkel PoW in this aircraft 25 Jan 1917; marked 'K'
1994/16	von Tutschek
2004/16	

Siemens-Schuckert DI/DIII

3753/16	arrived 27 Mar 1917
3754/16	arrived 12 Apr 1917

Pfalz DIII/DIIIa
4024/17

Albatros DV/DVa

1072/17	Wintrath KIA 25 Sep 1917; blue, white and green bands
2080/17	W von Bülow KIA in this aircraft 6 Jan 1918
2086/17	Papenmeyer's aircraft; yellow fuselage
2098/17	Black tail with small white symbol; Reichenbach's crash 8 Oct 1917
2346/17	Lange WIA 20 Oct 1917; dark tail with black and white band
2376/17	
4409/17	Bäumer's aircraft; white 'edelweiss' and red stripes
4430/17	Bäumer's aircraft
4578/17	Böhme's aircraft; white 'B' on green fuselage band
5235/17	
5373/17	
5375/17	Papenmeyer flew this aircraft 4 Jan 1918; yellow fuselage with a white band with a black 'B'
5395/17	
5398/17	
5405/17	Müller's aircraft; black comet on fuselage; KIA in this aircraft 9 January 1918
5410/17	Bäumer's aircraft; yellow fuselage with two black bands
5654/17	

Halberstadt CII

6382/17	Unit 'hack'

Fokker DV

2730/16	Conversion machine

Fokker Dr.I

128/17	
129/17	
130/17	
157/17	
162/17	
190/17	Löffler's aircraft; yellow fuselage band edged white, later with Jasta 27
191/17	
195/17	Vallendor's aircraft; large white 'V' on fuselage
203/17	Plange's aircraft; shot down 19 May 1918 while with Jasta 36
204/17	Bäumer's aircraft; red, white and black fuselage band
209/17	Bäumer's aircraft; large red 'B' on fuselage
212/17	Gallwitz's aircraft

213/17	Kempf's aircraft; large yellow 'K' on fuselage, the name KEMPF on top wing and the legend 'kemnscht mi noch?' (do you remember me?) across middle wing
214/17	Papenmeyer's aircraft; destroyed in air raid 13 Mar 1918; black/white/black fuselage band
409/17	Papenmeyer's aircraft; KIA 28 Mar 1918
413/17	Bolle's aircraft; later to Jasta 19; yellow fuselage band edged white/black

Pfalz DVIII

| 124/18? | Operational assessment, flown by Bäumer and marked with his red black and white fuselage band; black and white cowling |

Fokker DVII

| 332/18 | White 'lightning bolt' design on fuselage |
| 4453/18 | Lindenberger's aircraft: black & yellow striped fuselage |

Jasta Markings

By 1917 Jastas had begun to mark their aircraft for personal recognition and for unit identity. The more successful pilots wanted to ensure that observers of their successful combats, when asked to witness/confirm a victory claim, could easily say the German aircraft they saw had such-and-such a colour, letter or marking on it. There was also the morale-boosting unit marking or markings, usually a special colour or colours on specific parts of the aeroplane – engine cowling or tailplane for example.

In late 1916 Jasta 2 marked some of its machines with a pilot's initial, or part of a name. Reimann for example carried an 'R' while Büttner had 'Bü' on his Albatros DII and Höhne had 'Hö'. Von Richthofen's Albatros Scout was identified with the colour red once he moved to Jasta 11, red already featuring while he was with Jasta 2, although the 'red' on early Albatros fighters was more of a maroon/brown colour, which was actually an attempt at camouflage. RFC pilots who engaged such aircraft were more inclined to write about a 'red' coloured aircraft than try to describe this shade of reddish/brown.

In 1917 Jasta B selected a unit marking of a white tail on their Albatros DIIIs, while individual markings were at the whim of pilots. Some still marked their machines with a letter denoting their name, while Leutnant Noth marked his green painted aircraft with a covering of yellow spots! Hermann Frommherz had his Albatros painted a pale blue all over, including spinner, wheel covers and struts, with just the tail assembly in white, plus a personal black and white diagonal fuselage band aft of the cockpit. Gerhard Bassenge had his yellow fuselage encircled with a black band, thinly edged in white and another horizontal black line from the band to the nose, also edged in white. The 'yellow' fuselages of most of these Albatros Scouts was merely clear dope on plywood, giving it a yellow appearance.

Werner Voss, of course, had a very distinctive Albatros, its 'yellow' fuselage carrying a red heart (edged in white) on the fuselage sides and on the top decking, followed by a white swastika sign (a good luck symbol long before the Nazi Party made it theirs) surrounded by a green laurel wreath tied with a blue band at the bottom, and a red spinner, plus the white tail.

With the coming of the Fokker Triplanes Jasta B had its Prussian colours of half white, half black tails and elevators, and black engine cowlings with white 'faceplates'. Again individual markings varied, Hermann Vallendor carrying a large white 'V' on the fuselage sides, Kempf a large 'K'. Karl Bolle had a yellow band around the fuselage of his Dr.I which was edged in white and red. The yellow referred to his former Kürrassier-Regiment von Seyditz Nr.7. Paul Bäumer carried a large 'B' on his machine, and later changed this to a red, white and black fuselage band, while the wing-tips were painted black with a thin white inboard edging. The two lower wings also had a thin red edging next to the white.

Hermann Vallendor had a fuselage band of black and white diamond shapes and his main wing struts had a sort of black and white saw-tooth pattern on them. Some of the Dr.Is had the white rudder edged in black and while most had white rear fuselages up to the cross marking, Frommherz's machine was different, being painted black.

By the time the Fokker DVII biplanes arrived, Jasta B's pilots were marking their machines very distinctively, and so quickly that most of the serial numbers were obliterated, making it almost impossible for future historians to discover which aircraft carried which serial. The DVIIs still carried white fronts to their engine cowlings and white tails, but black became more prominent, especially for the engine compartment. Bolle still carried his yellow fuselage band edged in black and white but apart from the tail and cowling, the fuselage and wheel covers were black.

Otto Löffler's engine was also black and although he retained most of the fuselage's lozenge fabric, he had a white band around the fuselage on which was a black zig-zag pattern. Alfred Lindenberger's DVII was totally yellow and black diagonal lines, plus yellow wheel covers. The DVIIs still had the usual black and white elevators as their unit marking.

Appendix E

Combat Claims

Pilot's own running total under 'vic' in far right column. Reference to 'ds' and 'js' refers to 'jenseits' (other side, i.e. Allied side) and dieseits (this side, i.e. the German side of the lines). Zlg or Zlgzw means 'zur landung gezwungen, i.e. 'forced to land' – generally meaning forced to land inside Allied lines relatively undamaged. The abbreviation vL indicates a forced landing between or close to the lines.

Date	Pilot	Aircraft Type	Allied Sqn	Location of combat/crash	Time	Vic
1916						
2 Sep	Hpt O Boelcke	DH2	32	NE Thiepval ds	18.15	20
8 Sep	Hpt O Boelcke	FE2b	22	Flers js	18.25	21
9 Sep	Hpt O Boelcke	DH2	24	SW Bapaume js	18.40	22
14 Sep	Hpt O Boelcke	Sopwith 1½	70	Morval ds	09.15	23
14 Sep	Hpt O Boelcke	DH2	24	Driencourt ds	10.10	24
15 Sep	Hpt O Boelcke	Sopwith 1½	70	Herbécourt ds	08.00	25
15 Sep	Hpt O Boelcke	Sopwith 1½	70	Eterpigny js	08.15	26
16 Sep	Ltn O Höhne	FE2b	11	Manancourt ds	18.00	1
17 Sep	Ltn E Böhme	Sopwith 1½	70	NW Hervilly ds	07.45	2
17 Sep	Ltn H Reimann	FE2b	11	S Trescault ds	11.35	2
17 Sep	Hpt O Boelcke	FE2b	11	Equancourt ds	11.35	27
17 Sep	Ltn M v Richthofen	FE2b	11	Villers Plouich ds	11.40	1
19 Sep	Hpt O Boelcke	Morane V	60	Grévillers ds	19.30	28
22 Sep	Ltn O Höhne	BE12	19	Combles ds	am	2
22 Sep	OfStv L Reimann	BE12	19	S Sailly-Saillisel	am	2
22 Sep	Ltn H Reimann	BE12	19	Le Transloy ds	am	3
23 Sep	Ltn M v Richthofen	G100	27	S Beugny ds	09.50	2
23 Sep	Ltn H Reimann	G100	27	Bus ds	09.50	4
27 Sep	Hpt O Boelcke	G100	27	NE Ervillers ds	am	29
27 Sep	Jasta B	G100	27	SW Tolloy ds	am	–
30 Sep	Ltn M v Richthofen	FE2b	11	Frémicourt ds	11.50	3

Total victories for the month = 21

Date	Pilot	Aircraft Type	Allied Sqn	Location of combat/crash	Time	Vic
1 Oct	Hpt O Boelcke	DH2	32	NW Flers vL	am	30
7 Oct	Ltn M v Richthofen	BE12	21	Equancourt ds	10.10	4
7 Oct	Hpt O Boelcke	Nieuport XII	F.24	E Morval js	15.00	31
10 Oct	Hpt O Boelcke	DH2	32	NE Pozières js	am	32
10 Oct	Ltn E Böhme	FE2b	18	E Longueval js	09.50	3
10 Oct	OfStv M Müller	DH2	24	Vraucourt ds	11.00	1
10 Oct	Ltn H Imelmann	Sopwith 1½	70	Lagnicourt ds	pm	1
16 Oct	OfStv L Reimann	BE2c	34	SW Thiepval js	14.05	3
16 Oct	Hpt O Boelcke	BE2c	15	E Hébuterne js	14.20	33
16 Oct	Ltn M v Richthofen	BE12	19	Ytres ds	17.00	5
16 Oct	Hpt O Boelcke	DH2	24	NE Beaulencourt	17.45	34
16 Oct	Ltn J Sandel	BE12	19	N Ypres	17.00	u/c
16 Oct	OfStv M Müller	'Vickers'	?	Le Sars	17.50	u/c
17 Oct	Hpt O Boelcke	FE2d	11	W Bullecourt ds	12.10	35
17 Oct	Oblt S Kirmaier	FE2d	11	NE Bapaume ds	12.10	4
20 Oct	Hpt O Boelcke	FE2b	11	W Agny js	10.30	36
20 Oct	Ltn E Böhme	FE2b	11	NW Monchy ds	10.30	4
20 Oct	OfStv M Müller	BE12	21	Grévillers Wood ds	17.50	2
21 Oct	Oblt S Kirmaier	BE2c	12	Ecoust St Mein ds	am	5
21 Oct	OfStv L Reimann	BE2c	12?	Courcelette js	am	4
22 Oct	Hpt O Boelcke	Sopwith 1½	45	Beaulencourt ds	11.50	37
22 Oct	Ltn E Böhme	Sopwith 1½	45	Lesboeufs ds	11.50	5
22 Oct	OfStv L Reimann	BE12	19	SE Lagnicourt ds	14.00	5
22 Oct	Hpt O Boelcke	BE12	21	SW Grévillers ds	15.40	38
22 Oct	Ltn H Imelmann	FE2b	11	Bailleul ds	17.40	2
25 Oct	Ltn M v Richthofen	BE12	21	SW Bapaume ds	09.35	6
25 Oct	Ltn O Höhne	BE2d	7	Gommecourt ds	11.50	3
25 Oct	Hpt O Boelcke	BE2c	4	Miraumont ds	12.10	39
26 Oct	Ltn H Imelmann	Nieuport XVII	60	Serre js	16.30	3
26 Oct	Hpt O Boelcke	BE2c	5	SW Serre js	16.45	40
26 Oct	Oblt S Kirmaier	DH2	29	Le Transloy js	16.50	6
26 Oct	Oblt S Kirmaier	BE2d	5	N Grandcourt ds	17.20	7

Total victories for the month = 30 Aggregate total = 51

1 Nov	Oblt S Kirmaier	BE2e	9	Le Sars	15.40	8
3 Nov	Ltn M v Richthofen	FE2b	18	NE Grévillers	14.10	7
3 Nov	Ltn O Höhne	BE2c	?	Hébuterne js	14.35	4
3 Nov	OfStv M Müller	FE2b	22	SE Bapaume ds	15.20	3
3 Nov	Ltn E König	FE2b	22	Barastre ds	15.25	1
3 Nov	Ltn H Imelmann	Nieuport XVII	60	Douchy ds	16.45	4
9 Nov	Ltn M v Richthofen	BE2c	12	Beugny ds	10.30	8

Date	Pilot	Aircraft Type	Allied Sqn	Location of combat/crash	Time	Vic
9 Nov	Ltn H Imelmann	DH2	29	Haplincourt ds	10.30	5
9 Nov	Oblt S Kirmaier	BE2c	12	Mory ds	10.30	9
9 Nov	Ltn O Höhne	Nieuport XVII	60	Flers js	10.50	5
9 Nov	Ltn H Wortmann	Nieuport XVII	60	SW Le Transloy js	10.55	1
9 Nov	Ltn E Böhme	FE8	40	Arleux ds	15.10	6
16 Nov	OfStv M Müller	BE2c	9	Flers, zwdl	10.45	4
16 Nov	Oblt S Kirmaier	Sopwith 1^1/$_2$	70	S Bancourt ds	15.45	10
17 Nov	Ltn O Höhne	DH2	24	SE Bapaume ds	11.30	6
20 Nov	Oblt S Kirmaier	BE2c	15	N Miraumont ds	09.00	11
20 Nov	Ltn M v Richthofen	BE2c	15	S Grandcourt vL	09.42	9
20 Nov	Ltn M v Richthofen	FE2b	18	Grandcourt ds	16.15	10
22 Nov	Ltn E Böhme	Morane LA	3	Longueval js	14.10	7
22 Nov	Ltn E König	FE2b	11	Hébuterne js	16.50	2
23 Nov	Ltn D Collin	DH2	24	N Le Sars js	11.00	1
23 Nov	Ltn M v Richthofen	DH2	24	S Ligny ds	15.00	11
27 Nov	Ltn W Voss	Nieuport XVII	60	Miraumont ds	09.40	1
27 Nov	OfStv M Müller	Nieuport XVII	?	Hébuterne js	09.45	5
27 Nov	Ltn W Voss	FE2b	18	S Bapaume ds	14.15	2

Total victories for the month = 25 Aggregate total 76

11 Dec	Ltn M v Richthofen	DH2	32	Mercatel ds	11.55	12
20 Dec	Ltn M v Richthofen	DH2	29	Monchy ds	11.30	13
20 Dec	Ltn M v Richthofen	FE2b	18	Noreuil ds	13.45	14
20 Dec	Ltn H Imelmann	FE2b	18	NE Beugny ds	13.45	6
20 Dec	Ltn H Wortmann	FE2b	18	Saspignies ds	13.45	2
21 Dec	Ltn W Voss	BE2d	7	Miraumont ds	11.00	3
26 Dec	Ltn E König	DH2	5	Beaulencourt ds	11.15	3
26 Dec	Ltn D Collin	DH2	24	E Morval js	11.20	2
26 Dec	Ltn E Böhme	DH2	24	Courcelette js	15.15	8
27 Dec	Ltn M v Richthofen	DH2	29	Ficheux js	16.25	15

Total victories for the month = 10 Aggregate total = 86

1917

4 Jan	Ltn M v Richthofen	Sopwith Pup	8(N)	Metz-en-Coûture	16.15	16
7 Jan	Ltn E Böhme	DH2	32	W Beugny ds	12.30	9
25 Jan	Flgmt G Kinkel	FE2b?	?	Moislains js	11.30	1

Total victories for the month = 3 Aggregate total = 89

Date	Pilot	Aircraft Type	Allied Sqn	Location of combat/crash	Time	Vic
1 Feb	Ltn W Voss	DH2	29	Essarts ds	17.30	4
4 Feb	Ltn E Böhme	DH2	32	Le Transloy js	15.05	10
4 Feb	Ltn E Böhme	BE2e	15	NW Puisieux js	15.30	11
4 Feb	Ltn E König	BE2e	16	NW Neuville js	15.30	4
4 Feb	Ltn W Voss	BE2d	16	Givenchy js	15.40	5
10 Feb	Ltn E Böhme	FE2b	20	W Gommecourt js	12.20	12
10 Feb	Ltn W Voss	DH2	32	SE Serre js	12.25	6
11 Feb	Ltn E König	BE2c	13	N St Laurent vL	15.30	5
25 Feb	Ltn E König	DH2	29	St Catherine js	14.45	6
25 Feb	Ltn W Voss	DH2	29	St Sauveur js	14.55	7
25 Feb	Ltn W Voss	DH2	29	Arras js	15.00	8
26 Feb	Ltn W Voss	BE2c	16	Ecurie js	16.50	9
27 Feb	Ltn W Voss	BE2c	8	Blaireville js	10.45	10
27 Feb	Ltn W Voss	BE2c	12	St Catherine js	16.48	11

Total victories for the month = 14 Aggregate total = 103

Date	Pilot	Aircraft Type	Allied Sqn	Location of combat/crash	Time	Vic
4 Mar	Ltn W Voss	BE2c	53	S Berneville ds	11.30	12
6 Mar	Oblt A v Tutschek	DH2	32	N Beugnâtre ds	16.30	1
6 Mar	Ltn W Voss	DH2	32	Favreuil ds	16.35	13
11 Mar	Ltn W Voss	FE2b	22	Combles js	10.00	14
11 Mar	Ltn W Voss	Nieuport XVII	60	SW Bailleul ds	14.30	15
17 Mar	Ltn W Voss	FE2b	11	NE Warlencourt ds	12.15	16
17 Mar	Ltn W Voss	DH2	32	SW Bapaume js	12.25	17
18 Mar	Ltn W Voss	BE2d	8	Neuville ds	18.40	18
18 Mar	Ltn W Voss	BE2d	13	Boyelles ds	18.50	19
19 Mar	Ltn O Bernert	RE8	59	NE Mory ds	09.25	8
19 Mar	Ltn W Voss	RE8	59	St Léger ds	09.30	20
24 Mar	Ltn W Voss	FE2b	23	SE St Léger js	16.10	21
24 Mar	Ltn O Bernert	BE2e	8	NE Vaulx js	16.30	9
24 Mar	Ltn W Voss	BE2c	8	SE Mercatel js	16.45	22
31 Mar	Oblt A v Tutschek	Nieuport XVII	?	NW Loos js	09.00	2

Total victories for the month = 15 Aggregate total = 118

Date	Pilot	Aircraft Type	Allied Sqn	Location of combat/crash	Time	Vic
1 Apr	Ltn O Bernert	Balloon	5 Wg	Villers au Fins js	10.45	10
1 Apr	Ltn W Voss	BE2e	15	E St Léger js	11.45	23
2 Apr	Ltn O Bernert	Nieuport XXIII	60	Quéant ds	08.30	11
3 Apr	Ltn O Bernert	Balloon	5 Wg	Ervillers js	19.10	12
3 Apr	Ltn O Bernert	Balloon	5 Wg	N Bapaume js	19.10	13
6 Apr	Oblt A v Tutschek	FE2d	57	Anneux ds	08.30	3
6 Apr	Ltn W Voss	BE2c	15	S Lagnicourt js	09.45	24

Date	Pilot	Aircraft Type	Allied Sqn	Location of combat/crash	Time	Vic
6 Apr	Ltn O Bernert	RE8	59	Roeux ds	10.15	14
7 Apr	Ltn O Bernert	Nieuport XXIII	29	S Roeux ds	17.20	15
8 Apr	Ltn O Bernert	BF2b	48	SE Eterpigny ds	15.10	16
8 Apr	Ltn O Bernert	BE2c	4	N Bailleul ds	15.15	17
11 Apr	Ltn H Frommherz	Spad VII	23	Cuvillers ds	09.00	1
11 Apr	Ltn O Bernert	Morane P	3	Arras js	12.30	18
11 Apr	Ltn O Bernert	Spad	23	NW Lagnicourt js	12.40	19
14 Apr	Ltn H Frommherz	BE2f	10	Ribécourt ds	09.30	2
24 Apr	Ltn O Bernert	Sopwith 1^1/$_2$	70	S Vaucelles ds	08.30	20
24 Apr	Ltn O Bernert	BE2e	9	N Joncourt ds	08.40	21
24 Apr	Ltn O Bernert	BE2c	9	N Leverqies ds	08.42	22
24 Apr	Ltn O Bernert	BE2c	9	S Bellicourt ds	08.45	23
24 Apr	Ltn O Bernert	DH4	55	W Bony js	08.50	24
30 Apr	Ltn F Kempf	BE2e	9	SW Le Pavé ds	07.45	1

Total victories for the month = 21 Aggregate total = 139

7 May	Ltn W Voss	SE5	56	Etaing ds	19.25	25
9 May	Ltn W Voss	BE2e	52	Havrincourt js	14.00	26
9 May	Ltn W Voss	Sopwith Pup	54	Lesdain ds	16.45	27
9 May	Ltn W Voss	FE2b	22	Le Bosquet ds	16.50	28
14 May	Hpt F Walz	DH2	32	N Séverin-Fé ds	11.15	7

Total victories for the month = 5 Aggregate total = 144

| 5 Jun | Ltn F Kempf | Sopwith Pup | 54 | Masnières ds | 08.40 | 2 |

Total victories for the month = 1 Aggregate total = 145

July victories = nil.

| 17 Aug | Ltn J Wintrath | Sopwith Camel | 70 | Spermalie ds | 08.15 | 1 |
| 19 Aug | Ltn J Wintrath | Camel | 70 | E Dunkirk zlg | 17.45 | ? |

Total victories for the month = 1 Aggregate total = 146

9 Sep	Uffz P Bäumer	RE8	52	W Mannekensveere js	15.25	4
19 Sep	Ltn E Böhme	RE8	9	Boesinghe js	10.47	14
20 Sep	Ltn W Lange	Camel	10(N)	SW Stade ds	12.10	1
20 Sep	Uffz P Bäumer	Camel	9 (N)	Ramskapelle js	15.10	5
21 Sep	Ltn E Böhme	RE8	53	Comines ds	08.52	15

Date	Pilot	Aircraft Type	Allied Sqn	Location of combat/crash	Time	Vic
21 Sep	Uffz P Bäumer	Camel	70	Boesinghe js	17.50	6

Total victories for the month = 6 Aggregate total = 152

Date	Pilot	Aircraft Type	Allied Sqn	Location of combat/crash	Time	Vic
5 Oct	Ltn E Böhme	BF2b	20	N Dadizeele vL	08.15	16
8 Oct	Vfw Reichenbach	RE8	7	S Terland ds	09.40	?
(probably not confirmed due to his crash at Rumbeke airfield this date.)						
9 Oct	Ltn K Gallwitz	Sop Triplane	?	N Zeecote ds	18.15	3
10 Oct	Ltn E Böhme	Nieuport XXVII	29	N Zillebeke js	07.25	17
13 Oct	Ltn E Böhme	Sopwith Pup	54	S Couckelaere ds	08.50	18
14 Oct	Ltn E Böhme	Nieuport XXVII	29	Wieltje js	07.42	19
14 Oct	Ltn K Gallwitz	RE8	34?	S Wieltje js	07.42	3
16 Oct	Ltn E Böhme	Nieuport XVII	29	Magermairie ds	09.25	20
20 Oct	Ltn F Kempf	Camel	70	Gravenstafel js	12.20	3
20 Oct	Ltn G Bassenge	Camel	70	E Passchendaele	12.20	1
27 Oct	Ltn K Gallwitz	SE5a	56	Polterryebrug ds	12.10	4
31 Oct	Ltn E Böhme	SE5a	84	SE Zillebeke Lake	17.15	21

Total victories for the month = 11 Aggregate total = 163

Date	Pilot	Aircraft Type	Allied Sqn	Location of combat/crash	Time	Vic
5 Nov	Vfw P Bäumer	Camel	45	S St Julien js	12.50	7
6 Nov	Vfw P Bäumer	Spad VII	19	E Zonnebeke vL	08.25	8
6 Nov	Ltn R Plange	SE5a	60	S Passchendaele	08.45	1
6 Nov	Ltn E Böhme	Camel	65	Scherminkelmolen	11.50	22
6 Nov	Vfw P Bäumer	Camel	65	Vierlawenhoek ds	11.50	9
6 Nov	Ltn G Bassenge	Camel	65	Stade ds	11.50	2
7 Nov	Vfw P Bäumer	RE8	4	SW Moorslede vL	08.10	9
7 Nov	Ltn M Müller	Spad VII	19	SW St Julien js	09.30	30
8 Nov	Vfw P Bäumer	Camel/SE5	60?	N Zonnebeke js	16.45	11
8 Nov	Vfw P Bäumer	Camel ?	?	N Zillebeke js	16.45	12
11 Nov	Ltn M Müller	DH5	32	Wieltje js	12.20	31
18 Nov	Vfw P Bäumer	RE8	?	NE Zillebeke js	09.20	17
18 Nov	Ltn W Papenmeyer	Spad VII	23	NE Langemark	11.00	1
19 Nov	Vfw P Bäumer	RE8	?	NW Dixmude js	16.00	13
20 Nov	Ltn E Böhme	Nieuport XVII	5me	Oostkerke js	10.30	23
28 Nov	Vfw P Bäumer	RE8	7	N Gheluve ds	14.00	14
29 Nov	Ltn E Böhme	Camel	?	Zonnebeke js	12.55	24
29 Nov	Ltn M Müller	DH4	?	Schaep Baillie ds	16.10	32

Total victories for the month = 18 Aggregate total = 181

Date	Pilot	Aircraft Type	Allied Sqn	Location of combat/crash	Time	Vic
2 Dec	Ltn M Müller	DH4	57	NW Menin ds	09.45	33
5 Dec	Ltn O Löffler	Nieuport XVII	1	E Houlthulst ds	10.30	1
5 Dec	Ltn M Müller	SE5a	?	SW Poelkapelle js	14.40	34
7 Dec	Ltn M Müller	Spad VII	19	Moorslede ds	11.55	35
7 Dec	Vfw P Bäumer	Spad VII	23	Zonnebeke js	11.55	14
16 Dec	Ltn M Müller	Camel	70	Passchendaele js	14.10	36
16 Dec	Vfw P Bäumer	RE8	9	N Boesinghe js	14.10	16
18 Dec	Vfw P Bäumer	Camel	?	W Becelaere zlg	16.00	18

Total victories for the month = 8 Aggregate total = 189

1918

Date	Pilot	Aircraft Type	Allied Sqn	Location of combat/crash	Time	Vic
4 Jan	Ltn W Papenmeyer	SE5a	60	Geluveld ds	12.45	2
18 Jan	Ltn K Gallwitz	Camel	65	Passchendaele ds	11.20	5
19 Jan	Ltn K Gallwitz	Camel	65	Wyfwegen ds	14.45	6
22 Jan	Ltn R Plange	Camel	?	Langemark js	11.40	2
22 Jan	Ltn K Gallwitz	BF2b	20	Oostnieuwkerke	12.05	7
22 Jan	Ltn T Camman	BF2b	?	St Julien js	12.05	1

Total victories for the month = 6 Aggregate total = 195

Date	Pilot	Aircraft Type	Allied Sqn	Location of combat/crash	Time	Vic
3 Feb	Ltn O Löffler	DH4	25	SE Mariakerke ds	10.40	2
3 Feb	Ltn P Schröder	Camel	?	E Moorslede ds	15.10	1
3 Feb	Ltn H Vallendor	Camel	?	E Moorslede ds	15.10	1
24 Feb	Ltn W Papenmeyer	RE8	4	St Julien js	15.45	3
26 Feb	Ltn R Plange	Spad VII	19	Warneton ds	11.10	6

Total victories for the month = 5 Aggregate total = 200

Date	Pilot	Aircraft Type	Allied Sqn	Location of combat/crash	Time	Vic
9 Mar	Vfw P Bäumer	Camel	?	N Zonnebeke js	11.10	19
23 Mar	Vfw P Bäumer	Camel	46	SE St Léger vL	13.30	20
23 Mar	Vfw P Bäumer	RE8	5	N Tilloy js	15.45	21
23 Mar	Vfw P Bäumer	RE8	?	N Beugnâtre js	16.15	22
26 Mar	Ltn R Plange	Dolphin	19	Grévillers Wd ds	17.15	3
27 Mar	Ltn K Gallwitz	BF2b	20	S Albert vL	11.00	8
27 Mar	Ltn R Plange	RE8	16	SW Albert ds	pm	4
27 Mar	Ltn R Plange	SE5a	56	SW Albert ds	pm	5
27 Mar	Ltn H Vallendor	SE5a	56	NW Albert ds	pm	2
28 Mar	Ltn W Papenmeyer	RE8	5	Arleux-en-Gohelle	am	4

Total victories for the month = 10 Aggregate total = 210

Date	Pilot	Aircraft Type	Allied Sqn	Location of combat/crash	Time	Vic
21 Apr	Ltn K Gallwitz	Camel	203	W Bailleul ds	13.50	9
25 Apr	Ltn K Bolle	Camel	73	SE Wulverghem ds	14.24	6
29 Apr	Ltn R Plange	Spad VII	Spa68?	Westoutre js	20.15	6

Total victories for the month = 3 Aggregate total = 213

Date	Pilot	Aircraft Type	Allied Sqn	Location of combat/crash	Time	Vic
3 May	Ltn K Bolle	Camel	73	SE Bailleul ds	13.45	7
3 May	Ltn K Bolle	DH9	98	Ypres ds	14.10	8
8 May	Ltn K Bolle	SE5a	1	St Eloi ds	08.20	9
8 May	Ltn K Bolle	Camel	43	W Steenwerck ds	14.20	10
8 May	Ltn F Kempf	Camel	43	Steenwerck ds	14.20	4
19 May	Ltn K Bolle	DH9	206	SW Zonnebeke ds	08.20	11
29 May	Ltn K Bolle	Spad VII	Spa99	Soissons ds	?	12
31 May	Ltn A Lindenberger	Bréguet XIV	?	Villers Cotterets js	?	5
31 May	Ltn E Bormann	Bréguet XIV	?	Taille Fontaine js	?	zlg

Total victories for the month = 8 Aggregate total = 221

Date	Pilot	Aircraft Type	Allied Sqn	Location of combat/crash	Time	Vic
1 Jun	Ltn A Lindenberger	Bréguet XIV	?	Priez ds	?	4
2 Jun	Ltn J Heemsoth	Bréguet XIV	?	SW Chévillon ds	?	1
3 Jun	Lt K Bolle	Spad VII	?	Faubourg	?	13
3 Jun	Ltn H Frommherz	Spad VII	?	Ancienville vL	?	3
4 Jun	Ltn K Bolle	Bréguet XIV	?	Fresnes	?	14
9 Jun	Ltn K Bolle	Spad	?	Dampleux	?	15
9 Jun	Ltn H Frommherz	Spad	?	Vauxbuin ds	?	4
14 Jun	Ltn K Bolle	Bréguet XIV	Br29	Laversine ds	?	16
16 Jun	Ltn J Heemsoth	DH9	27	S Roye ds	am	2
16 Jun	Ltn W Suer	DH9	27	S Roye ds	am	1
16 Jun	Ltn K Bolle	DH9	27	Bus-la-Mésière ds	am	17
24 Jun	Ltn K Bolle	Bréguet XIV	?	S Saponey ds	?	18
28 Jun	Ltn K Bolle	Spad VII	?	Longpont vL	?	19

Total victories for the month = 13 Aggregate total = 234

Date	Pilot	Aircraft Type	Allied Sqn	Location of combat/crash	Time	Vic
3 Jul	Ltn E Bormann	Spad XIII	N471	Noroy ds	?	1
5 Jul	Ltn H Frommherz	Nieuport 28	95th	Courchamps ds	?	5
5 Jul	Ltn K Bolle	Nieuport 28	95th	Courchamps ds	?	20
15 Jul	Ltn H Frommherz	Nieuport 28	95th	Château-Thierry js	?	6
15 Jul	Ltn K Bolle	Camel	54	Dormans ds	14.30	21
16 Jul	Ltn K Bolle	DH9	49	Soilly ds	pm	22
16 Jul	Ltn E Bormann	DH9	98	NE Soilly ds	pm	2

Date	Pilot	Aircraft Type	Allied Sqn	Location of combat/crash	Time	Vic
16 Jul	Ltn H Frommherz	DH9	98	Vassy ds	pm	7
18 Jul	Ltn K Bolle	Bréguet XIV	?	Ferte-Henelles	?	23
18 Jul	Ltn K Bolle	Spad XIII	Spa159	Beuvardes ds	?	24
22 Jul	Ltn K Bolle	Camel	73	Coincy ds	19.10	25
24 Jul	Ltn H Frommherz	Spad XIII	Spa83	Acy ds	?	8
25 Jul	Ltn K Bolle	Camel	43	Fère-en-Tardenois	pm	26
25 Jul	Ltn K Bassenge	Camel	43	Fère-en-Tardenois	pm	3
25 Jul	Ltn H Frommherz	Camel	43	Mareuil-en-Dole ds	pm	9
28 Jul	Ltn H Frommherz	Salmson 2A2	12th	Sergy js	pm	10
28 Jul	Ltn K Bolle	Salmson 2A2	12th	Villers-sur-Fère ds	pm	27
31 Jul	Ltn K Bolle	Spad XIII	?	Courtemain		28

Total victories for the month = 18 Aggregate total = 252

Date	Pilot	Aircraft Type	Allied Sqn	Location of combat/crash	Time	Vic
9 Aug	Ltn K Bolle	RE8	6	Rosières ds	pm	29
9 Aug	Ltn O Löffler	AWFK8	35	Maricourt js	pm	3
11 Aug	Ltn K Bolle	Spad XI	88th	Villesavage	?	30
18 Aug	Ltn E Bormann	AR2	Ar268	Nouvron	?	3
18 Aug	Ltn A Lindenberger	Bréguet XIV	?	Moulin-sous-Touvent	?	6
20 Aug	Ltn A Lindenberger	AR2	?	W Champs	?	7
21 Aug	Ltn O Löffler	Bréguet XIV	?	W Champs	?	4
22 Aug	Ltn E Bormann	Spad XIII	?	S Neufheuse	?	4
26 Aug	Ltn F Heinz	Camel	17th	Bourlon Wood ds	pm	1
26 Aug	Oblt K Bolle	Camel	17th	W Beugny ds	pm	31
31 Aug	Ltn A Lindenberger	RE8	6	Haynecourt ds	pm	8

Total victories for the month = 11 Aggregate total = 263

Date	Pilot	Aircraft Type	Allied Sqn	Location of combat/crash	Time	Vic
1 Sep	Ltn E Bormann	BF2b	62	S Lécluse ds	pm	5
2 Sep	Ltn O Löffler	Camel	148th	Palluel ds	pm	5
2 Sep	Ltn E Bormann	Camel	148th	Sauchy-Lestrée	pm	6
2 Sep	Ltn F Heinz	Camel	148th	Boiry ds	pm	2
2 Sep	Ltn E Bormann	Camel	148th	SW Drury ds	pm	7
2 Sep	Ltn E Bormann	Camel	148th	W Havrincourt ds	pm	8
2 Sep	Ltn O Löffler	Camel	148th	Beugnâtre ds	pm	6
2 Sep	Ltn O Löffler	Camel	148th	S Pelves ds	pm	7
3 Sep	Ltn O Löffler	DH9	98	Epehy ds	16.25	8
3 Sep	Ltn A Lindenberger	BF2b	20	Combles js	18.05	9
4 Sep	Ltn E Bormann	SE5a	64	Pelves ds	11.00	9
5 Sep	Ltn P Bäumer	BF2b	20/88	S Douai	18.40	23
6 Sep	Ltn O Löffler	BF2b	11	N Bourlon ds	am	9
6 Sep	Ltn P Bäumer	BF2b	11	W Cantaing ds	am	24

Date	Pilot	Aircraft Type	Allied Sqn	Location of combat/crash	Time	Vic
6 Sep	Ltn E Bormann	Camel	208	NW Bourlon ds	pm	10
6 Sep	Ltn A Lindenberger	Camel	?	Lagnicourt js	pm	10
14 Sep	Ltn P Bäumer	RE8	?	W Cantaing	?	25
16 Sep	Ltn P Bäumer	DH4	?	NE Hénin-Liétard ds	?	26
16 Sep	Ltn O Löffler	DH4	98	Haveluy ds	am	10
16 Sep	Ltn O Löffler	DH4	98	NE Arras js	am	11
16 Sep	Ltn F Hoffmann	BF2b	?	SW Cambrai	?	1
20 Sep	Ltn P Bäumer	Camel	203	E Rumaucourt ds	15.50	27
21 Sep	Ltn P Bäumer	DH4	57	E Bourlon ds	18.45	28
21 Sep	Ltn P Bäumer	DH4	205	E Lagnicourt ds	18.45	29
21 Sep	Ltn P Bäumer	DH4	205	E Morchies ds	18.45	30
24 Sep	Ltn P Bäumer	Camel	?	Sailly	?	31
24 Sep	Ltn P Bäumer	DH9	49	SW Clary ds	am	32
24 Sep	Ltn O Löffler	DH9	49	W Cambrai ds	am	12
26 Sep	Ltn E Bormann	Camel	203	N Cambrai ds	?	11
27 Sep	Ltn P Bäumer	SE5a	?	W Cambrai ds	?	33
27 Sep	Ltn P Bäumer	SE5a	?	W Cambrai ds	?	34
27 Sep	Ltn H Vallendor	Camel	73	Marquion ds	08.25	3
27 Sep	Ltn H Vallendor	Camel	?	N Bourlon ds	08.25	4
27 Sep	Ltn P Bäumer	DH4	25	SE Oisy-le-Verger	?	35
27 Sep	Ltn E Bormann	Camel	54?	E Epinoy	?	12
27 Sep	Ltn E Bormann	Camel	?	Ecourt St Quentin	?	13
27 Sep	Uffz K Fervers	Camel	?	Aubencheul	?	1
27 Sep	Ltn G Bassenge	SE5a	56	Noyelles ds	17.35	4
28 Sep	Ltn O Löffler	SE5a	?	Epinoy ds	?	13
28 Sep	Ltn G Bassenge	Camel	203	Ham-Langelet ds	08.35	5
28 Sep	Uffz K Fervers	Camel	?	Epinoy ds	?	2
29 Sep	Uffz P Keusen	BF2b	22?	E Irony ds	?	1
29 Sep	Uffz K Fervers	BF2b	22?	Cagnoucles ds	?	3
29 Sep	Ltn P Bäumer	RE8/BF2b	?	Marcoing	?	36
29 Sep	Ltn P Bäumer	Camel	46	Bourlon Wood ds	?	37
29 Sep	Ltn P Bäumer	Camel	46	SE Sailly ds	?	38

Total victories for the month = 46 Aggregate total = 309

Date	Pilot	Aircraft Type	Allied Sqn	Location of combat/crash	Time	Vic
3 Oct	Ltn P Bäumer	BF2b	?	Rumilly ds	14.30	39
4 Oct	Ltn P Bäumer	BF2b/DH4	25?	Cambrai ds	?	40
4 Oct	Ltn G Bassenge	SE5a	85	Joncourt ds	?	6
4 Oct	Ltn P Bäumer	SE5a	85	Montbréhain ds	?	41
5 Oct	Ltn G Bassenge	Camel	?	Crevecoeur	?	7
8 Oct	Uffz K Fervers	Camel	?	Cagnoucles ds	?	4
8 Oct	Ltn P Bäumer	Camel	?	Bantigny	?	42
9 Oct	Ltn P Bäumer	BF2b	62	Preseau ds	am	43

Date	Pilot	Aircraft Type	Allied Sqn	Location of combat/crash	Time	Vic
9 Oct	Ltn H Vallendor	DH9	107	Sebourg ds	14.40	5
9 Oct	Ltn O Löffler	DH9	107	Thulin ds	14.40	14
29 Oct	Ltn E Bormann	Camel	3	E Valenciennes ds	am	14
29 Oct	Ltn P Blunck	Camel	3	Valenciennes ds	am	2
30 Oct	Ltn O Löffler	DH9	98	N Quievrain ds	am	15
30 Oct	Ltn P Blunck	DH9	98	Fayet ds	am	3
30 Oct	Ltn Schlack	DH9	98	Blaton ds	am	1
30 Oct	Ltn A Lindenberger	SE5a	32	Harchies ds	am	11
30 Oct	Ltn E Bormann	SE5a	32	N Neuville ds	am	15
30 Oct	Oblt R v Griesheim	SE5a	32	Fresnes ds	am	1

Total victories for the month = 18 Aggregate total = 327

Date	Pilot	Aircraft Type	Allied Sqn	Location of combat/crash	Time	Vic
1 Nov	Oblt K Bolle	SE5a	32	W Harchies ds	13.25	32
1 Nov	Ltn A Lindenberger	SE5a	32	SW Harchies ds	13.25	12
1 Nov	Ltn H Vallendor	SE5a	32	Fresnes	13.25	6
4 Nov	Vfw P Keusen	BF2b	62	Villerau ds	am	2
4 Nov	Oblt K Bolle	Snipe	4 AFC	Englefontaine	10.15	33
4 Nov	Oblt K Bolle	Snipe	4 AFC	Englefontaine	10.15	34
4 Nov	Ltn K Bormann	Snipe	4 AFC	W Renaix ds	13.20	16
4 Nov	Oblt K Bolle	Snipe	4 AFC	N Tournai ds	13.20	35
4 Nov	Oblt K Bolle	Snipe	4 AFC	Esconouffles ds	13.20	36

Total victories till the Armistice = 9 Total victories for the war = 336

Appendix F

Combat Victories of Oswald Boelcke

Vic	Date	Aircraft type	Sqn	Crew	Location	Time
1915 FA62						
1	4 Jul	Morane L	MS15	Lt M Tetu KIA Lt LeComte G de la R Beaulicourt KIA	Valenciennes	

(Boelcke's observer in this action was Ltn Heinz von Wühlisch)

Vic	Date	Aircraft type	Sqn	Crew	Location	Time
2	19 Aug	Bristol			Front-lines	eve

(possibly a BE2 of 2 Sqn RFC forced to land near Arras with its fuel pipe shot through – Capt J G Hearson and Capt Barker both OK.)

Vic	Date	Aircraft type	Sqn	Crew	Location	Time
3	9 Sep	Morane 2/S	?	?	Douai	eve
Brieftauben Abteilung Metz						
4	25 Sep	Farman	MF16	S/Lt P Moulières MIA MdL P Samarcelli MIA	Pont-à-Mousson	
5	16 Oct	Voisin B1 (V839)	VB110	Cpl G Frepillom MIA Sgt R Cadet MIA	St Souplet	am
6	30 Oct	Voisin B1	MF8	Lt A Dullin KIA Lt Leclerc KIA	S Tahure	am
1916 FA62						
7	5 Jan	BE2c (1734)	2	2/Lt G C Formilli PoW Lt W E Somervell PoW	N Harnes	am
8	12 Jan	RE7 (2287)	12	2/Lt L Kingden KIA Lt K W Gray PoW	NE Turcoing	10.40
9	14 Jan	BE2c (4087)	8	2/Lt J H Herring WIA Capt R Erskine	Nr Flers	am

Vic Date	Aircraft type	Sqn	Crew	Location	Time
Kek Jametz					
10 12 Mar	Farman	MF63?	MdL J Cellière Adj-Ch G Loviconi	S Fort Marre	11.30
11 13 Mar	Voisin	?	?	Emalancourt	13.00
12 19 Mar	Farman	MF19	Sgt P Galiment KIA Lt J Libman	Forges	13.00
13 21 Mar	Voisin (V1417)	VB109	Lt J Antonioli KIA Capt F LeCroart KIA	Le Fosses Wd	11.15
14 28 Apr	Caudron	C53?	?	S Vaux	am
15 1 May	French m/c	?	?	Poivre	eve
16 18 May	Caudron	C56	MdL H Cagninacci KIA S/Lt L Vivien KIA	S Ripont	eve
17 21 May	Nieuport Sct	N65	Adj H Brion WIA	S Morte Homme	am
18 21 May	Nieuport Sct	N65	Sgt G Kirsch WIA	Bois de Hesse	eve
FA62					
19 27 Jun	Nieuport	?	?	Douaumont	eve
Jasta 2					
20 2 Sep	DH2 (7895)	32	Capt R E Wilson PoW	NE Thiepval	18.15
21 8 Sep	FE2b (4921)	22	Lt E G A Bowen KIA Lt R M Stalker KIA	Flers	18.25
22 9 Sep	DH2 (7842)	24	Lt N P Manfield KIA	SW Bapaume	18.40
23 14 Sep	Sop 1½ St (A897)	70	2/Lt J H Gale KIA Sap. J M Strathy KIA	Morval	09.15
24 14 Sep	DH2 (7873)	24	2/Lt J V Bowring PoW	Driencourt	10.10
25 15 Sep	Sop 1½ St (A895)	70	Capt G L Cruickshank KIA Lt R A Preston KIA	Hesbécourt	08.00

Vic	Date	Aircraft type	Sqn	Crew	Location	Time
26	15 Sep	Sop 1^1/$_2$ St (A1903)	70	2/Lt N Kemsley KIA 2/Lt C J Beatty KIA	Eterpigny	08.15
27	17 Sep	FE2b (7019)	11	Capt D B Gray PoW Lt L B Helder PoW	Equancourt	11.35
28	19 Sep	Morane V (A204)	60	Capt H C Tower KIA	Grévillers	19.30
29	27 Sep	G.100 (A1568)	27	Capt H A Taylor KIA	NE Ervillers	am
30	1 Oct	DH2 (A2533)	32	Capt H W G Jones OK	NW Flers	am
31	7 Oct	Nieuport XII	F24	Capt M Challe MIA S/Lt H Mewuis MIA	E Morval	15.00
32	10 Oct	DH2 (A2539)	32	2/Lt M J J G Mare-Montembault OK	NE Pozières	am
33	16 Oct	BE2c (6745)	15	Sgt F Barton KIA Lt E M Carré	E Hébuterne	14.20
34	16 Oct	DH2 (A2542)	24	Lt P A Langan-Byrne	NE Beaulencourt	17.45
35	17 Oct	FE2b (7670)	11	2/Lt Lt W P Bowman KIA 2/Lt G Clayton KIA	W Bullecourt	12.10
36	20 Oct	FE2b (7674)	11	Lt R P Harvey WIA 2/Lt G K Welsford KIA	W Agny	10.30
37	22 Oct	Sop 1^1/$_2$ St A1061	45	Sgt P Snowden KIA 2/Lt W F H Fullerton KIA	Beaulencourt	11.50
38	22 Oct	BE12 (6654)	21	2/Lt W T Wilcox PoW	SW Grévillers	15.40
39	25 Oct	BE2d (5831)	7	2/Lt W Fraser KIA 2/Lt B T Coller DoW	Miraumont	12.10

Vic	Date	Aircraft type	Sqn	Crew	Location	Time
40	26 Oct	BE2d (5781)	5	2/Lt J S Smith WIA Lt J C Jervis KIA	SW Serre	16.45

Bibliography

A Yankee in the RAF, Ed. J H Morrow Jr & E Rogers, University Press of Kansas, 1996.

Air of Battle, W M Fry, Wm Kimber & Co, 1974.

An Airman's Outings, A J Bott MC ('Contact'), Blackwood & Sons, 1918.

An Aviator's Field Book, Oswald Boelcke, 1917. The Battery Press, 1991.

Flieger im Feuer, Kurt Jentsch, Karl Josef Sander Verlag, Magdeburg, 1937.

Hawker VC, Tyrell Hawker, Mitre Press, 1965.

Jagdstaffel Boelcke, Karl Bolle, from "In der Luft Unbesiegl."
    J F Lehmanns Verlag, Munich, 1923.

Knight of Germany, Prof Johannes Werner, John Hamilton Ltd, 1933.

Sopwith Camel Fighter Ace, Robert M Todd, Ajay Enterprises, 1978.

Squadron 95, Harold Buckley, Arno Press, 1972.

The Jasta Pilots, Franks, Bailey and Duiven, Grub Street, 1996.

The Red Air Fighter, Manfred von Richthofen, 1917. Greenhill Books, 1990.

The Sky their Battlefield, Trevor Henshaw, Grub Street, 1995.

The War in the Air, H A Jones (& W A Raleigh), The Clarenden Press, 1922-37.

War Bird, Burke Davis, University of North Carolina Press, 1987.

Various issues of *Cross & Cockade* and *Over the Front*.

Index